THE REPUBLICAN PARTY
IN THE AGE OF ROOSEVELT

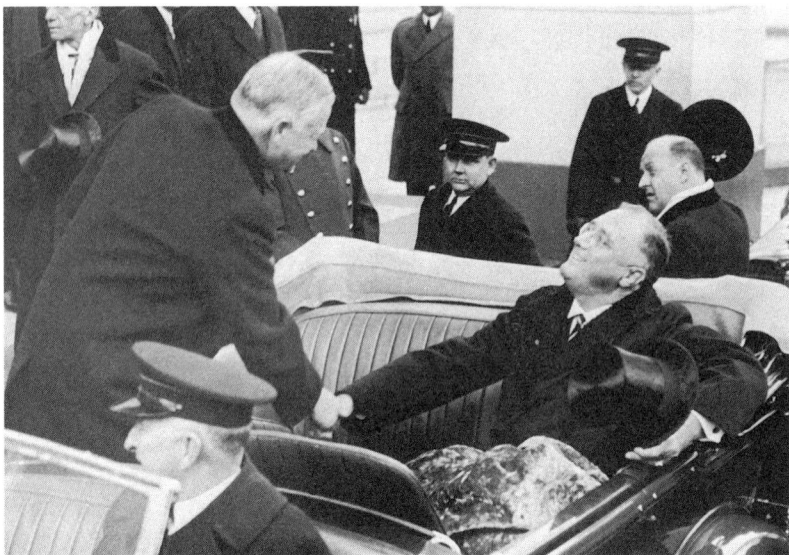

THE REPUBLICAN PARTY IN THE AGE OF ROOSEVELT

SOURCES OF ANTI-GOVERNMENT CONSERVATISM IN THE UNITED STATES

ELLIOT A. ROSEN

UNIVERSITY OF VIRGINIA PRESS
CHARLOTTESVILLE AND LONDON

University of Virginia Press
© 2014 by the Rector and Visitors of the University of Virginia
All rights reserved
Printed in the United States of America on acid-free paper

First published 2014

9 8 7 6 5 4 3 2 1

Library of Congress Cataloging-in-Publication Data
Rosen, Elliot A.
  The Republican party in the age of Roosevelt / Elliot A. Rosen.
      pages   cm.
  Includes bibliographical references and index.
  ISBN 978-0-8139-3554-6 (cloth : alk. paper) — ISBN 978-0-8139-3555-3 (e-book)
  1. Republican Party (U.S. : 1854–)—History—20th century. 2. Conservatism—
United States—History—20th century. 3. United States—Politics and government—
20th century. 4. Roosevelt, Franklin D. (Franklin Delano), 1882–1945. 5. New Deal,
1933–1939. I. Title.
    JK2356.R49 2014
    324.273409′043—dc23

                                                                              2013034295

Frontispiece: Hoover congratulates FDR at his first inaugural, March 4, 1933. Within
the year, the former president drafted the "Ark of the Covenant," which served as an
ideological foundation for opposition to the New Deal. (AP Images)

All illustrations unless otherwise noted courtesy of the Franklin D. Roosevelt
Presidential Library and Museum, Hyde Park, New York.

For Carol Mendes Rosen

CONTENTS

PREFACE

I N A SENSE, this book had its inception during the Great Depression, when my father, a stitcher of fancy women's shoes, became sporadically employed due to declining demand and the migration of such work to Italy. When he was employed occasionally as a piece worker, I recall that he was paid two and a half cents a pair for sewing slippers. As a result, my mother turned to sewing to keep the family in food and shelter. Frances Moley, one of her first customers, delighted in bouncing me on her knee and explaining that her fingernails were red because she ate her carrots. In due course, I became the delivery boy for the establishment signed in our apartment window as "Fancy Dressmaker," its location just off Manhattan's Gramercy Park.

The Moley apartment on East End Avenue near Gracie Mansion, the mayor's residence, was a frequent destination. When I was in college or graduate school at New York University, Frances, noting that "Ray likes history too," proposed, "Why don't you have lunch with him?" Finally gathering up the courage, I headed to the Newsweek Building, then just off Times Square. Raymond Moley and I dined occasionally at his huge desk and discussed English history, with our talk turning most often to Burke, Disraeli, and Maitland's *History of the Common Law*.

Both Burke and Disraeli represented to me conservatism tempered by subsuming contemporary ideas while retaining the most worthwhile institutions of the past. Then again, Disraeli also drew the underclass into the political process. Growing up and maturing in the 1930s and 1940s, I entered the workplace at age sixteen earning forty cents an hour, and I regarded self-sufficiency, personal provision, and hard work as critical to advancement. As a doctoral candidate and novice academic, I did not question the need for the economy to recover in a downturn largely through competitive energy, research, and entrepreneurship.

Upon meeting Rexford Tugwell—an expert in agrarian economics and government, and, like Moley, a Roosevelt adviser—and editing his *The Brains Trust* (1968), I felt no need to abandon traditionalist ideas; I simply adapted them to changed conditions. Like Tugwell, I observed—in concert with institutional economists—that government needed to assume a larger managerial role than before in a national and international economy more complex than acknowledged by Herbert Hoover's American System. Thus Social Security protected the individual against the penury of old age, and unemployment insurance against seasonal and cyclical layoffs. Further, as I understood institutionalism, the individual could no longer bargain as an equal with the large corporation.

In the fall of 1956, Raymond Moley asked me to write a review of Russell Kirk's *The Conservative Mind* (1954). Evidently satisfied, in February 1957, he invited me to lunch. Would I collaborate on a memoir of his participation in the 1932 presidential campaign, the Hoover-Roosevelt interregnum of November 1932 to March 1933, the shaping of the Hundred Days legislation, and his participation in the international Monetary and Economic Conference held in London in the summer of 1933? I might utilize his earlier *After Seven Years* as an outline, he proposed when I explained that I had never taken a course that more than touched on the New Deal era, but he desired to rectify the acerbic view of Roosevelt he had published in 1939, which he attributed to his then assistant. While working on the initial draft of *The First New Deal* (1966), I undertook my own version of the input of the brains trust assembled by Moley in 1932. Ray further contributed to my understanding in taped discussions that are available at both the Hoover and Roosevelt presidential libraries.

The bulk of my lifetime has been spent in an effort to evaluate Depression causation and examine economists' proposals for its remediation and the extent to which such ideas impacted the political process. More than a half century later, after spending a productive and pleasant year in Iowa at the Hoover Presidential Library and several winters and summers at Hyde Park; examining the papers of Neville Chamberlain in his role as chancellor of the Exchequer at Birmingham University; and studying several dozen collections scattered about the United States, I offer my reflections as follows: Depression causation was complex and is not explained by one or two issues. Monetary and fiscal policy operating independently or in tandem can stabilize an economy in depression or severe contraction. But full recovery requires remediation of deep structural problems, which accordingly requires a decade or more. The critique offered by the radical scholarship of the 1960s and 1970s, which insisted that Roosevelt should have adopted a more radical program, ignores the strength of the antistatist sentiment in American society represented particularly in the Congress. Austerity in such a crisis is counterproductive. And the political economy of the Age of Roosevelt cannot be understood in a framework of two or three discrete New Deals; it was a continuum.

This book is the last of three volumes assessing the New Deal and its opposition. In light of their interconnection, both foreign and domestic economic policies are included. *Hoover, Roosevelt, and the Brains Trust* (1977) dealt with the contentious transition from Hoover's administration to Roosevelt's, particularly the defeated president's effort to fasten his unsuccessful policies on the president-elect, notably maintenance of the deflationary gold standard that served as a major factor in Depression causation. The book focused on the structuring of the early New Deal program by the original Brains Trust assembled by Moley, a group of Columbia University academics aided by outside specialists, who with FDR formulated a legislative program designed to restore the banking system and to achieve a better income balance between agriculture, labor, and industry and among the nation's regions.

Roosevelt, the Great Depression, and the Economics of Recovery (2007) analyzed at greater length Depression causation and the contrasting approaches of Hoover and Roosevelt toward recovery. Domestic contraction can be tied partially to external problems including the deflationary gold standard and the shrinkage of agricultural exports as desperate nations structured their economies and monetary policies for self-sufficiency designed to save hard currencies and for the possibility that there would be a reenactment of the Great War.

The Smoot-Hawley Tariff of 1930 exacerbated economic nationalism in America and worldwide. In the United States, income failed to match capacity to produce. Deflated price levels and a dear dollar made it impossible for debtors to meet their obligations to creditors, impaired consumption, and helped to bring down the financial system. Millions of agrarians were displaced by the application of technological innovations to agriculture. While productivity growth restored corporate profitability to 1929 levels by 1937, it induced technological unemployment. The Federal Reserve followed a procyclical monetary policy in a deflationary environment. And no economic rationale existed for fiscal stimulus as a

policy until the late 1930s, when it was opposed by the Republican minority and the business community.

Infrastructure investment by government, one of the most important
developments of the 1930s recovery program, was nurtured initially by
Republican Progressives in the Hoover presidency, yet was opposed by
party stalwarts. The Roosevelt administration promoted a better balance
in the national economy through the provision of federal transfers from
prosperous sections, particularly the industrial Northeast, toward impoverished raw-materials producers in the South and Midwest. Once a
modicum of recovery was achieved, Roosevelt embraced minimal social
guarantees, notably Social Security in old age and unemployment insurance in the event of temporary loss of wages. Recovery was accorded pri-
ority, and reform followed, not the reverse. In short, Roosevelt assigned
the federal government an activist role in the economy in order to stem
the economic contraction. The Republican Party leadership opposed this
approach, opting for austerity.

Overriding Hoover's insistence on adherence to the gold standard in
January 1934, the Roosevelt administration secured legislation that depreciated the dollar by reducing its gold content. Subsequently, with recovery under way in the late 1930s, FDR unwisely abandoned a policy
of modest fiscal stimulus under pressure from the business community,
which feared inflation. Budget balancing and the Federal Reserve's tight-
ening of credit led to the "Roosevelt recession" of 1937–38, which featured a collapse of lending and declining price levels and employment. A
hard-won partial recovery was reversed at the insistence of conservative
advocates of a deflationary fiscal policy.

The current volume documents the Republican Party's opposition to
the New Deal and to American involvement in the Second World War
by focusing on the party's leadership. It denotes the GOP's transition
from the Party of Progressivism and a strong central government to a
party hostile to Washington and advocating a devolution of power to the
states. It documents the preference of conservatives for budget balance
and austerity in depression. On the foreign front, it points to the party
leadership's acceptance of Nazi dominance of Europe and its terms of
trade, which depended on autarchy or self-sufficiency. And it introduces
Wendell Willkie as an interloper who challenged the party's resistance to
advanced thought in foreign affairs and domestic issues. Among the issues Willkie pressed were civil rights, acceptance of industrial unionism,

and the necessity for American leadership in the shaping of international structures to preserve the peace after the Second World War.

This has been a long journey, and many institutions and individuals afforded assistance. Grants by the American Philosophical Society for research expenses started me on my way. The Rutgers Research Council provided a summer fellowship, a one-year faculty fellowship, and a number of research grants enabling me to devote my energies to research and writing. The Graduate School–Newark funded my research in the papers of Neville Chamberlain. The Dirksen Congressional Center supported my research in Everett McKinley Dirksen's papers at Pekin, Illinois, and subsequently in the papers of Robert Taft at the Manuscript Division, Library of Congress. The Eleutherian Mills-Hagley Foundation provided several grants for research at the Hagley Library in Wilmington, Delaware. The National Endowment for the Humanities awarded a fellowship for College Teachers and Independent Scholars as well as travel grants. Appointment as a Hoover Library Fellow and stipends as a Hoover Library Scholar for research at West Branch by the Hoover Presidential Library Association afforded the opportunity to spend a year in Iowa, where I examined a number of collections, benefited from midwestern hospitality, and made warm friendships that have lasted a lifetime. Finally, several FDR Freedom Foundation Research Awards and a grant by the Eleanor Roosevelt Institute enabled me to scour the Roosevelt Library collections and meet a cluster of helpful archivists over the years.

I confess that I have failed to keep a log of the many archivists who have aided me in my work over the years. I do feel obliged to single out Dwight Miller, former chief archivist at the Hoover Presidential Library, and to thank the late Bill Emerson, who knew much about FDR and who insisted that I invest time in a much-neglected collection at the library, that of Alexander Sachs, a brilliant economist whose papers enabled me to attain a richer understanding of the economics of the Age of Roosevelt. I am also indebted to Lawrence Gelfand, then at the University of Iowa, who suggested that I summarize my year's research in a paper, "The Midwest Opposition to the New Deal," published by the Center for the Study of the Recent History of the United States (1983). That essay served as an introductory statement to the work that would follow.

My research in the Post-Presidential Individual files at the Hoover Presidential Library began shortly after the library opened and ended in 1981. Accordingly, my notes follow an old system that since has been changed from file numbers to box numbers. Wherever possible I have changed my citations to the newer arrangement found on the Internet as follows: box number, PPI. In a few instances, as I was unsuccessful, I retained my old system: PPI, followed by file number. In the instance of Wendell Willkie's papers, my research was undertaken when his correspondence was alphabetized; there were no box numbers.

I am obliged to two friends who were exceptional in their willingness to edit the manuscript and who challenged my conclusions without hesitation, indeed with ardor, Carl Siracusa and Kendrick Clements. Carl is a former colleague who utilized much red ink and deliberation in connection with the original manuscript and offered wise counsel along the route to its realization. Ken and I labored together for a time in the Hoover Archives at West Branch and exchanged views on Hoover and the interwar era in the process and more recently in connection with this book. I benefited much from his insights and editorial comments. Finally, I am indebted to an anonymous reader for several profoundly thoughtful and helpful suggestions. Needless to say, while grateful for their labors on my behalf, I am solely responsible for the observations in the pages that follow.

THE REPUBLICAN PARTY
IN THE AGE OF ROOSEVELT

INTRODUCTION

We are moving toward two Americas with two contrasting—and increasingly codified—concepts of liberty. Can such a nation long endure?

—Charles Blow, "Lincoln, Liberty and Two Americas," New York Times, November 24, 2012

THIS BOOK situates the genesis of the Tea Party movement in the Age of Roosevelt. It suggests that determination by Republican Party conservatives to undo major components of the New Deal originated with Herbert Hoover's Ark of the Covenant (1934), resumed with the Goldwater phenomenon and Reaganomics, and culminated with the Tea Party movement. All were committed to limiting the dimension of federal intrusion into the rights of the states, corporations, and the individual. Objectives included curbing of welfare-state legislation, pursuit of balanced budgets, and in the process stemming public investment in the economy. While social insurance for old age and unemployment found reluctant acceptance, it was proposed that their scope and level of expenditures, though federally subsidized, would be determined at the state level with emphasis placed on individual responsibility. Regulation of business would be confined largely to antitrust enforcement. In the event of an economic downturn, private-sector investment would serve as the principal source of recovery, necessitating a low tax structure for private wealth and corporations.

However timid in its conception and implementation in the view of radical historians a generation ago, the Roosevelt program and policies proved disconcerting to those who managed the post–World War I consensus, one that rested on private ordering of the market, private management and investment, modernized labor relations that implied reliance on compliant company unions, and allocation of the income stream by a corporate elite. The genius of the Founding Fathers, traditionalists argued in their desire to retain the status quo that existed before the Depression, had effected a balance between central and local authority that should not be set aside for a "passing headache," Herbert Hoover's appraisal of the Great Depression.

The prestigious economist Wesley Clair Mitchell explained the nature of business cycles in a framework of automatic built-in correctives to a downward cycle marked by lower interest rates and reduced wage levels. "Unemployment," Hoover claimed in accepting his party's 1928 presidential nomination, "in the sense of distress is widely disappearing." Indeed, recent analysis by conservative revisionists suggests that the Depression's depth and persistence can be attributed to Roosevelt's interventionist policies, which induced "regime uncertainty."[1]

Long before other observers, while campaigning against Franklin D. Roosevelt in 1932, Herbert Hoover discerned the intention of the squire of Hyde Park to bring about a revolution in the role of the federal government. Once defeated, the ex-president spent the rest of his days in a crusade to reverse the New Deal. This effort commenced with the "Ark of the Covenant," as he termed it in 1934. Hoover objected to the willingness of party moderates in the Congress such as Everett McKinley Dirksen, Bronson Cutting, and Senate Minority Leader Charles McNary to accept certain essentials of the early Roosevelt program. Accordingly, he laid down a set of principles that resurfaced decades later in the Great Recession that erupted in 2008–9.

The Hoover orthodoxy offered austerity as the remedy for the Great Depression and subsequently for the economic contraction of the early twenty-first century. Proponents of business-confidence theory argued that lower taxes and diminished public expenditure would yield lower interest rates and encourage business investment. Then again, Hoover and other opponents of the New Deal also genuinely believed that Roosevelt planned to institute a dictatorship based on the model that typified European governments in the 1930s, which, once established, resisted reversal.

Hoover, Ohio's Robert Taft, and Michigan's Arthur Vandenberg, the party leaders, joined by antistatist economists and business luminaries urged a return to the gold standard. Such a policy would curb the Federal Reserve's capacity to expand credit and the currency supply, limiting social investment in the process. The retention of a "dollar as good as gold," it should be noted, would have initiated a return to a procyclical monetary policy followed by the Federal Reserve System before the Depression, one which stimulated the economy in the recovery cycle and further depressed the economy in a recessionary cycle. Another feature of limited government included curbing the growth and reach of independent federal agencies. Achieving these ends, Hoover insisted, dictated the purging from the GOP of those who offered cooperation and compromise with those across the aisle.

Roosevelt and Hoover offered distinctly different approaches to reversing the Great Depression. Funded by his business and financial supporters, Hoover's anti–New Deal program remains the foundation of the GOP's aspirations to decentralize the national government and allocate its functions in a complex global economy to the states. Interestingly, our society still wavers between the Hoover ethic and its stress on individual responsibility as opposed to economic intervention at the federal level. The issue remains whether preservation of an unfettered marketplace and our liberties remain inseparable, or whether a global economy requires enlargement of governmental functions. Decades later we return to the inception of the debate.

The New Dealers, in their response to the economic collapse, assumed that the New Economic Era of the 1920s needed to give way to a strong presidency and a regulatory state vested with authority to institute policies that assured prevention of future depressions through federal investment in the economy during a downturn. The Roosevelt entourage of academic and financial advisers embraced the notion of an organic economy with interrelated parts, one that required structural reforms to assure a permanent recovery from the Great Depression. Economic disequilibrium pointed to the need for major transfers from the industrial, advanced economies of the Northeast to underdeveloped regions of the United States, notably the South, the Midwest, the Southwest, and the Pacific Northwest through the device of regional valley development. Expanded public investment in weakened banks and insurers, and in federal recovery agencies, fell under the aegis of the Reconstruction Finance Corporation (RFC), created in the closing year of Hoover's presidential tenure. "We wanted recovery, we wanted a balanced economy, we wanted to institutionalize the balance and prevent future depressions," Rexford Guy Tugwell explained.[2]

Following the congressional election of 1938, Taft and Vandenberg shared informal leadership of the GOP. Taft, an expert in budgetary issues, assumed direction of domestic matters; Vandenberg served as shadow secretary of state. Taft served with Hoover in the wartime Food Administration, the American Relief Administration, and at the Paris Peace Conference. He lauded Hoover's *The Challenge to Liberty* (1934), which enunciated the principles of the Ark of the Covenant, for it expressed the "essential principles of government." Taft's political career was built on opposition to excessive government expenditure, curbing the accretion of centralized authority under Roosevelt, and limiting the growing power of industrial unions. Like Hoover before him, Taft relied on a narrow ideological base consisting of close associates who concurred with his views.

Taft's most notable success came in 1943, when New Deal economists presented a postwar plan, *Security, Work, and Relief Policies,* for establishment of a welfare state on the European model. The effort of the Harvard economist Alvin Hansen and the National Resources Planning Board (NRPB), these proposals would have broadened the nature of economic and social sustenance provided to individuals by government and would establish a postwar works program. The NRPB's *Post-War Plan and Program* suggested government-business partnership in key industries after the war, indicating the likelihood of an industrial policy. The NRPB proposals were defeated in Congress at the hands of conservative legislators, with Republicans and southern Democrats led by Taft. Indeed, the southern Democratic–GOP antistatist alliance based in the South, the Mountain states, and the Midwest that took shape in Roosevelt's second term foreshadowed the future composition of the Republican Party's base.

Just as the nationalism of the Party of Lincoln morphed into the states' rights agenda of the modern GOP, so the internationalism of Theodore Roosevelt morphed into "insulism," reflecting Arthur Vandenberg's belief that a self-sufficient United States could fend for itself in an interdependent world. The senator from Michigan was convinced that profiteers bore responsibility for the United States' involvement in the Great War and contested Secretary of State Cordell Hull's view of a peaceful world based on open trade primarily on these grounds. Tariff protection, in Vandenberg's view, also promised to insulate the American standard of living, the world's highest even during the Depression, by sustaining corporate profits and the wages of labor. Then, should Europe venture into a second continental conflict, a self-contained United States could avoid the risk of involvement in another bloody war.

According to hegemonic theory, since the inception of the Industrial Revolution, the world's dominant economy provides international stability for the global economy to its benefit. The coming of the Second World

War and the issue of American intervention should be considered in this context, namely as a contest between two hegemons, Nazi Germany and the United States. It is proposed here that in the event of American neutrality, Germany would have dominated the postwar world, and would likely, in partnership with Japan, control vital strategic resources and dictate the terms of international trade to the detriment of the United States.[3] Yet, with the fall of France, and the United Kingdom transparently incapable of challenging Hitlerite Germany's control of a considerable portion of the European landmass, the Republican Party leadership conceded Berlin's dominance of the international economy. After all, the anti-interventionists argued, only 5 percent of the American economy was impacted by its imports and exports. Accordingly, they opposed aid to Britain, including the destroyer-bases agreement and Lend-Lease.

Once the United States became embroiled in the Second World War, Vandenberg moderated, transitioning from "insulist" to nationalist and serving as mediator between the party's former anti-interventionist component, centered in the Midwest, and the eastern internationalists. Vandenberg was determined to protect American interests in a postwar arrangement for peace and to maintain party unity, yet he intended to avoid transmission of sovereignty to an international organization created for the prevention of war. Beginning in 1943, Vandenberg, Vermont's Senator Warren Austin, and John Foster Dulles, who represented Thomas Dewey, the GOP's likely 1944 presidential nominee, worked with Secretary of State Cordell Hull on behalf of the administration to shape American membership in the United Nations.

Vandenberg offered major concessions to Austin's internationalist predisposition, treading carefully in the face of the widespread belief that the Republican Party's opposition to United States membership in the League of Nations accounted for a renewal of war in Europe. Yet, in the last analysis, Vandenberg remained a nationalist, declining to serve in the conferences that shaped postwar international economic institutions. Taft went further, actively opposing United States funding of these institutions and even American membership.

Commencing with his receiving the Republican Party's nomination for the presidency in 1940, Wendell Willkie served as provocateur in connection with the comfortable ideological assumptions of his adopted party. (It needs to be kept in mind that Hoover's diktat included acceptance of minority status by the Grand Old Party so long as ideological purity was maintained.) The Hoosier business executive who headed Commonwealth and Southern (C&S), a private utility, emerged as a spokesman for free enterprise in the 1930s, when he fought the Tennessee Valley Authority's incursion into C&S territory. Though recently a Democrat, Willkie won the 1940 Republican presidential nomination by acclaim and went on to mount a serious challenge to FDR in the latter's quest for a third term, winning more votes by far than Hoover or Alf Landon, the 1936 candidate. Disinclined to go along with his isolationist colleagues in 1941, Willkie supported Roosevelt's defense policy and measures designed to sustain Britain.

During the Second World War, Willkie continued in the role of thorn in the side of his adopted party, convinced that Hoover and reactionary businessmen pulled the strings behind the pliable Thomas Dewey, regarded as the likely nominee in 1944. An avid internationalist, Willkie used his *One World,* published in midwar after a round-the-world trip, to press the GOP nationalists to acknowledge international economic interdependence, the end of colonialism, and the necessity for United States commitment to a strong postwar United Nations capable of preventing a third world war. Willkie also pursued a civil-rights agenda including the ending of racism; urged the acceptance by business of industrial unionism, including broader union representation in government; and distinguished between legitimate and excessive corporate profits.

In the last analysis, Willkie, who died in late 1944, lost the fight against the party reactionaries. The Pews of Sun Oil Co. dominated the National Committee. He was shut out of the Mackinac Island Conference, which shaped party policy regarding the degree of commitment to a postwar United Nations, and ignored at the 1944 convention, which nominated Thomas Dewey to oppose FDR's fourth term, with the interloper's views unwelcome. Hoover lived to a ripe old age, continuing the struggle to undo the New Deal agenda.

In the course of the Great Recession, the strictures articulated by Hoover were reprised along the lines of the 1920s New Economic Era, which featured limited government, the nostrum of a stable currency, and pliant unions. Once again the party's ideologues opposed interventionist measures that focused on monetary and fiscal policy. Once again Republicans who cooperated with the other party were regarded as collaborators who should be reined in or opposed in the primaries. Unwilling to be silenced, some moderates quietly withdrew. The conflicting views of Hoover and Roosevelt, long submerged under mass consumption funded by excessive public and private debt, surfaced once again. In an environment marked by economic deleveraging, the GOP viewed fiscal austerity and economic contraction as the cure, though it is axiomatic that such a remedy would induce further retrenchment, consequent revenue loss, and still more retrenchment and revenue decline.

Considering the nation's unacceptably high levels of public and private debt, Americans needed to contemplate increased taxes at all income levels and reduced entitlements over the long run. But in the face of long-term structural deficiencies beginning with education, they also should contemplate public investment in human capital in a bank modeled on the Reconstruction Finance Corporation. Partnering with private capital, such a federal entity should finance the upgrading of public transportation and roadways, research and development, renovation of decaying urban sewage and water systems, modernization of the electric grid, and other such projects, many of which can repay their cost over time.

Economic recovery cannot be achieved in an environment of political radicalism of Left or Right. Can politicians cooperate across party lines as they did in the early 1930s? Or will they instead engage in ideological warfare? Unwillingness to compromise will result in a low-level, long-term recession and threaten the very democratic institutions that the heirs of Edmund Burke presume to protect—feeding extremes in the United States resembling those that infected Europe in the 1930s, the sort of conflict that usually attracts the disenfranchised and those who feel threatened by change they do not understand. This inquiry concludes that—counter to cyclical theory, which assumed a natural or organic recovery—the Great Depression and the Great Recession are akin in nature and require a partnership of government and the private sector for remediation of deep, long-term structural problems.

1 | HERBERT HOOVER AND THE ARK OF THE COVENANT

A S THE Democratic Party's National Convention opened on June 28, 1932, Herbert Hoover broached the issue of his likely opponent with his press secretary, Theodore Joslin. "Do you think Roosevelt will be nominated?" the president inquired. Joslin assured him that the governor of New York would overcome his projected one-hundred-vote deficit on an early ballot. Less sanguine about Franklin D. Roosevelt's chances, Hoover noted: "I am afraid of Baker. . . . He's a strong second choice of the convention and would be a harder man for me to beat." The strength of Ohio's Newton D. Baker depended on his reputation for eloquence, intelligence, and probity. Woodrow Wilson's secretary of war, Joslin conceded, would succeed if Roosevelt lost momentum by the fourth or fifth ballot. There seemed "one way to nail him [Baker]. [William Randolph] Hearst hates him," Joslin said, referring to the newspaper magnate's abhorrence of Baker's internationalist views.

Joslin suggested a telephone call by the Hoover aide Lawrence Richey to Louis B. Mayer, vice president of Metro-Goldwyn-Mayer and vice chairman of the California State Republican Central Committee. Mayer would be asked to warn the isolationist Hearst against the growing likelihood of a Baker nomination. The notion of selecting the weaker of Hoover's two potential opponents in the coming campaign sounded appealing, and the call was made. Hoover exulted: the scheme worked "to perfection." "If Baker isn't stopped, it will not be the fault of Hearst."[1]

This is not to suggest that Herbert Hoover had a hand in the choice of his adversary in the 1932 presidential contest, but rather to shed light on his strategy. Hoover's actions seem to suggest that he ascribed to the "boy scout," or squire, theory—a belief shared by many who served with Roosevelt in the Wilson administration and popularized in the columns of Walter Lippmann, which held that the governor of New York was shallow, pliant, eager to please all comers, and possessed of few if any convictions. This view was misguided. Unhindered by dogma, amenable to ideas that challenged economic orthodoxy, and surrounded by advisers who discarded traditional approaches to previous economic downturns, Roosevelt shed Hoover's measured view of the role of the central government and the presidency in managing the economy.[2]

While the squire of Hyde Park assumed an experimental approach to the Great Depression, Hoover, despite such innovations as the Reconstruction Finance Corporation, no longer seemed the modernizer he had been during his service at Commerce in the New Economic Era of the 1920s. "Full of information," Raymond Moley recounted, Hoover was "imprisoned by his knowledge." Indeed, when the Republican governor of Iowa, Daniel Webster Turner, called on the president in 1931 and offered his appraisal of agrarian sentiment, "Mr. Hoover brought the interview to a close with the brusque statement, 'That's not my information.'"

Surrounded by supporters who tended to revere him and confirm his appraisal of the economic and political outlook, and given to a growingly defensive frame of mind, Hoover was shrewdly evaluated by fellow Republicans. The Kansas congressman Clifford Hope observed: "No one could ever discuss anything with Hoover while he was president because he very distinctly gave the impression that his mind was already made up." Verne Marshall, the outspoken editor of the *Cedar Rapids Gazette-Republican,* admonished Hoover in May 1933 that his miscues had often resulted from information provided him by associates who were "too sympathetic or too dumb to give it to you as you should have had it." One needs only to compare the "yes-men" who surrounded Hoover with the often diverse, even discordant, advisers who served Roosevelt.[3]

No sharp line demarcated Hoover's viewpoint on economic and political matters before and after the Great Depression. His economic ideology, shaped when he served as secretary of commerce, rested on the principle of voluntarism. Government regulation and control of business, he believed, was clumsy, incapable of adjusting to changing economic needs. It produced results more abusive than the problems to be remedied. The vast and harmful tide of such legislation could be avoided by the "organization of business itself," by business leadership operating through voluntary associations, which would preserve initiative and foster progress. Cooperation would eliminate waste in the form of destructive competition, business-labor strife, extremes of the business cycle, unemployment, and lack of synchronized standards. He viewed business, in sum, as the process of passing from extremely individualistic action to a period of associational activity managed by trade associations, chambers of commerce, craft unions, professional groups, and farmers' cooperatives. Collective action through self-governing industrial groups would stabilize output and employment, and move society toward industrial democracy.[4]

A devolutionist, Hoover held that "the American people have not forgotten how to take care of themselves" and "should not delegate their welfare to distant bureaucracies," namely Washington. Thus originated the Republican theology applied by Hoover, Robert Taft, and Arthur Vandenberg to a host of economic and social issues during the Age of Roosevelt.[5]

When the Great Depression descended on his administration, Hoover relied on the findings of the President's Conference on Unemployment of 1921, which he had chaired. As he had in the postwar recession, he urged state and local acceleration of public works, along with community and business efforts to sustain employment and provide relief. The creation of a bank of public works, proposed in the prosperous 1920s, never materialized. When public revenues evaporated and deficits grew in late 1931 and in 1932, Hoover and Treasury Secretary Ogden Mills sought cuts in expenditures and revenue enhancement. Nor did business prove able to maintain employment or investment levels as requested by the president and pledged at sundry White House meetings as the downturn deepened. When the states proved unable to fund public works, their customary role in that era, the administration offered loans through the Reconstruction Finance Corporation. The states, however, subject to the requirement that they declare virtual insolvency in order to receive the loans, hesitated to borrow. Local communities and charities proved unable to meet welfare needs. Hoover, unwavering, insisted on adherence to voluntarist principles and minimal government intervention in the economy and a sharply delimited concept of executive power. The threat to the nation, he asserted during the 1932 campaign, came less from the Depression than from the prospect of Franklin D. Roosevelt's proposed New Deal.

Though initially anticipating victory—he appraised his opponent as intellectually incapable of surviving the rigors of a national contest—as the campaign progressed, the president exhibited increasing signs of distress, sensing a fundamental challenge to the American System as he had defined it. Ready to concede the immediate contest, he determined to fight for his concept of the American dream. Still the defender of principles originally set out in his *American Individualism* (1922), Hoover urged reliance on individual initiative, cooperation by organized groups of citizens for sustenance in periods of joblessness, and, when required, dependence on the states and the local community for social and economic remedies. Hoover viewed American society and its political system as unique and distinct from that of Europe. His was a secular religion based on immutable principles that applied equally to the New Economic Era of the 1920s or the Great Depression. Determined that his ideology should outlast that of the New Deal and aware that more than a customary shift in political management at the White House was under way, Hoover took full aim and let loose at Madison Square Garden on October 31, 1932.

The American System, the president intoned, "had been builded up by some 150 years of the toil of our fathers." It was the unique accomplishment of our race and its experience. The United States had created on this continent a civilization superior to any other in the history of mankind. The Depression, he insisted, was a fleeting episode, nearly ended. To embark at that point on the course proposed by his opponent would undermine and destroy the nation's basic institutions and achievements. Hoover preferred "self-government by the people outside of Government," the best approach to the nation's malaise, since it would dissolve with the Depression's end. Roosevelt's proposals portended the enlargement of the federal bureaucracy, its power, and its budget at the expense of the people, local government, and the states. Tyranny and incompetence would ensue. "You cannot extend the mastery of government over the daily life of a people," he insisted, "without somewhere making it master of people's souls and thoughts." Free speech would die with the suffocation of free enterprise. More by implication than by concrete proposals, he warned ominously, his opponent planned a profound change in American life. Following defeat at the polls in November, Hoover devoted the balance of his years to shaping the Republican Party as a vehicle for undoing the "collectivist" state.[6]

Hoover's political ideology remained fixed to the end of his days. Insistent on individual, local, and state responsibility, he contended that the federal government should step in only as a last resort. The function of government, he urged following his defeat in the contest with Roosevelt, "lies in the State directing its activities to the prevention of the abuse of the right of property and to act as an umpire between property holders to see that they do so. That is the spirit of the Constitution."[7] Upon repairing to Palo Alto, California, Hoover undertook the task of checking the Roosevelt administration's "march to Moscow." The abandonment of the gold standard and consequent dollar devaluation, he insisted, defrauded savers and investors and inhibited capital investment leading to inflation and social instability. Instead, Hoover offered:

> When I organized the country in 1931 it was done upon the basis of a long experience based on the principles: (a) that administrative responsibility must be lodged in voluntary non-partisan agencies directed locally by leading citizens; (b) that the state and local authorities must contribute something; (c) that the state, and finally the federal government, should be present only as *contributors* to these organizations. In no other way was it possible to eliminate politics and corruption, secure economy, and at the same time maintain the important spiritual element that these were neighbors helping their neighbors. In no other way could supply be adjusted to personal need and community standards.[8]

Similarly, Hoover condemned the transfer of income to farmers under acreage allotment and subsidies as destroying their independence. Farmers, he believed, could best survive by cooperative activity and government credit. He opposed the National Industrial Recovery Act on the ground that it substituted "regimentation" for cooperative activity. He regarded the Tennessee Valley Authority as socialist, substituting government ownership, generation, distribution, and sale of electric power for private ownership and operation. He wanted to see the "disloyal demagogues" of his party purged, meaning the western Progressives—George Norris, Hiram Johnson, Robert La Follette Jr., and Bronson Cutting—while winning over to the GOP those Democratic Party conservatives such as Carter Glass, James Warburg, and Lewis Douglas who opposed the Roosevelt policies. The result, the ex-president hoped, would be a two-party system based on clearly delineated ideological lines, with the GOP committed to the prevention of dictatorship, which he defined as the centralization of power in the federal government.

Hoover opposed the reciprocity program fostered by Secretary of State Cordell Hull on the ground that it would induce job losses in the United States and represented a transfer of authority from the legislative to the executive branch. When it appeared in the early 1930s that another

European conflagration was a distinct possibility, he was determined that the United States should keep out of it. He insisted that the Congress reassert control of the national agenda, which it had abdicated to the executive branch during the domestic emergency and in foreign affairs.[9]

When Hoover proposed a statement of principles for the GOP, drafted in the fall of 1933, he ran into a brick wall. The initial blow came from the party's eastern internationalists, a small group largely situated in downtown Manhattan and relatively powerless in the nationalistic 1930s. Former secretary of state Elihu Root agreed that the western Progressives constituted a hostile bloc within the party. But the GOP, he insisted, "had abused the tariff," a clear allusion to the party's high-tariff policies in the 1920s, Hoover's signing of the Smoot-Hawley Tariff, and his protectionist views. Henry L. Stimson, Hoover's secretary of state, soon added his own demurrer to the ex-president's economic agenda. He did not oppose FDR's experiment in inflation, he observed, noting that many of his acquaintances in the financial district agreed. In the event, he supported the concept that recovery depended on increased price levels. This required a cheaper dollar in relation to gold in order to achieve reflation to pre-Depression price levels and recovery, a position Hoover abhorred as immoral and unprincipled.[10]

Aware that he needed to build support well beyond his base in Southern California's reactionary Republican politics for a rematch with Roosevelt, and that a return of the Midwest to the GOP fold was critical to the party's aspirations for 1936, Hoover met in late September 1933 with Chicago's Strawn group, some forty to fifty bankers, food processors, economists, and publishers hostile to the New Deal recovery program and led by Silas Strawn, senior member of the law firm of Winston, Strawn & Shaw and a power in the Windy City's financial community. (Strawn was also a powerful figure in the state's party structure, the American Bar Association, and the United States Chamber of Commerce.)

The Strawn cohort, which supported Hoover's presidential ambitions and promoted his ideological views, launched a movement among conservative economists aimed at preventing Roosevelt from depreciating the dollar by reducing its gold content. By devaluing the dollar, Roosevelt aspired to stem the deflationary spiral by inducing a rise in prices, spending, profits, and business investment. Hoover claimed instead that both Great Britain and the United States should commit to gold, each nation purchasing the yellow metal in the open market at the established legal price of $20.70 and £4.2s.[11]

His policies, Hoover claimed after defeat in 1932, had turned around the Depression, whereas Roosevelt's had proved destabilizing. The time had come "to fix the value of the dollar today, make it convertible in gold payable in coin over the counter," resulting, he believed, in a quick recovery. More likely it would have created a still more disastrous deflationary cycle. It is fitting in this context to note, by way of contrast with Hoover's analysis, the abandonment of J. P. Morgan partner Russell Leffingwell's faith that the gold-exchange standard would restore price stability and promote recovery.[12]

Following World War I, Leffingwell regarded a return to London's management of the gold-exchange standard as critical for improvement from the dislocations visited by the European conflict. Indeed, Morgan & Co. supported the United Kingdom's return to gold at a prewar parity of $4.86 in April 1925, or a currency redeemable at a fixed value, on the basis of the City of London's prewar role as banker to the world and its willingness to exchange pounds into other currencies in relation to gold. In order to assist the British Treasury in its return to gold, Leffingwell proposed Morgan & Co. leadership in a banking syndicate that would provide a $300 million credit for two years. This enterprise was also based on a cheap-money policy of the Federal Reserve banks intended to protect London's gold stock. Presumably, according to Leffingwell, the resumption of the prewar gold-exchange system would foster world trade and, if need be, could be defended by deflationary mechanisms such as lowering wages or the dole as well as by tolerating reduced employment in England. If successful, the Wall Street banker believed, the Bank of England management would fend off the "monetary nostrums fostered by Keynes in England and Yale's Irving Fisher in America as well as by politicians."

The system worked well as long as there was minimal pressure on Britain's gold reserves. It collapsed in mid-1931, when *The Macmillan Report* revealed the extent of sterling balances convertible to gold and *The May Report* claimed the existence of unacceptable budget deficits incurred by the Labor government. In September 1931, Britain abandoned gold and soon moved to a depreciated currency pricing the pound at $3.40. While such a policy was designed to improve exports from the United Kingdom, it also resulted in a dear dollar. With the United Kingdom leading the way, forty-four nations imposed special tariffs, twenty-six import quotas. In this environment, the Hoover administration and the Federal Reserve focused on the retention of the gold standard in the United States.

Initially, Leffingwell concurred on the ground that national currencies required a common denominator, namely gold. He ascribed the Great Depression and the accompanying massive deflation to the economic dislocations imposed by World War I; excessive nationalism, which fostered a high tariff regime; postwar debts and reparations; the excessive creditor status of the United States; a cheap-money policy that induced inflation beginning in 1927; and the disequilibrium between agricultural prices and other prices. Leffingwell's cure resembled that offered by Hoover: restoration of confidence by means of a return to the gold-exchange standard managed in London and supported by the United States. He deplored "Keynes's theory that England's return to gold standard is at the bottom of the depression." He endorsed budget balance achieved by increased taxation and reduced public expenditure—though Leffingwell saw merit in expansion of credit by the Fed to the extent of "the limits allowed by the gold standard."

By late October 1932, the Wall Street banker had reversed course, deciding to vote for "Frank." He now judged Hoover as "a desperate man who wished to continue desperate remedies for a desperate situation, created by his party's persistence for fourteen years in policies of political and economic isolation which he wishes to continue." Specifically, he maintained that the Fordney-McCumber and Smoot-Hawley Tariffs and the abandonment of the gold standard by Great Britain, which had led to gold hoarding, were largely responsible for the country's current distress.[13]

Leffingwell's subsequent support of Roosevelt's embargo of gold exports, then dollar depreciation in relation to gold, was based on an analysis of the precipitous collapse of agricultural prices and prices in general. Although Leffingwell regarded monetary stability as essential to general recovery, this needed to wait on a satisfactory level of wages and prices. Pressures for a return to the old gold standard were "simple-minded."

The views of Leffingwell likely had considerably more influence on Roosevelt's decision in late December 1933 to fix the dollar at $35.00 to the ounce, or at 59.6 percent of its former value, than those of monetary cranks such as Cornell's Robert F. Warren. While in the past, according to Leffingwell, the gold standard and stable currencies facilitated commerce, in the current autarchic climate, they were a force for instability. Closed economies required monetary management keyed to restore internal price levels. In this environment, gold was a drag on recovery.[14]

Roosevelt's monetary policy, based on price reflation for raw-materials output and manufactures in the hope that reflation would provide solvency for producers and their creditors, was a major Hoover complaint. Ample credit existed in the banking system, according to the ex-president. Indeed, he held further, Congress had delegated its legislative powers to the president, a situation resembling, as he saw it, the accretion of authority to the center in fascist, socialist, and communist Europe. Unwilling to accept the centralizing tendencies of the modern economy and the complexities of the Great Depression, Hoover nevertheless could rely on the unswerving support of antistatist conservatives beyond the reactionary Strawn group in Chicago. These included loyalists who had worked with him as chairman of the American Commission for Relief in Belgium, created to feed that country's populace following Germany's invasion; subsequently as food administrator in the Wilson presidency; and then in his service at Commerce and in the White House. In the process, he built a reputation as "the Chief," a superbly skilled administrator capable of recruiting the best minds in order to meet the challenges of that era.

Lacking warmth, distant in personality, and a poor public speaker, Hoover nevertheless fit well the mold of the New Economic Era delineated by the economist Thorstein Veblen, notably management of business by engineers for efficient production and widespread benefits as opposed to the financial manipulations of late-nineteenth-century industrial buccaneers that created wealth exclusively at the top. The Depression undermined the respect accorded the Great Engineer.

Challenged by western-based insurgents in the party—the "wild jackasses of the desert"—on the level of expenditure for public works and farm relief, as well as on federal control of the distribution of electric power generated by giant dams in the public domain, Hoover turned increasingly to the GOP's Old Guard. In the course of his presidency and the early New Deal years, he relied on the support of Senators Simeon Fess (Ohio), George Moses (New Hampshire), Lester Dickenson (Iowa), Frederick Walcott (Connecticut), David Reed (Pennsylvania),

Felix Hébert (Rhode Island), Henry Hatfield (West Virginia), and Bertrand Snell, the party's leader in the House. Hoover continued to rely on this group even after many were swept from office following the 1932 and 1934 elections. With Roosevelt ensconced in the White House, Hoover also turned to antistatists in the business establishment, especially in the upper Midwest and California, as well as to the Crusaders, a group of younger anti–New Deal and upwardly mobile business types. And he found support in anti–New Deal publications, especially the widely circulated *Saturday Evening Post*.

Dismayed by the unwillingness even of the party's die-hards in Congress to challenge the panoply of New Deal legislation, Hoover devoted the early months of 1934 to writing, in his words, the "Ark of the Covenant." A set of fundamental principles, it was intended to bind the Republican Party to his philosophy of limited government and to further his ambition for another crack at Roosevelt in 1936. Titled *The Challenge to Liberty*, it would, Hoover hoped, rein in the GOP's congressional remnant, especially those who had accommodated the New Deal program. "If the Republican Party does not grasp it," he predicted, "then its destiny will be as swift as that of the Whig Party."[15]

In a curious twist of subsequent American historiography, Hoover has since then been situated by some academicians as the originator of the interventionist state. Yet from the onset of his public career, his mission was to place curbs on the powers of the central government. The claim that Hoover accepted deficit financing is a fiction, as it resulted from declining revenues and not from increased expenditure. Equally fallacious is the claim that there existed no substantial difference in their monetary policies other than Roosevelt's willingness to detach the dollar from gold, which distorts their fundamental differences on the subject of money and credit.[16]

The Challenge to Liberty (1934) evinces continuity with Hoover's earlier views on limited government. He decried Roosevelt's inflationary program; massive expenditures for public works, relief, and agriculture; creation of public corporations that impinged on private enterprise; establishment of production controls as well as minimum wages ("regimented industry") under the aegis of the National Recovery Administration; output controls introduced under the Agricultural Adjustment Administration; and the lowering of tariffs, especially under the reciprocal trade agreements program. Hoover opposed any extension of federal power, including provision of social services. Accordingly, old-age pensions should be contributory, the responsibility of the individual though supplemented by taxpayer subsidies and managed by private insurers. He claimed that the central government's legitimate functions were limited to regulatory legislation for banks and stock exchanges, transportation, utilities, and natural-resource industries. Otherwise, state and local government and, with them, individual liberty would be undermined.[17]

Hoover viewed the 1934 midterm congressional election and its result with mixed feelings. Contrary to previous experience, the Democrats made substantial gains in both the House and the Senate. He deplored the defeat of his principal supporters in the Senate—Reed, Fess, Hébert, and Hatfield—and attributed their loss to the New Deal's fiscal largesse in the form of relief and payments to farmers, or as he put it, the nationalizing of Tammany's corrupt practices. He envisaged the 1934 defeat of the radical Democratic nominee for the California governorship, Upton Sinclair, as providing a model for an alliance of "sane" Democrats and Republicans, a result he claimed to have managed from behind the scenes. Presumably, such an alliance across both parties in tandem with *The Challenge to Liberty* would serve as a guide for the GOP's resurgence. At the same time, he observed, "forty-five percent of the vote was cast against the New Deal," and further, some 8 million fewer votes were cast than in the recent presidential election. "There would appear to be a very large group yet open to be worked upon."

Convinced that "democracy cannot function absent an adequate opposition and adequate debate of every public question," and dismayed by the failure of the GOP's legislative remnant in the Congress to defend his administration and challenge the Roosevelt program as unconstitutional and threatening economic ruin, the ex-president decided to take on the New Deal "from the outside."[18]

Particularly irksome to Hoover was the unwillingness of the Senate minority leader, Oregon's Charles McNary, to challenge New Deal legislation. "The Democrats are continuously feeding Senator McNary applesauce," Joslin related to Hoover. Actually, McNary, a shrewd politician and a moderate, had been fed something more substantial: federal development of the Columbia River Valley. Indeed, in the early New Deal years, McNary endorsed much of Roosevelt's recovery program. "Our country is on the upgrade," he offered in a public statement in August 1933. "The program of President Roosevelt supported by the Congress has inspired confidence and courage" and was responsible for "a decided movement upward, more business, improvements in wage scales, hours of labor, and volume of sales." McNary boasted of the "fine spirit of cooperation between the Republican minority and the president." Like Hoover, the Senate minority leader opposed Cordell Hull's reciprocal trade agreements program. But on agricultural price supports, social security, and public power, McNary differed substantially from Hoover's narrow construction of federal authority in light of the economic crisis of the early 1930s. In fact, the majority of Senate Republicans, including those comprising the party's conservative wing as well as southern Democrats, proved unwilling to challenge the Roosevelt program in the early stages of the New Deal.[19]

In pursuit of the 1936 nomination, Hoover needed to broaden his base beyond the loyal band of followers who had served under him in the past. Organization of the Chicago group—which included grain processors bitterly opposed to agricultural legislation that raised commodity prices and the bankers and law firms that serviced them—served as a source of funding for the party but hardly carried weight even in southern Illinois, let alone the Midwest.[20] An early sign of Hoover's weakness surfaced in June 1934, when the Hoover forces and those of the New York GOP boss Charles Hilles contested the appointment of a party chairman. The eastern Old Guard, commanded by Hilles, drafted a platform written by Ogden Mills, a hard currency proponent and a supporter of Kansas governor Alf Landon. It then selected Henry Prather Fletcher—a Bull Mooser grown reactionary and a former diplomat—as party chairman over the objections of Hoover's representatives at a meeting of the National Committee in Chicago. Fletcher, like Hoover, was a budget hawk and a sharp critic of the Republicans in Congress who lodged no objections to the Roosevelt program. Although he regarded the New Deal as unconstitutional, Fletcher was tied to the eastern conservative wing that financed the national committee. This group was convinced early on that the 1936 candidate should be chosen from a state west of the Appalachians and east of the Rockies.[21]

Despite the capture of the party machinery by the Hilles group, Hoover was convinced that the GOP would not accept leadership from New York. Scarcely a realist in these matters, Hoover developed a strategy for winning the GOP's 1936 presidential nomination. As a fellow engineer and Hoover's longtime intimate Edgar Rickard noted, the ex-president

desired the nomination but "will not go after it." There were critical obstacles to a draft. He had been beaten badly in 1932 and, justly or not,
was tethered to the Great Depression. In the course of his presidency,
he had alienated the Progressive wing of the party. As William Allen
White noted: "That territory is normally Republican but it is also . . .
intransigently committed to a rather militant and liberal idealism. . . .
And the major mistake that the president made was to outlaw these militant long horn statesmen from the Northwest."

Hoover had no intention of seeking reconciliation with the Progressives. In an address at Lincoln, Nebraska, during a swing through the
western states, he remained faithful to his principles and the claim that
he was not an ordinary politician. The party's titular leader criticized subsidies provided in the Agricultural Adjustment Act despite the conviction held by agrarians that the tariff system favored eastern industry. He
also suffered from past opposition to McNary-Haugenism, a high-tariff
dumping scheme for the nation's agricultural surplus. Hoover's unwillingness to accommodate the interventionist-welfare state and the broad
appeal of the New Deal program scarcely matched that of younger GOP
legislators. Centrists such as Everett McKinley Dirksen demonstrated
willingness to go partway with FDR both as a matter of conviction and in
response to their need for political survival.[22]

"Dead set on the presidency," Hoover countered the widely held view
that he was responsible for the Great Depression with the claim that he
had reversed the economic collapse by the early summer of 1932. He also
held that Roosevelt was responsible for the winter of 1932–33 bank clo-
sures in the absence of a clear commitment during the interregnum to
both gold and budget balance. William Starr Myers and Walter H. Newton reiterated that claim in the "Origins of the Banking Panic of March 4,
1933," published by the *Saturday Evening Post* on June 8, 1935. They dated
the panic from Roosevelt's inauguration and explained the collapse in a
framework of public anxiety concerning his policies, a position that GOP
congressional leaders and the national committee ignored to Hoover's
dismay.[23]

In the early months of 1935, John D. M. Hamilton, the ultraconserva-
tive Kansas state GOP chairman, planned the midwestern "Grass Roots"
Republican Conference. (Arthur Hyde, Hoover's agriculture secretary,
was present at the organizing committee.) In Hoover's mind, the conference held in Springfield, Illinois, in early June demonstrated a deter-

mination by the party's constituency to shape the content of the 1936 platform and thereby to override the pusillanimous congressional Republicans who collaborated with the Roosevelt agenda. Ashmun Brown, editor of the *Providence Journal* and Hoover confidant-spokesman, echoed this view: "These [GOP leaders in the Congress] had nothing to do with the conference and it is very apparent the conference had nothing to do with them. . . . The 'Grass Rooters' in effect have repudiated their own senators and representatives who supported the acts that the conference condemned."

Though the Springfield conference adopted the constitutional concerns expressed in *The Challenge to Liberty*, Hoover lost out on the critical issue of opposition to a federally subsidized farm program when the midwesterners endorsed the principle of the equality of agriculture with industrial producers, a foreshadowing of Alf Landon's 1936 effort. The party was "safely anchored to the Right," and its agenda "cannot be formulated by any group in the Congress," a satisfied Hoover crowed. While Hoover correctly judged the outcome, the Springfield principles hardly ran counter to Landon's plan as likely nominee to cement a union with the party's eastern reactionaries.[24]

Often serving in the capacity of honest broker between the Hoover and Landon interests in these prenomination maneuvers, William Allen White, editor of the *Emporia Kansas Gazette*, rendered the following insights as the 1936 nominating process began. Regular Republicans, he noted, would clamor for a return to the "good old days" of Republican rule. "There are two crowds who are now potential Republicans for next year: one crowd that wants us to be as far to the left as Roosevelt has gone—and I am in that crowd." The other would "revert to Coolidge. . . . And I won't write nor sign my name connected with any program which does not set up a definite promise of a new social order." This required a rise in the standard of living, specifically a more equitable distribution of income to the lower two-fifths of industrial labor by pressing industry in the direction of more responsible social behavior.[25]

In a maneuver designed to accommodate the views of the eastern and western wings of the party, the dark-horse candidate Frank Knox, publisher of the *Chicago Daily News;* Charles "Barney" Goodspeed; and Sun Oil's J. Howard Pew funded a newly created Western Headquarters in Chicago. Ominously for Hoover, it quickly became evident when the financiers of the Chicago headquarters put Hamilton in charge that they contemplated a Landon nomination.[26]

Hoover's ambition to mount a challenge to Roosevelt's interventionist state now depended on a plan to head off Landon's lead by stalemating the Cleveland convention through uninstructed state delegations. Convinced, further, that someone needed to "preach the gospel," confront Roosevelt's "march to Moscow," and stir up a cautious congressional GOP, Hoover took to the stump. In a series of major policy addresses in 1935 and 1936, he embraced the assignment with relish.

In May 1935, Walter F. Brown, an Ohio politician who had played a major role in securing the 1928 nomination for Hoover, began the process of recruiting former officeholders and followers of "the Chief" for a try at capturing the grand prize in Cleveland. While Brown contemplated a long journey, it ended abruptly. Hoover's last hurrah occurred with a stunning victory in the California party primary by his allies, who secured an uninstructed delegation over pro-Landon forces supported by the newspaper magnate William Randolph Hearst, Townshendites who advocated a national pension scheme, and Governor Frank Merriam, who had his own national ambitions. Hoover quickly lost momentum when his Ohio supporters lost out to a favorite-son delegation, a setback compounded by the state committee's public request that he refrain from pursuit of the 1936 nomination.

By the close of 1935, it was an open secret that Hoover's treasury secretary, Ogden Mills, favored Landon's nomination, and that congressional Republicans regarded the ex-president as a political liability. Close associates, among them Rickard, Kuhn Loeb's Lewis Strauss, the publisher Arch W. Shaw, the columnist Mark Sullivan, and the California banker Henry Robinson, privately at least, favored a Hoover disavowal of candidacy. As in the Hoover presidency, however, none of his intimates appeared ready to suggest an unequivocal withdrawal from the contest. As William Allen White observed, "People will tell him what they think he wants to hear or what they like to feel is the truth and not the truth."[27]

Still open to a draft, unrealistic and ambivalent about his chances, and deeply hurt, Hoover committed to checkmating Landon's presidential quest on the ground that the Kansan and those around him failed to endorse his policies and his philosophy. To no avail. In the end, the conservative anti–New Deal bankers, attorneys, and business leaders who financed the National Committee, joined by the eastern Old Guard led by Hilles, were determined to attract the Midwest to the GOP by anointing a challenger to Roosevelt from that region.

As for Hoover, the National Committee refused either to defend his administration or to finance publication of his "addresses on the American road." Nor did the claim that the Hoover administration had turned around the Depression in mid-1932 appear in the party platform. "This he will not tolerate," in the words of John Callan O'Laughlin, a Hoover supporter and editor of the *Army and Navy Journal*. The ultimate blow came when the New York delegation, abetted by Ogden Mills, a principal in the financial community, deferred to the Midwest's preference for Landon as party standard-bearer in 1936. Rejected by his party and embittered, Hoover nevertheless remained influential with its conservative, antistatist, and isolationist wings.

THE 1936 CAMPAIGN would lead to "a rendezvous with destiny," Franklin D. Roosevelt predicted in his acceptance of the Democratic Party's nomination for the presidency. The phrase seems, in retrospect, to apply to both major parties. The massive defeat suffered by the Republican Party dictated a reevaluation of its future course: either compromise with the New Deal's basic premise that the Great Depression required government to assume an expanded role in the economy, or remain true to the GOP's antistatist tradition begun by Warren Harding and Calvin Coolidge. Their policies, which promised a largely noninterventionist central government, were elaborated during the economic crisis of the early 1930s in Herbert Hoover's Ark of the Covenant, which outlined the restorative processes inherent in the business cycle. As a practical matter, it also remained critically important to retain the party's traditional dominance in the area extending from the Appalachians to the Rocky Mountains where it had been founded.

A later generation of New Left historians in a quest for a radical tradition judged the New Deal as timid in its approach to the capitalist system, which in their view consisted of internal dominance of both the government and the economy and reliance on external expansion to feed its ravenous appetite for overseas markets. The more recent revisionist movement, nurtured initially in the nation's interior and now joined by southern conservatives, again regarded government as a threat to free institutions. Both extremes misjudged the nature of the New Deal's quest for equilibrium between the public and private sectors.

Although Herbert Hoover proved to be an ineffective public speaker, his views are clearly recorded in surviving diaries and memoirs. Connecting the dots is not as readily accomplished in the case of Roosevelt, who rarely revealed his innermost convictions. Rather one turns for insight to advisers, who often held no formal office in his administration, to his addresses, and ultimately to his actions. For FDR's was a strong presidency, one that reversed traditional nineteenth-century economics, which held that a depression would be reversed automatically through lower wages and interest rates. In the face of opposition from the Federal Reserve and Treasury officials, the squire of Hyde Park initiated an effort to reverse the ruinous deflation of the early 1930s by departing from the lock hold of both the old gold standard and pound sterling and by enacting legislation designed to increase industrial and farm price levels. Release from the burdens of the gold standard served as the first step in Roosevelt's strategy for achieving economic recovery. It liberated domestic policy from needlessly high, deflationary interest rates, credit restriction, and budget balance. This in turn would stimulate profits, wages of labor, and farm income, and enable debtors to repay their creditors, notably the banks.

The New Deal was not an exercise in political theory. And for all of Roosevelt's delight in relating to Raymond Moley his conviction that historians would have difficulty in fathoming the reasoning behind his re-

The Great Depression in rural America. Principal causes of the Depression included the deflationary gold standard; trade and currency warfare; pro-cyclical Federal Reserve policies; demand deficiency and insufficient public investment; and technological unemployment on farm and in factory.

Great Depression in the city.

covery program, it was basic in its outline. It treated the collapse of farm prices for staples such as corn, wheat, cotton, hogs, and tobacco—which commenced with the postwar depression and eventually fell below the cost of production—as the initial cause of the Depression. Demand collapsed as Europe replaced its own lost agricultural output after the Great War, partially to protect gold reserves. Subsequently, in 1932, the Ottawa Agreements created preference for raw materials exports to Great Britain from Canada and Australia at the expense of the American farmer. Then, too, millions of farmers and farm laborers, some 40 percent of the population, were displaced by new techniques introduced to agriculture, including scientific farming, greater use of machinery, seed hybridization, and better cultivation practices. When the Depression struck, those displaced could no longer find employment in the cities. Thousands of country banks collapsed in the process.

The New Deal agricultural program, initially based on production allotments and subsidies for managed output, later by removal of marginal land and reforestation, was fashioned by two agrarian economists, Rexford Tugwell at Columbia University and Millburn Lincoln Wilson at Montana State University. The practicalities originated with M. L. Wilson, the theory with Tugwell, who preached the notion of a concert of interests or an organic economy of interrelated parts. If business could tailor output to the market, agrarians empowered by government could also achieve reasonable prices.

Planning for industry from the top, Tugwell's overhead economic management proved a failure in the early New Deal years. While a minority of industrialists initially welcomed federally sponsored efforts to balance output with demand, federal intrusion in the realm of labor-management relations quickly soured that relationship. Evidently the American experience was not conducive to sustaining Tugwell's vision of government allocation of resources, capital investment, and industrial production except in wartime. Instead, Roosevelt turned government intervention in the direction of public works programs aimed at infrastructure development, modernizing of impoverished regional economies, and temporary relief. These measures were designed to achieve a better-balanced national economy.

Public investment in infrastructure proved to be one of the enduring features of the New Deal. Public-works programs, which absorbed more than half of expenditure at the federal level, funded valley resource development and regional economic diversification; highways and air-transport facilities; public buildings; electric-power generation and transmission, especially for underdeveloped rural areas; water supply and sewers; flood control; and national-park facilities. In the process, such programs maintained skills essential to industrial recovery. While public investment in the shape of federal interregional transfers from the industrialized Northeast to the South and West facilitated a better-balanced economy and society, it also created financial resentment organized by the Du Ponts, as Delaware, for example, paid in $228.4 million to the federal coffers and received $40.9 million in return by way of federal-to-state transfers.[1]

In an era of modest national budgets, accelerated public expenditure could have a measurable economic impact. But it was insufficient to attain a full-employment economy. Overall federal nonrecoverable relief or pump-priming expenditure for the period from March 4, 1933, through December 31, 1937, in the United States and its territories amounted to

The Civilian Conservation Corps (CCC), Rock Creek, California, 1933. Roosevelt's earliest reemployment project, the CCC was aimed at youth. The Public Works Administration and Works Progress Administration were also intended to maintain and develop skills as well as modernize infrastructure.

$17.153 billion. A substantial percentage of the nation's budget in these years was distributed through such programs as the Agricultural Adjustment Administration, Civil Works Administration, Federal Emergency Relief Administration, Civilian Conservation Corps, Bureau of Public Roads, Public Works Administration, Works Progress Administration, and Emergency Relief Appropriation Acts of 1935 and 1936. This sum does not include loans amounting to $14 billion made by the Reconstruction Finance Corporation, the Farm Credit Administration, and other federal lending agencies. Federal expenditures for FY 1933 through 1937 totaled more than $34 billion, half pump-priming and redistributive, half ordinary.

Traditionalists shuddered at these sums and concluded that they impeded a private-sector recovery. Yet, as Alexander J. Field demonstrates, the 1930s proved to be the most technologically progressive decade in American history. This progress facilitated American productivity during the Second World War, and it played an important role in establishing the foundations for postwar prosperity. While industrial advances of the Depression years, according to Field, "resulted largely from private initiative and creativity," it is equally evident that technological advance in the public and private sectors complemented one another. Innovations in automobile production, petrochemicals, communications, and public utilities in the private sector were complemented by construction of dams, tunnels, and bridges, which led to advances in concrete and steel output.[2]

Provision for social security and unemployment insurance reflected several considerations. Old Progressives had long sought to soften the vulnerability of the individual in the new industrial age to occupational injury; seasonal unemployment or that caused by technological advances; and the penury that often accompanied old age. Social programs also promised to furnish a cushion against future depressions.

As the 1936 presidential contest approached, the Republican Party needed to cope with Roosevelt's introduction of a major transformation in the role of government in the nation's economy. In the early summer, Alfred Mossman Landon, the Progressive governor of Kansas, manifestly a dark horse in the upcoming contest with Roosevelt, was selected to define the Grand Old Party's response to the New Deal. Once nominated, Landon could attempt to pull the Republican Party out of the nineteenth century and at the least in the direction of the nation's ideological center, paving the way for another chance at the brass ring in 1940 against a potentially less formidable foe. Or he could defer to the party's Old Guard, considering that it brought him to the altar as a sacrificial lamb potentially capable, at the least, of restoring the nation's midsection to the GOP fold. In the event, while contesting the presidency with one of the most proficient campaigners in the American political tradition, Landon's campaign managed to lurch from one set of advisers and one point of view to another.

A mediocre student at the University of Kansas and its law school and born to the oil business—his father served as a superintendent at the Union Oil Company—Alf Landon made a comfortable living as an independent oil and gas producer. His investments, like his personality, proved deliberate, and by 1930 he became a director of the Independent Producers Association. Father and son were Bull Moose Progressives, with Alf gradually emerging as a bridge between the feuding conservative and liberal wings of the GOP in the Sunflower State.

Active in business and local politics, Landon was selected as a harmony Republican candidate for governor in 1932 and handily defeated his opponent, the incumbent Democrat Harry Woodring. Equally compelling to the eastern group that subsequently bestowed the nomination on him at Cleveland, he was the only Republican governor to survive the 1934 Democratic onslaught. In office, Landon cooperated with the bulk of the New Deal program and cleverly balanced the state budget by shifting the relief burden to localities and to Washington. Yet his lack of experience, and that of his advisers at the national level, seemed all too evident.[3]

"Still apologizing for Landon," Herbert Hoover sniffed in an acerbic marginal note upon reading William Allen White's studied evaluation of the governor upon his nomination. He was decent and courageous, the editor of the *Emporia Gazette* observed: "Whether he will crumble or crystallize under the tremendous heat and pressure of the White House, God knows." On talking over this very same question on the front porch of Landon's Topeka residence, the governor and the editor conceded that they themselves did not know the answer.

The first indication of Landon's strategy and inability to control advisors surfaced in the months before the party's convention. In an effort to mend the East-Midwest party split, Landon designated White, a stout supporter of Theodore Roosevelt's 1912 Bull Moose campaign and a liberal internationalist who also supported Roosevelt's domestic programs, to fuse the interests of midwestern farmers with the reactionary Ogden Mills, a deflationist who was dedicated to reversing the New Deal economic program. Mills dominated economic policy in the run-up to the nomination and well into the campaign. In the interim, with the singular exception of agricultural policy, the party's Old Guard controlled the platform committee despite White's chairmanship.

White's problems in dealing with Mills and the eastern Old Guard surfaced on several occasions. He was not well, and he proved insufficiently tough in the hurly-burly of a presidential campaign. A moderate, he was gradually squeezed out of the Topeka entourage of Landon advisers. In part, his difficulties reflected his change of heart since 1932. Despite reservations about centralized power in Washington, the editor had come to regard Roosevelt as substantially more than the lightweight described in Walter Lippmann's widely read 1932 newspaper columns. "I was for Hoover with all the ardor I could summon in my middle sixties," White confided to Theodore Roosevelt Jr. Yet with the dire economic and social situation in the winter of 1932–33, he felt obliged to "go along" with FDR, and was later amazed by the president's successes. "I used to think it was luck. For a long time . . . I feared that he would revert to type, pull off his whiskers and goggles and be the rather mediocre governor of New York." In due course, White made up his mind: "Liberty in this modern world may only be guaranteed by a considerable amount of fundamental security that is established by a more equitable distribution of income than we have today." Why then support the Landon candidacy?[4]

White conceded that the governor, hardly a political heavyweight, would be no match for his upcoming opponent. Yet, as a widely syndicated editorialist and the best-known Kansan in the nation, he suspected that opposition to Landon would have been fatal to his candidacy. He also knew that Landon was neither a social nor an economic liberal. Given the political climate of the 1930s in Europe, however, White was wary of the tendency toward accretion of power to Washington.

With White in poor health and unsure about economic policy, Mills became a substantial force in shaping the economic and financial priorities of the party platform and, in time, the Landon campaign. An advocate of economic orthodoxy and a nationalist, FDR's Hyde Park neighbor sought to contain the New Deal tide. As Hoover's treasury secretary, Mills endorsed the deflationary policies adopted by the Federal Reserve System at the depth of the Depression, extolled budget balance, and proposed a diplomacy designed to restore the gold standard. Landon invited Mills to address the Kansas Day Club on January 29, 1934, likely because of the latter's influence with the dominant right wing of the New York State Republican Party, his knowledge of fiscal and monetary matters, and because his views reflected Landon's own recent turn to the right.

At Topeka, Mills excoriated the New Deal as "an unconstitutional attempt to extend the powers of the federal government beyond the limits contemplated by law." While he accepted as a fait accompli recent dollar devaluation with passage of the Gold Reserve Act of January 1934, he insisted on dollar stabilization as essential to business activity. Mills deplored the New York Federal Reserve Bank's shift of ownership of gold to the Treasury Department since it facilitated its backing for deficit spending. As for Roosevelt's policy of reflation to pre-Depression price levels, Mills feared a government policy focused on increased price levels as economically and socially destabilizing. Mills also judged Roosevelt's budgets as excessive and, like his monetary policy, inflationary. Remarkably, Landon viewed Mills's speech as a model of liberal Republicanism.[5]

In the ensuing months, Mills portrayed the New Deal as collectivist and comparable to contemporary Europe's fascist plague. He urged renewed world trade, yet favored a tariff that reflected differences in cost of production, meaning a high-tariff policy. His underlying philosophy was one of a return to a Constitution that conferred the residue of power on the states. He deplored the delegation of congressional power to the executive. He bitterly opposed the New Deal's generous interpretation of NRA's Section 7(a), which fostered unionism and offered a narrow interpretation of federal authority under the interstate power clause.

As for social issues, Mills regarded unemployment as uninsurable, favoring provision for the unemployed by the states on a charity basis. He preferred old-age pensions based on annuity rather than social-justice principles, effectively turning Roosevelt's proposed social-security scheme into an investment vehicle. Landon's campaign for the presidency mirrored these views, especially fiscal prudence, currency stabilization, and reliance on the states for social programs. Thus began the rightward drift of the Republican campaign of 1936—away from the Wisconsin Progressives who shaped national social legislation; the public power Progressives led by George Norris of Nebraska; William Wesley Waymack, editor of the *Des Moines Register,* a Cowles brothers publication; Bronson Cutting of New Mexico; Charles Taft; and Charles McNary.[6]

Landon's recruitment of Wall Street and other business and banking opponents of meaningful federal intervention in the economy was occasioned by more than the need for funding that could not be furnished by his local supporters. While Landon was occasionally identified as a Theodore Roosevelt Progressive in the 1936 contest, his positions more nearly reflected the traditionalist nature of Kansas Progressivism. Radical Progressives in the mold of the La Follettes of Wisconsin, Iowa's Smith Brookhart, the Farm-Laborites of Minnesota, and North Dakota's Non-Partisan League never prospered in Kansas, where farm organizations were dominated by classical liberals. William Allen White's cosmopolitan views played well at the national level but carried little weight at home. Kansas Progressives, Landon included, favored low taxes, minimal public expenditure and investment, and clean government, and held fundamentalist religious views.[7]

Landon's Kansas Day address before the Topeka Club in January 1936 set the tone for his presidential quest and served to recruit some of the nation's prominent reactionaries. "Change," he argued, alluding to the New Deal, "does not necessarily mean progress. A social philosophy is not always bad because it is old, nor good because it is merely new." The Constitution had been flouted by "executive evasion" and "loose legislation." Establishing one of the major themes of his challenge to Roosevelt, Landon accused the administration of financial extravagance and waste through relief programs and the Works Progress Administration, which were projected by Roosevelt to cost $5 billion over the next few years. Unemployment insurance and old-age pensions in the form recently legislated by Congress, Landon claimed, were unworkable. And agriculture's recovery would come through the application of the principles of soil conservation and land-use management, presumably to be substituted for the subsidies provided by New Deal legislation.[8]

Well aware of a drift among the party's power brokers toward an anti–New Deal stance, Landon recruited bankers, high-profile attorneys, business leaders, and conservative writers and economists to his cause. Winthrop Aldrich of Chase Bank pledged substantial financial support and extended to Landon the services of Benjamin Anderson, an antistatist economist and author of the *Chase Economic Bulletin*. The group that supported Landon included George Davison, chairman of the board of Central Hanover Bank of New York; Henry Ford; Henry Itlleson of New York, a business associate of Ford; Colby Chester of General Foods and president-elect of the National Association of Manufacturers; Robert Lund of the Lambert Co. (Listerine), also a major player in the NAM; William Bell of American Cyanamid; Ernest Weir, the reactionary head of Weirton Steel; Howard Heinz, who with Bell helped to secure Landon's nomination; and the Du Ponts, who contributed substantially to the effort to unseat Roosevelt. The Pews of Sun Oil funded John D. M. Hamilton, Landon's campaign manager, and then picked up the pieces following Landon's crushing defeat. In addition to the Du Ponts, several of this group were members of the bitter-end anti–New Deal Crusaders, close to Hoover, and associated with the American Liberty League.[9]

Landon's shift from Bull Mooser, which implied a strong government at the center, to modification of the social and economic changes introduced by the New Deal is illuminated by his contacts with Stanley High, a liberal Republican and former editor of the *Christian Herald*. Employed as a commentator by the National Broadcasting Company, High exchanged views with Landon from late 1935 to early 1936. A Republican victory in 1936, High insisted, might well convince the party's reactionaries that they could successfully dismantle the New Deal, an undesirable result. Landon concurred: It was "impossible to go back to where we started in 1933." Rather, the party's nominee, once elected, would need to "work out" New Deal experiments such as the Federal Deposit Insurance Corporation, which Landon opposed in principle. Corporate leaders and bankers, Landon felt assured, were fully prepared to support a "constructive program." What these possibilities entailed was never spelled out in Landon's pursuit of the nomination and the presidency. But Landon was clear in the assertion that a continuation of the Roosevelt policies spelled "ruin."

High riposted that Landon's nomination on a decentralist platform might well enable the "old gang" to return to the "old game." "The old deal is dead and done for," High insisted, and the country would not vote for its return. While agreeable, Landon claimed: "I do feel that it has never been so important in the history of the country to defeat a president as to defeat Roosevelt," whose program would result in the destruction of representative institutions. Improvident, Tammany-style financial policies had proved fatal to every government in the history of civilization, he intoned. Instead he would take a middle way between government by bureaucracy and government by plutocracy, wherein both parties would adopt a number of the New Deal's principles. As wealthy contributors began to channel their energy and funding toward a Landon candidacy, High dispatched a friendly letter: he intended to use his talents in support of Roosevelt's reelection. Upon resigning from NBC, he became a speechwriter for FDR, one of several liberal Republican defections from the Landon crusade.[10]

Landon's fundamental conservatism on economic and social issues is further illustrated in his exchanges with Raymond Gram Swing, an editor of the *Nation*. When Swing proposed funding Social Security, old-age pensions, and unemployment insurance by general taxation graduated to impact the upper brackets more heavily, Landon opposed: Power should be kept "close to our old system of government—which is the local unit—in a modern industrial civilization." Swing countered that social insurance could not be met at the local or state levels, adding, pointedly, "The cry to 'get back' to local government, when raised by the Liberty League, is merely a cry to be left alone." In the end, at Milwaukee in the course of the campaign, Landon proposed federally subsidized old-age pensions in the form of supplementary payments that assured a minimum income, too often in reality a means test and a return to classic poor laws.[11]

Landon's prospects for a strong showing depended on regaining the Midwest, historically a GOP bastion, from the Democratic Party. This objective required a satisfactory plan for replacing the subsidies provided by the Agricultural Adjustment Act of 1933, declared unconstitutional by the Supreme Court in *United States v. Butler* (January 1936). The Court declared that taxation could not be used for the specific purpose of regulation of agriculture, since this function was exclusively the preserve of the states. The Roosevelt administration responded with the hastily drafted Soil Conservation and Domestic Allotment Act of 1936, which was based on the general welfare clause of the Constitution. Funded by general taxation, the law subsidized farmers (through the states) who curtailed output by planting crops that restored the soil. In search of a substitute plan, Landon turned to the Kansas representative Clifford Hope, who had been involved since the 1920s in the principal measures designed to boost farm income.[12]

Until the great drought of the 1930s, Hope's Seventh Congressional District, located in the state's southwestern counties, produced one-tenth of the nation's total wheat output. Initially elected to Congress in 1926, Hope urged parity for agriculture with industry through the same tariff protection gained by manufacturers after the First World War. Developed by George N. Peek, who was associated with Bernard Baruch and the War Industries Board, the tariff equivalent had been featured in the unsuccessful McNary-Haugen bills of the 1920s. At a meeting of agrarian economists held in Chicago in July 1932, Hope converted to domestic allotment, in effect acreage controls. Rexford Tugwell, a member of the original Brains Trust, also in attendance, recruited Roosevelt to the concept, resulting in the candidate's endorsement of acreage allotments at Topeka in the autumn campaign.

Like his congressional colleagues, Hope judged the New Deal program largely in the context of its benefits to his constituency. He pursued tariff protection for wheat producers and the southern Kansas oil independents. He favored economy in government, excepting only subsidies

for agrarians on the ground that protective tariffs for industrial producers raised the cost of farmers' necessities. Anticipating increased consumption of foodstuffs, he favored old-age pensions and unemployment
insurance. In search of a centrist candidate, Hope, White, and Henry
Haskell, editor of the *Kansas City Star,* invested their aspirations in the
Landon candidacy.[13]

Impressed with a native Kansan, Earl "Zack" Taylor, an associate editor of the *Country Gentleman,* Landon proposed that Hope and Taylor
collaborate on a program for agricultural relief. Swayed by George Peek's
views, the two experts shaped the GOP's farm plank and Landon's major
campaign speech on agriculture at Des Moines, Iowa. Their proposal, a
"tariff equivalent farm subsidy" based on the transfer of tariff collections
to farmers, would theoretically equalize farm income with the profits of
industrial producers. Significantly, however, such subsidies were pre-
mised on budget balance at the national level, an unlikely event.

The tariff equivalent harked back to Hope's ties to Peek's earlier program for bartering and exchange controls, key features of a self-sufficient
agriculture and one component of a self-contained economy. Imports
of livestock and dairy products would be excluded upon failure to meet
the health and sanitary requirements imposed within the United States,
a familiar protectionist device. While such a scheme entailed government planning and monetary management, Landon never evidenced a
grasp of the contradiction between the Hope-Taylor plan and his small-
government outlook.[14]

There were other problems with the Hope-Taylor proposal. Land-use
management in the form of marginal-land acquisitions, soil conservation
and reclamation, reforestation, drought relief, and crop insurance, which
it recommended, required an unbalanced federal budget, which Landon
condemned. Based on the presentation of his agriculture program at Des
Moines, economists, according to the *New York Times,* projected a cost of
$2.3 billion for paying a tariff equivalent on the domestically consumed
portion of exportable crop at a time when federal government receipts
(fiscal 1936) totaled just over $4 billion. Customs receipts, intended to
fund the tariff equivalent, came to only $387 million.[15]

Landon's Minneapolis address, which immediately followed his presentation of the Hope-Taylor scheme, provoked a deep fissure in the
Republican Party and precluded an alliance with anti–New Deal internationalist Democrats. The latter included Wilsonians such as Newton

Baker, Woodrow Wilson's secretary of war; Lewis Douglas, Roosevelt's budget director; James Warburg, an unofficial adviser to the United States delegation to the Monetary and Economic Conference held at London in the summer of 1933; Will Clayton of Clayton, Anderson, the world's leading cotton broker; and Dean Acheson, who served at Treasury under Roosevelt. Internationalists identified with Secretary of State Cordell Hull's program for trade reciprocity based on multilateral, unconditional, most-favored-nation trade agreements in the belief that the Depression's end and avoidance of another worldwide conflagration depended upon open markets unhampered by protectionism.

Minneapolis represented a turning point, the beginning of a bitter debate that extended into the twenty-first century. Opposed to Hull's pursuit of lowered tariffs were nationalists given to protectionism. George Peek and his disciples, Hope, Taylor, and Arthur Vandenberg among them, favored bilateral trade agreements that gave "the American farmer and industrial worker the full benefit of the American market." An American (higher) standard of living necessitated tariffs, quotas, and bartering, which required, in Peek's view, management of imports and exports by a foreign trade authority independent of the Hull free traders who dominated the State Department. A self-styled Jeffersonian, Peek was in reality a corporatist and an isolationist who espoused an economy managed by a business elite. The notion of a protected domestic market and bartering offended open-market internationalists in the Republican camp: Henry Stimson, John Foster Dulles, Benjamin Anderson, H. Alexander Smith, William Wesley Waymack, and Charles Taft, several of whom were directly involved in the Landon campaign.

Liberal internationalists were particularly distressed by Landon's assertion that the reciprocal trade agreements program had destroyed farmers' overseas markets and "sold the farmer down the river." Trade agreements were acceptable, according to Landon, "only when noncompetitive commodities were exchanged between the two nations concerned." While theoretically desirable, he added, unconditional most-favored-nation treatment under the Trade Agreements Act of 1934 had led to concessions to foreign nations at the expense of American producers. Specifically, Landon decried the recent trade agreement made with Canada, presumably at the expense of dairy farmers and the livestock industry. And he opposed the current procedure whereby reciprocal trade agreements were negotiated without public hearings or legislative approval. Counterattacks by Cordell Hull and Henry Wallace could be anticipated. Hull defended the reciprocity concept, and Wallace aired his ever-normal granary plan, later enacted into law. The reaction of the internationalists portended future internecine party strife as the United States became more engaged in world affairs.[16]

Wilsonian internationalists viewed Roosevelt's decision at the London Economic Conference (summer of 1933) to nationalize the dollar as destabilizing for the world economy. Besides, closed markets clearly made impossible international cooperation elsewhere. James Warburg, a Manhattan banker and outspoken critic of Roosevelt's unilateralist monetary policy, broke with the president and joined the Republican critics of the Gold Reserve Act of 1934. When Mills assigned campaign speech drafts relating to finance and international economic relations, Warburg, the author of two widely circulated anti–New Deal tracts, was asked to provide an address on foreign relations. A convinced internationalist, Warburg viewed the Republican platform's promise of economic nationalism as "inconsistent with . . . peace." He could undertake an address, Warburg pointedly wrote Landon, only if "I find myself in basic agreement with the position to be taken" with respect to tariffs and economic nationalism. Whether Landon replied is not clear, though his secretary offered that the candidate "is not one who is given to precipitate action." Warburg nevertheless proceeded with a draft focused on the need to prevent future warfare by ending the search for economic advantage among nations. He condemned tariffs, quotas, embargoes, currency depreciation, and other weapons of economic warfare.[17]

When Warburg insisted on a "reconciliation" of Landon's protectionist address at Minneapolis with his speech draft that pledged economic internationalism, clearly an impossibility, Landon demurred. Upon deciding that the policy gap could not be bridged, Warburg posted a letter to Secretary Hull endorsing the Roosevelt administration's recent turn toward currency stabilization and reciprocal trade agreements. "National self-sufficiency," he stated as he returned to FDR's embrace, "means a permanent government-directed economy" as opposed to the current administration's move in the direction of economic liberalism. This analysis was correct. Peek's proposals for quotas and bartering with Germany required currency controls similar to those instituted by Hjalmar Schacht at the Reichsbank. Accordingly, Warburg declared his intention to cast his vote for Roosevelt.[18]

Dean Acheson concurred with Warburg. When as undersecretary of the Treasury he refused, on the ground of their questionable legality, to endorse the late 1933 gold purchases conducted by the Reconstruction Finance Corporation and financed by Treasury, Roosevelt asked for his resignation. Opposed to the centralizing tendencies of the Roosevelt program, Acheson attended the infamous Liberty League dinner held at Washington's Mayflower hotel in January 1936. Yet upon receipt of Warburg's communication, torn between his distaste for Roosevelt's erosion of a federal system based on the states and Landon's foreign policies, Acheson declared for Roosevelt. Landon's attack on the Hull program represented a challenge to Cordell Hull's effort to revive international trade: "I must be on his [Hull's] side."[19]

Still more embarrassing for Landon's cause, Henry Haskell, editor of the *Kansas City Star* and one of candidate's earliest supporters, offered editorial support for the Hull agreements "as one of the really constructive achievements of the New Deal." Denying Landon's claim that trade reciprocity lowered farm prices, Haskell reported that the United States–Canadian trade agreement was followed by increased exchanges between the two nations and increased commodity prices for domestic farm output.[20]

Appalled by Landon's approach to the Hull trade program, Charles Taft and William Allen White attempted, as White put it, to "take the curse off the Minneapolis speech." Taft, son of the former president and a civic reformer when mayor of Cincinnati, had published a campaign manifesto, *You and I—and Roosevelt,* in the spring of 1936. A moderate, he lauded the model offered by Britain's Conservative Party: acceptance by government of responsibility for maintenance of a basic living standard. Taft also praised the so-called Reading Formula embraced by the National Labor Board and enshrined in the 1935 Wagner Act. Bitterly opposed by business groups, the formula required that employers recognize the bargaining unit selected by a majority of employees. Summoned by Landon to Topeka, Taft agreed to help draft the party platform and became a speech writer, especially on the subjects of foreign affairs, labor, and social insurance.

Landon's foreign-policy speech, delivered at Indianapolis late in the campaign, was designed to appease the Republican internationalists. It proved too little, too cautious, too replete with contradictions, and too late. It was a mishmash like most Landon speeches that were filtered through the hands of conservative advisers domiciled in Topeka. The best hope for preventing a conflict in Europe, Taft's book advised his fellow Republicans, rested on the end of economic isolationism. America's position as a creditor nation enabled greater acceptance of imports and assumption of the responsibility of international citizenship in the form of trade agreements negotiated by the State Department. Landon's foreign-policy speech drafted by Taft and William R. Castle, Hoover's undersecretary of state, mysteriously reverted instead to the legalisms and vague assurances formulated in the previous decade: a call for disarmament; arbitration and mediation among nations to prevent another war; United States willingness to engage in conferences—without commitment to any course of action; and the desirability of trade. But it offered no endorsement of trade reciprocity.[21]

Invited to participate in the Landon campaign trips and to confer with his Topeka advisers, William Allen White demurred. "I did not want to be part of a compromise which would go nowhere, stultify me, and . . . leave me no liberty of action." With tariffs regarded as instruments of economic warfare, Wilsonians of both parties organized the following year under the banner of the Economic Policy Committee and opted to promote the Hull policies. Most were Republicans. Charles Taft served as a founding member and organizer. And when, in 1940, the Committee to Defend America by Aiding the Allies was formed, its membership list was based partly on the Economic Policy Committee.[22]

Landon's domestic agenda extolled individual responsibility, fiscal restraint, efficiency, and government decentralism. Congress, he believed, had abdicated its authority to the executive; representative institutions were under siege. Speaking at Chicago on October 9, he pledged budget balance as "absolutely imperative" to restore business confidence. Corporations would be granted tax relief, and destabilizing inflationary policies would be avoided. "The spenders must go," he insisted, reinforcing his reputation as a budget balancer.[23]

Landon's desire to return to states' rights was also reflected in his approach to social policy. Whereas Charles Taft urged acceptance of social insurance under the parameters legislated in 1935, Landon condemned the law as paternalistic, discouraging individuals from saving for their own needs in old age. Landon proposed old-age pensions based on supplementary payments made to the needy administered by the states and funded in part by federal taxation for that purpose. Unemployment insurance, he suggested, was "an appropriate area for experimentation by the states," not the responsibility of Washington. States, in fact, shied away from taxing employers and employees for this purpose lest they lose out to those that did not do so.[24]

With the founding of the Congress of Industrial Organizations in 1935, growing labor-management tensions in the steel industry, and confronted by pressures for labor organization on an industrywide basis, the GOP candidate conceded political support by industrial unions, including their funding and membership, to Roosevelt and the Democratic Party. Industrial conflict in the mid-1930s concentrated on establishing the right to organize, and under what conditions. According to Landon, the right of employees to organize included choosing the type of union, which implied company unions; the right to join a union or not; and the absence of outside interference by any source, whether by fellow employees or employers.

Norman Thomas, the Socialist Party candidate for president, challenged Landon to define "freedom from interference" since employers commonly equated it with their right to prevent unions from organizing a nonunionized plant or industry. Specifically, Thomas wanted to know where Landon stood in connection with the ongoing strife between labor and the steel industry. When Thomas deplored the low wage structure and unsatisfactory working conditions for miners in Cherokee County, Kansas, Landon held that the State of Kansas could not interfere with local issues such as of wages, health, and safety.[25]

Precisely what Landon meant by these generalizations is difficult to say. Was he in effect throwing down the gauntlet to the industrial unions that supported Roosevelt? Was he condoning company unions financed by employers? Was he willing to define coercive tactics beyond legal proscriptions against violence already in effect? As an example, blacklists were shared by employers to avoid hiring pro-union employees. Landon never amplified his definition of a legitimate labor organization or what constituted unfair obstruction to the right to organize.[26]

The Roosevelt landslide in 1936 resulted in a House of Representatives consisting of 333 Democrats and 88 Republicans and a Senate of 75 Democrats and 16 Republicans, the balance "Others." Landon won only two states and lost by 11 million votes, a record. His running mate, Frank Knox, a Chicago newspaper publisher, and John Hamilton, the party chairman, both extremely conservative, ran their own campaign against the New Deal. Landon was abandoned by powerful members of his own party: Senators Robert La Follette Jr. (Wisconsin) and George Norris (Nebraska), who headed the Progressive National Committee for Roosevelt. Senators James Couzens (Michigan) and Peter Norbeck (South Dakota) supported FDR. Others in the GOP Senate contingent, William E. Borah (Idaho), Hiram Johnson (California), Gerald P. Nye (Nebraska), and the Senate minority leader, Charles McNary (Oregon), went fishing.

Landon was simply out of his depth in a contest with the foremost American politician of the twentieth century. His defeat was made still worse by the inability of a well-meaning politician to muster the support of a divided and disorganized party. Then again, he never settled on a theme or a cluster of ideas, instead offering contradictory messages. Roosevelt's unprecedented victory was based on the mass support of workers who turned to government as an agency for economic provision of a basic living standard when superannuated or discarded by the industrial system, and also on agrarians caught in a market dominated by oversupply. The GOP, it appeared, was condemned to long-term minority status.

For the GOP to mount a serious challenge to the New Deal, it would need to reconsider many of its traditional positions. A monetary policy based on the deflationary gold standard induced unemployment and international monetary instability. A high-tariff regime based on self-sufficiency lowered living standards. The growth of giant corporations suggested that business could not be regulated exclusively through antitrust or at the state level. The working class needed to share the benefits of the industrial advances of the 1920s and the technological revolution that began in the 1930s. And in foreign affairs, the party needed to shed its insularity.[27]

T HE BUSINESS-GOVERNMENT partnership associated with early New Deal legislation faded with the fostering of the union movement under Section 7(a) of the National Industrial Recovery Act and subsequent passage of the Wagner Act. Republican Party financing by the Du Ponts and the Pews of Sun Oil—the principals as well behind the American Liberty League—in the 1936 and 1940 elections suggests that a considerable number of industrialists viewed the GOP as a vehicle for anti–New Deal, anti-union policies. The Du Ponts and the Pews, who favored company unions, gave the Republican National Committee $1 million toward a total of $8.8 million expended in 1936. Other substantial contributors included William Randolph Hearst and John D. Rockefeller Jr. Forty-four percent of contributors to the National Committee came from the banking and brokerage communities. Other organizations, including the National Association of Manufacturers, the United States Chamber of Commerce, and the chemical, petroleum, and steel industries, followed suit. Alternatively, the Democratic Party increasingly relied on funding and foot soldiers furnished by organized labor, particularly the emerging industrial unions.[1]

The Du Ponts ascribed America's standard of living, the world's highest, to its business leadership. Elected political leaders, they argued, were hardly qualified to manage a modern economy or provide for the nation's workforce. Rather, American workers generally, and those of E. I. du Pont de Nemours in particular, were beneficiaries of their firm's managerial and technical skills. Nor, in the Du Ponts' view, did they require unions as intermediaries between labor and management. Equally important, investment, technological advance, economic growth, and general economic well-being were impeded by excessive taxation of personal wealth (the income tax) and corporate income. Whatever the merit of their arguments, the Du Ponts proved inept in the world of politics, unaware that their contempt for politicians would eventually backfire in 1936 as it had in 1932, when Roosevelt and Cordell Hull recaptured the Democratic Party organization from Wilmington's financial control.

The Liberty League's approach to government originated in Pierre S. du Pont's resentment toward the antitrust prosecutions leveled at his firm's corporate acquisitions by the administration of Theodore Roosevelt. His antipathy to politicians grew when Woodrow Wilson's secretary of war, Newton D. Baker, opposed the Wilmington firm's bid to take over the generation of electricity in the Tennessee Valley, Du Pont claimed, for defense purposes. His hostility to the Congress quickened when anti-interventionist western Progressive legislators labeled E. I. du Pont de Nemours a profiteering munitions maker in wartime. Since government had proven inimical to DuPont's interests, Pierre concluded, "I can't see how the company can stay out of politics these days when political conflict is a matter of life and death." This attitude permeated the top ranks of the DuPont Corporation, the nation's largest and most profitable.

At war's end in 1918, DuPont diversified beyond explosives and munitions, a process facilitated by huge wartime profits made in furnishing munitions to the Allies and the American military. Guided by the financial acumen of John J. Raskob, Pierre and his brothers, Lammot and Irénée, invested in General Motors, United States Rubber, Phillips Petroleum, and a host of other corporate entities. The ambitious Raskob, son of an immigrant cigar maker and orphaned like Pierre at an early age, had joined Pierre as his personal secretary and quickly rose to become treasurer and chairman of DuPont's powerful finance committee.

Pierre's retirement as company president in the 1920s afforded him the time to dwell on the issue, as he saw it, of government's unwarranted intervention in business affairs. He judged the Sixteenth (income tax) Amendment as unfair to those who generated employment. Pressures for a child labor amendment, he held, served as an example of a growing tendency of Progressives to enact intrusive social and economic policies the responsibility for which belonged with the states. Not unreasonably, the Du Ponts fancied themselves as entrepreneurs who conveyed the benefits of a mass-market economy and new technologies to an upwardly mobile middle class geared to the consumption of appliances, automobiles, plastics, and the other accoutrements of modern life. At the same time, capitalizing on its extraordinary profitability and an innovative managerial and scientific culture, the firm introduced cellophane, rayon, and a host of other products.

Highly profitable even in the Great Depression (earnings advanced from $26 million in 1932 to $90 million in 1936), DuPont provided its workers with sickness, retirement, and death benefits as well as a savings and stock investment plan. Its emphasis on workplace safety, a model for industry, was vital given the nature of its continued investment in explosives. Workers were also kept content through employees' councils, or company unions, in which they could voice their grievances directly to their supervisors. The creation of Christiana Securities in 1915 cemented voting control of the corporation in the hands of Pierre, who owned 50 percent of the stock. To further protect its interests, DuPont negotiated patent cross-licensing agreements. Jointly with General Electric, Westinghouse, General Motors, American Telephone and Telegraph, Bethlehem Steel, Goodyear, International Harvester, New Jersey Standard, and Irving Trust Company, DuPont founded the Special Conference Committee to coordinate economic policy and deflect pressures for unionization. Cartelist arrangements with I. G. Farben and Imperial Chemical Industries effected shared technologies in explosives and a division of world markets.

Considering the position of E. I. du Pont de Nemours at the apex of the corporate pyramid, highly profitable and able to dismiss employees and introduce technological advances at will, how does one explain Pierre's distress and determination to engage the political process as well? Pierre's estimate of the emergence of corporate capitalism resembled Rexford Tugwell's subsequent conceptualization of this development. As opposed to subsequent conclusions reached by revisionist historians of the Progressive movement, both viewed interpenetration, or the tension between the business and government, as undecided in outcome.

Tugwell, an institutional economist, preferred overhead economic management by government. The Great Depression, he explained, required government to rein in the economic chaos resulting from dominance by industry. It was in this framework that New Deal planners envisaged the National Industrial Recovery Act.[2] Pierre came to a starkly different conclusion. He resented interference by elected officials with what he considered legitimate business behavior, as politicians were not equipped for the task by training or experience. In the process, Pierre viewed the Eighteenth Amendment (Prohibition) as an attack on legitimate personal behavior and the opening wedge of state interference in property rights. Legalization and with it taxation of alcoholic beverages would establish a precedent for terminating intervention in the business system and would afford relief from the heavy income and corporate tax rates imposed in World War I and retained in the 1920s. He founded the Association Against the Prohibition Amendment, a forerunner of the American Liberty League, as an educational venture designed to disseminate the desirability of limited government and unhampered private entrepreneurship.

Shy and retiring, Pierre entered the political arena through the agency of Raskob. Raskob befriended Alfred E. Smith in 1926, when, following social forays to New York City, he was invited to join the governor's "golfing cabinet" and the Tiger Club, an assemblage of Irish-Catholic contractors and Democratic politicians devoted to imbibing, poker, business, and politics. Smith and Raskob had much in common: both were ambitious and rose from poverty to pinnacles of success. Raskob had been orphaned at a young age, supporting a widowed mother and his siblings and emerging as one of the nation's wealthiest entrepreneurs.

The DuPont executive managed Smith's 1928 presidential campaign, subsequently served as chairman of the Democratic National Committee, and bankrolled the party through the next four years. In the process, Raskob became a prominent New Economic Era spokesman for corporate liberalism: high wages, a five-day, forty-hour week, and three-day weekends in tandem with legal holidays. These steps, he proposed, would stimulate consumption and absorb industry's growing capacity for the production of durables. Also to this end, he originated installment sales for big-ticket items, founding the General Motors Acceptance Corporation.

Raskob persuaded a reluctant Roosevelt, still recovering from polio, to run for governor in 1928 in order to secure the Upstate New York Protestant vote for Smith at the top of the Democratic ticket. Raskob insisted that the economic collapse of the early 1930s was best reversed in an investment climate unfettered by government excepting only tariff protection for industry. Roosevelt's capture of the convention and party machinery in 1932 terminated this initial attempt by Raskob and the Du Ponts to enter the arena of politics at the national level.[3]

The replacement of Raskob as head of the Democratic National Committee by James A. Farley came about at the very time that Pierre was involved in assembling some of the New York region's corporate heads and bankers in an effort to frame an agenda for reversing the Great Depression. Meeting at the Metropolitan Club in New York in the spring and early summer, the group, sponsored also by Owen Young (General Electric) and Walter Teagle (New Jersey Standard), included Gerard Swope (General Electric), Pierre, Irénée, and Lammot du Pont, Thomas Watson (International Business Machines), Andrew Watson (Westinghouse Electric), Merlin Aylesworth (National Broadcasting Co.), Alfred Sloan (General Motors), Lewis Pierson (Irving Trust), Gordon Rentschler (National City Bank), Albert Tinney (Bankers Trust of New York), Walter Gifford (AT&T), W. W. Atterbury (Pennsylvania Railroad), and Eugene Grace (Bethlehem Steel). Several of the group continued their deliberations into the Roosevelt presidency as members of the Commerce Department's Business Advisory Council, the president's house capitalists. Corporate concerns included budget balance, credit expansion, forgiveness of foreign debts incurred by the Allies during World War I, reduced taxation, repeal of (or at a minimum clarification of) the antitrust laws, business self-regulation, and the stemming of pressures for unionization.[4]

Roosevelt's assurances of a balanced budget, Prohibition repeal, a beer tax, and subsequent passage of the National Industrial Recovery Act (NIRA) in June 1933, with its potential for corporate self-governance, appealed to the Du Ponts. According to Pierre, the NIRA offered an opportunity for different sections of industry to "work out their own ends under collective action." He now focused his quest for an economy administered by business luminaries through membership on the Business Advisory Council and the National Labor Board. This required, in his view, the mitigation of pressures for unionization of the nation's large industries.[5]

Since mass-production industries opposed negotiation with independent trade unions, conflicting interpretations of Section 7(a) of the National Industrial Recovery Act and consequent large-scale strikes unsettled the recovery process during FDR's first term in office. The National Labor Board (NLB), created in early August by executive order, was intended to "consider, adjust, and settle differences and controversies" between labor and management." The NLB consisted of three representatives each of labor and business, with one public member appointed by the president, Senator Robert Wagner of New York.

Fundamental issues dominated NLB proceedings. Would employers be required to deal exclusively with representatives elected by a majority vote of employees under Section 7(a); or could they deal separately with minority groups and individuals and thus divide their employees into distinct bargaining units? Would company unions consisting of employee representatives and their supervisors, termed employee representation or works councils, satisfy Section 7(a)'s language? Would NLB decisions carry weight in light of the board's reliance on the powers of suasion and public opinion?

The "Reading Formula" outlined NLB policy before Pierre's appointment to the board. In a contest between a large group of hosiery manufacturers—including H. W. Anthony Mills, Fashion-Made, and Berkshire Knitting Mills—and the American Federation of Full-Fashioned Hosiery Workers, the union won recognition as the result of majority vote conducted by secret ballot and was found to be entitled to a written contract on behalf of all employees. Yet, since the "Reading Formula" was created as an instrument of mediation, not arbitration, on the assumption of labor-business cooperation, the board had no legal authority to implement this precedent in subsequent cases and relied on an unsympathetic Justice Department for enforcement.[6]

It was not unusual for department heads in the administration to take positions counter to presidential policy, a situation Roosevelt tolerated. In this instance, General Hugh Johnson, chief administrator of the National Recovery Administration (NRA), and his deputy and NRA general counsel, Donald Richberg, scarcely sympathetic to organized labor, repudiated the Reading agreement. Nor did they concur with the NLB's finding for majority representation. At the same time, they regarded strikes as impeding recovery, as did Roosevelt.

Appointed to the National Labor Board in November 1933, Pierre du Pont sympathized with Johnson and Richberg, insisting on the constitutional legitimacy of minority rights in the workplace. This point of view reflected a major concern of employers at such industrial giants as DuPont, General Motors, General Electric, Westinghouse, United States Steel, and the dominant firms in the rubber tire and electrical industries, all of which faced a series of strikes for recognition launched by member unions of the American Federation of Labor under the aegis of Section 7(a). General Electric's Swope and Jersey Standard's Teagle, both powers in the Business Advisory Council, argued for the "right to manage." According to Swope, "business should remain free of governmental influence and control," meaning unions as well. Teagle insisted that employee representation, meaning company unions, was a bona fide form of collective bargaining.

Pierre, passionate on the subject, adopted what he believed to be a principled position. The DuPont firm contended that no employee-management antagonism existed in its widespread operations and that works councils, made up of equal representation of labor and management, could more effectively sort out differences and needs than the confrontational mechanism of a strike. Employees, Pierre contended, were not necessarily disposed toward a walkout called by union heads, and union officials were not accountable to the workers they purportedly represented. Indeed, like employers, unions should be required to incorporate and be financially accountable.[7]

Prior to passage of the Recovery Act, William Green, president of the American Federation of Labor, concurred with the DuPont executive's notion of business-labor harmony but on a substantially differing set of assumptions: that he could persuade industry's leadership to see the light regarding the desirability of unionization. Influenced by social Christianity, Green subscribed to the view that cooperation served as the keystone of a capitalist economy. He abhorred the strike as confrontational and potentially violent. Management, once open to conferring on the subject, would willingly share the benefits of industrialization with its workforce, for higher wages would build a consumption-based middle class instead of a proletariat. Like Pierre, he viewed the enactment of the National Industrial Recovery Act as an appropriate vehicle for his aspirations. Green was frustrated and ultimately deeply disappointed when business reactionaries challenged his rationale for Christian capitalism.

When the chief executives of Weirton Steel and Budd Manufacturing—sensing that the National Industrial Recovery Act would not meet a constitutional test—announced with impunity that they would not abide by the decisions of the NLB, the industrial recovery program was seriously undermined. Section 7(a)'s key phrase—"Employees shall have the right to organize and bargain collectively through representatives of their own choosing"—lost its original purpose, at least as labor saw it. This view was reinforced when Johnson and Richberg insisted that Section 7(a) did not empower a majority of employees in a plant or larger unit to nullify the right of minority groups or individuals to deal separately with employers.

A series of NLB decisions favoring majority rule in the Denver Tramway Case, then in Houde Engineering and Budd Manufacturing, carried little weight in the business community. When unions won the vote of overwhelming numbers of workers, it was not uncommon for employers—as in the instance of the appliance manufacturer Servel in Evansville, Indiana—to disregard the authority of the NLB. While Roosevelt signed executive orders seemingly supporting majority rule, Johnson and Richberg continued to interpret them otherwise. Roosevelt's willingness to allow proportional representation on works councils in the auto industry further clouded the matter and led Wagner to turn to the legislative process to assure the rights of labor. While a labor disputes bill introduced in 1934 met no success in the absence of presidential support, the following year, when FDR once again stayed on the sidelines, Wagner won passage of the National Labor Relations Act. The National Labor Relations Board, created under the law, consisted exclusively of public members with the power to subpoena and to enforce its decisions.[8]

It is interesting to note that while the new mass-production industries proved subject to the unionization movement by their employees, the DuPont firm felt no need to capitulate to such pressures. DuPont employees represented an array of skills and groupings ranging from scientists and technicians to the unskilled, scattered at sites across the nation, making organization difficult. A corporate policy of mutuality of interests between capital and labor, in tandem with a policy of generous wages and benefits, also differentiated chemical producers from industrial employers. Firms pressured by mass unionization such as General Electric, General Motors, and United States Steel sought labor peace in exchange for stability of output and profits. Many industrialists hostile to the New Deal program who bemoaned the policies of the "traitor to his class" were not about to take on a popular president who acquiesced in the mass union movement of the mid-1930s. For Pierre, opposition to the movement evidently was a matter of constitutional principle, namely the government invasion of legitimate business interests.[9]

Federal tolerance and encouragement of the movement for unionization; provision for an incipient welfare state; securities legislation; the Public Utilities Holding Company Act, which regulated tiers of control; creation of the Tennessee Valley Authority; heavy taxation of corporations; fiscal excess; and congressional delegation of authority to the State Department for treaties involving trade reciprocity, all offended the Du

Ponts' sense of property rights. No less grating was the realization that the State of Delaware, in reality the Du Ponts, contributed heavily to federal coffers, subsidizing impoverished southern and western states through federal revenue transfers. Challenging one of the most astute and powerful politicians in the nation's history, the Du Ponts turned their attention to founding the American Liberty League (ALL) in August 1934 and to support of the Republican Party.[10]

A complaint written by Pierre's brother-in-law R. R. M. ("Ruly") Carpenter served as the catalyst for the founding of the ALL. The DuPont executive remarked on the Roosevelt administration's "purchase" of voters through employment in the Civilian Conservation Corps and the Civil Works Administration at wages higher than those available in the private sector. As an example, he cited "five negroes" at his South Carolina plantation who had quit for easy government jobs. Why, he inquired, would a man of Roosevelt's education and birth "carry on a campaign of labor against capital, and a campaign to eliminate wealth?" Raskob suggested the organization of businessmen intended to protect society from "communistic elements" who would lead the people astray in opposition to a sound money policy, universal access to wealth, and the objectives of the business community.

Formed as a federation of property owners—including stockholders, labor, homeowners, farmers, and women's organizations—to protect the Constitution and property rights, the principal objectives of the Liberty League, organized by Raskob, were the ouster of the Roosevelt administration, reduction of the scope of federal authority, and lessening the tax burden on corporations and individuals of substance, on the ground that inordinate taxation under the Revenue Acts of 1935 and 1936 inhibited investment and recovery. Founders included Pierre, Irénée, and Lammot du Pont; the former Democratic Party presidential candidates Alfred E. Smith and John W. Davis; Nathan Miller, who defeated Smith in the 1920 gubernatorial contest, now a Wall Street attorney; and Sewell Avery of Montgomery Ward. Jouett Shouse, former executive director of the Democratic National Committee and a principal in the effort to block Roosevelt's 1932 presidential aspirations at Chicago, was employed as the ALL president. Its Washington headquarters matched those of the Republican and Democratic National Committees in staff and funding.

A series of Liberty League publications hammered away at the Roosevelt program, including lawmaking by executive order and congressional delegation of its powers to the executive branch. Some 3.5 million copies of eighty-five pamphlets, supplemented by press releases, bulletins, and speakers, criticized government control of industry and agriculture, an inflationary monetary policy, a confiscatory tax system, and the introduction of planning. Noting "similarities to European dictatorships," the organization's publications insisted on "a return to sound fiscal principles consistent with the Constitution."

The Du Ponts and the ALL funded anti–New Deal books by Roosevelt's former monetary adviser James Warburg, who broke with the administration on its failure to remain on the gold standard, and his former budget director Lewis Douglas, who challenged New Deal expenditure. A National Lawyers Committee pursued New Deal legislation in the courts. Led by Raoul Desvernine, the group asserted the unconstitutionality of the Roosevelt program on the ground that the general welfare clause did not grant Congress "distinct and substantive power to provide for the general welfare," helping to undermine compliance with controversial New Deal legislation.[11]

Since the ALL agenda replicated the pronouncements of the National Association of Manufacturers, the most surprising feature of its effort was its inability to attract substantial support from the business community beyond Delaware, Pennsylvania, a handful of downtown Manhattan corporate attorneys, Detroit auto magnates, and the reactionary Chicago group of bankers and processors that bitterly opposed legislation for heightened commodity prices and abandonment of gold. Frustrated by his inability to reach funding goals, Raskob relied on his own bank account and the Du Ponts to meet the league's unfulfilled financial obligations.

A West Coast trip by Raskob, Irénée du Pont, and E. F. Hutton, a member of the finance committee, proved relatively unproductive. Consumer-related industries shied away from the Wilmington reactionaries. General Motors' Alfred P. Sloan originally insisted on keeping a low profile and then exited the cause in 1936, declaring that "politics and business do not mix." And the nabobs of Wall Street, practiced in the art of political survival in turbulent times, by and large kept their distance.[12]

The Du Ponts mustered support largely among die-hard opponents of social and economic change such as the Crusaders, tied to H. J. Heinz and Herbert Hoover; Raymond Pitcairn's Sentinels of the Republic; and the Jeffersonian Democrats. Unlike Roosevelt's domicile at Hyde Park, which was surrounded by rural poverty, the Brandywine estates and Delaware, virtually Du Pont fiefdoms, hardly opened the family to the realities of American life. This was evidenced by the infamous Liberty League dinner held at Washington's Mayflower hotel on January 25, 1936, marked by a parade of chauffeured men of substance in their evening attire. The event featured a lavish dinner and a succession of speakers who lectured Roosevelt on the abandonment of the 1932 party platform, which stressed economy and states' rights. Among the luminaries in attendance were James Warburg, Dean Acheson, and Lewis Douglas, the Chase bank's Winthrop Aldrich, Eugene Meyer, publisher of the *Washington Post,* Raskob, a dozen Du Ponts, and a clutch of former senators, congressmen, and government officials.

Now an unhappy warrior, Alfred E. Smith won deafening applause by invoking the Constitution and states' rights while asserting that Roosevelt had fomented class antagonism. "There can be only one capital," he intoned, "Washington or Moscow." Smith pointed to the 1932 platform's pledge to reduce government expenditure and bureaucracy and contain old-age and unemployment insurance under the umbrella of the states.

Smith's threat to take a walk proved to be meaningless. Having emerged from the poverty of immigrant newcomers, he had risen to the state's highest office. Subsequently Smith gravitated to a lavish lifestyle as president of the corporation that built the Empire State Building, thanks to his friendship with Raskob. Both had lost touch with their humble roots. Smith's supporters—self-styled Jeffersonian Democrats, former diplomats, and legislators who opposed institutional change—enjoyed virtually no following. The Mayflower hotel gathering was ridiculed in Congress and the press. Nevertheless, the Du Ponts, Raskob, and the Pew family of Pennsylvania (Sun Oil Co.), viewing the GOP as they would a corporate shell, served as the Republican Party's principal financiers.[13]

From the inception of the Liberty League, J. Howard Pew, Sun Oil Co.'s president, sat on its executive committee, became a major contributor, and pressed for an uncompromising anti–New Deal stance. The league, he advocated, should attack price fixing and government intrusion into the sanctity of private property. Pew promoted the sales tax as the principal source of revenue for the states and insisted on free competition in the marketplace, opposing both private and public monopoly. J. Howard and Joseph Pew inherited their views from a fearless and successful contest waged by their father with one of the nation's foremost monopolies, the Standard Oil Company. Sun Oil survived as an astute competitor in the marketplace, secured by a better-quality grade of (unleaded) gasoline, protected sources of product and transport, and high-grade refinery products. Bitter opponents of the Roosevelt administration, the Pews reflected the antistatist views of a successful, highly efficient family firm in a business dominated by majors administered by bureaucratic hierarchies. The Roosevelt presidency, in their view, heralded "the installation of a Russian order" in place of the business environment in which the Pew family had excelled.

Like the Du Ponts, the Pews were welfare capitalists, offering a stock purchase plan and life insurance through payroll deductions to "their men." While the Sun Oil firm was paternalistic and anti-union, it maintained employment and profitability in the face of the Great Depression, enjoyed steady growth, and introduced new technologies. Unions, the Pews held, intruded on their management. Purchase and control of publications such as the *Farm Journal* and Pew sponsorship of Sun Oil's *Three Star Extra,* broadcast nationally by the radio voice of Lowell Thomas, facilitated the dissemination of their antistatist views.

During the 1936 presidential contest, the Pews served as substantial benefactors of the Republican National Committee, including its chairman, John D. M. Hamilton, a dapper attorney and a former Speaker of the Kansas House of Representatives. A bitter opponent of the New Deal reforms, Hamilton was tied to the eastern Old Guard, and as a Pew amanuensis, campaigned independently of Landon. Characteristically, when the Democrats withdrew their candidates in deference to Minnesota's Farmer-Labor Party, the GOP chairman situated the decision "in line with President Roosevelt's quest for the support of Communists and other left wingers." Landon, it should be noted, ascribed the severity of his loss in part to Hamilton's antireform campaign speeches.[14]

Following the 1936 debacle, Hamilton remained party chairman while the Pews continued to finance the Republican National Committee. Yet it soon became evident that the congressional remnant, however small and weakened in numbers, would not defer to corporate outsiders, moneyed or not, on legislative strategy in an effort to checkmate the New Deal program. To Hamilton's consternation, when the Supreme Court crisis broke in the winter and spring of 1936–37, Charles McNary, the Senate minority leader; Idaho's William Borah; and Michigan's Arthur Vandenberg determined that Republicans would defer to conservative Democrats in the

Senate. When southern Democrats, distressed by much of the New Deal, perceived a threat to the racial status quo by the addition of liberal justices, it was agreed on both sides of the aisle that they would lead the opposition to FDR's attempt to enlarge the Court. Vandenberg so informed a dismayed party chairman, whose role was limited to financing the expenses of witnesses, usually Democrats, who testified against the Roosevelt proposal before the Senate Committee on the Judiciary.[15]

Prior to the 1938 congressional elections, Hamilton proposed a formal alliance of conservative Democrats and Republicans under the GOP banner, "to preserve the traditional form of the American government against the encroaching hand of those who would Russianize and Hitlerize our country." The proposal failed to gain traction. Southern politicians remained in the Democratic fold in order to retain seniority control of committee chairmanships.[16]

The forging of the Republican Party antistatist consensus in the 1930s and aspirations for a return to majority status rested on a difficult proposition: melding of corporate domination of the party structure featuring opposition to industrial unionism and midwestern emphasis on agrarian interests that dominated congressional policy making. Both groups, however, concurred on limitation of the powers of the central government. Checkmating of a Second New Deal rested on a cross-party coalition with southern Democrats. As Clifford Hope predicted, in time the nation's midsection would crawl out from under the tent of the New Deal party, which was based in the unions and the cities. At the same time, sit-down strikes did not sit well with the middle class, which viewed them as illegal seizures of private property. Republicans publicized abuses of the Hopkins relief program, charging the purchase of votes in 1936. They challenged the National Labor Relations Board as unfairly dominated by pro-labor membership.[17] Still, the party lacked a leader, and its legislative remnant hailed from safe districts, "tight little islands of thought . . . simply out of step with the thinking of the rank and file American voter."[18]

Until the 1938 congressional campaign reversed the party's fortunes, congressional leadership rested on the shoulders of McNary, Borah, and Vandenberg. McNary, the GOP Senate leader, a mild-mannered conciliator by nature, served as a bridge between the Progressives and the remnant of the Old Guard. Given his representation of Oregon and, in effect, the Pacific Northwest, McNary supported George W. Norris's crusade for federal ownership of waterpower potential in the nation's major river valleys, the Tennessee, Colorado, and Columbia. Generally, he had been since the 1920s a proponent of agricultural relief and old-age pensions and had voted for much of Roosevelt's domestic program. They parted ways on the issue of increasing the Court's membership and FDR's tolerance of the sit-down strikes of 1937.

In the early years of his Senate service, Idaho's William Borah, "the spearless warrior," as he was described by a biographer, had sponsored legislation for establishment of a federal labor department and supported the income tax amendment. The latter half of his public service was devoted principally to insulating the United States from Europe's affairs—opposition to ratification of the Versailles Treaty and membership in the League of Nations and the World Court, and even fierce opposition to reduction of the Allied war debts to United States. Generally, Borah in these later years had the reputation of a bull in a china shop.[19]

Of the three, Vandenberg alone was regarded as a potential leader at the national level. His involvement in Republican Party politics at the state level began while he was editor of the *Grand Rapids (Mich.) Herald*. Appointed to the Senate in 1928 by Michigan's governor to fill a vacancy, he was elected to a full term in 1934 on a platform largely supportive of the New Deal program. Vandenberg established his bona fides as a diligent legislator especially knowledgeable in banking and credit problems. As early as 1931, he pressed the Federal Reserve and the Hoover administration for credit expansion in order to assist troubled small-town banks and owners of home and farm mortgages. In 1933, collaborating with Virginia's conservative Democrat Carter Glass, the Michigan senator championed creation of the Federal Deposit Insurance Act, one of the major pieces of legislation passed by the Hundred Days Congress. Subsequently, he voted for securities regulation, payment of prevailing wages on public-works projects, and the Social Security Act.[20]

With the 1935–36 recovery, Vandenberg's support for early New Deal legislation gave way to opposition, like other GOP centrists who reversed course in the hope of a turnaround in party fortunes: Landon, McNary, and Michigan's James Couzens in the Senate; Hope and Everett McKinley Dirksen in the House. Vandenberg deplored expanded budget deficits, especially for the public-works and relief programs led by Harry Hopkins. Like Bernard Baruch, he preferred instead federal bonding of public works to be paid off annually over ten years. He condemned Cordell Hull's trade agreements program, advocating instead tariff protection for local producers. He insisted on decentralization of social and economic programs and, unlike McNary, opposed construction of public-power projects unless sustained by income from flood control. He opted for state administration of relief and other social programs. During and after the 1936 debacle, Vandenberg urged a tie-up with the Jeffersonian Democrats, effected when Republicans and southern Democrats formed a conservative coalition in order to check the Roosevelt program.[21]

Considering Vandenberg's reputation for intelligence, diligence, and a grasp of the credit crisis that led to the Great Depression, as well as his opposition to United States involvement in Europe's affairs, why then his failure to win the party's presidential nomination? Part of the problem was the floridity of his speech and prose: he was regarded by his peers as a doctrinaire windbag. The Senate Democratic leader Joe Robinson quipped that in the event of Vandenberg's nomination as GOP standard-bearer in 1936, "We would have vacuity, vacillation and Vandenberg."

Vandenberg did vacillate on substantive issues. He favored unionization of labor but opposed the National Labor Relations Act of 1935 on the ground that it put government in a position of fostering unionization and the closed shop. He supported work relief on a small scale but opposed the massive, $5 billion congressional authorization made in 1935 for creation of the Works Progress Administration, on the grounds of fiscal profligacy and congressional delegation of power to the presidency. While he viewed himself as a Hamiltonian and a Theodore Roosevelt Progressive, he was a self-described nineteenth-century "Constitutionalist" who supported Supreme Court decisions in 1935–36 that markedly curbed federal regulation of business.

This is not to suggest that Vandenberg's critique of the New Deal's antibusiness tendencies was entirely off the mark. Roosevelt's growing hubris exhibited in the Supreme Court crisis, the questionable economics behind burdensome corporate and estate taxes levied in the 1935 and 1936 revenue acts, and passage of the crippling Public Utilities Holding Company Act, outdated by reforms in private utilities structures and operations, afforded a wedge for the Republican Party. The subsequent tie with southern Democrats served as a legislative counterweight to the New Deal. But the GOP remained bereft of strong national leadership and lacked a broad program that addressed the massive technological unemployment and underconsumption that defined the 1930s.

Despite the wedge issues provided by FDR, the Republicans in the

1930s offered little beyond curbing state power and a return to a devastating deflationary monetary policy that exacerbated the depths of the Great Depression. The 1936 election result indicated the need for a program relevant to current conditions other than advocacy of classical principles and decentralism that no longer fitted economic interdependence at the national and international levels.[22]

D URING THE 1930s, the Republican Party divided between anti-interventionists and internationalists on America's proper role in world affairs and, increasingly, on the specific issue of Hitler's ambitions—what they were and what, if anything, should be done about them. In their depiction of these events, the so-called "court historians" considered the Second World War as fundamentally a contest between good and evil.

Revisionists challenged the liberal internationalist assessment of the conflict, treating United States involvement in the war as a continuation of American imperialism's chronic quest for markets. Others argued that, by pressuring the Western democracies to abandon appeasement and pledging material aid to the Allies, Roosevelt transformed unrelated regional conflicts in Europe and the Far East into a worldwide conflict and subsequently provoked Germany and Japan in order to gain a commanding seat at the peace table. In reality, the postwar reconstruction of Europe's industry facilitated modernization and its ability to compete with the United States. Nor did America require a global conflict to achieve industrial preeminence as measured by productivity and output. Economic primacy had been accomplished decades earlier.

It is helpful to observe that since the commencement of the industrial era, a dominant economic power has maintained international economic stability. By the middle of the nineteenth century, this role fell to Great Britain by dint of its innovative facilities for banking, shipping, insurance, and finance. While central bankers believed that gold assured currency stability, gold in fact fluctuated in value, promoted instability, and worse still, prompted a deflationary environment in depression. That the world economy functioned well was actually due to central bank cooperation and a sterling standard that afforded convertibility of other currencies to pound sterling or gold in London. In addition, British investment of profits abroad, including important contributions to United States infrastructure development, afforded income for London; and imported raw materials for local manufacture mitigated the imbalances that would have resulted from a one-way flow of capital.

Britain's leading manufacturing position began to erode relative to that of the United States toward the close of the nineteenth century. Commitment to older industries, failure to absorb and apply new technologies, sclerotic management, an outdated educational system, and American protection of local producers opened England to competition. The United States' lead over all advanced economies is explained by its availability of natural resources, advantages of scale, the link between universities and business, research and development, cheap land, large-scale immigration, and high fertility rates. Britain's financial situation deteriorated seriously with the costs associated with imperialism, massive expenditure prior to and during the First World War compelling liquidation of its overseas investment position, substantial borrowing on Wall Street, and subsequent loss of market share abroad to the United States, Germany, and Japan.

American labor productivity exceeded that of England even before the Great War. By 1913, the United States manufacturing output stood at over one-third of the world's total, Britain's at 17 percent. On the eve of the Second World War, Britain's share of manufacturing output on a worldwide basis fell to 9 percent while that of the United States remained at 36 percent and Germany's reached 15.7 percent.

Great Britain's inability to retain its historic position in finance led to its abandonment of gold and the substantial devaluation of the pound sterling in 1931. The institution of the equalization account designed to maintain a depreciated sterling at the expense of the gold-standard currencies including the dollar, creation of a closed sterling trading system by Chancellor of the Exchequer Neville Chamberlain in 1932, and the introduction of protectionist legislation designed to assure access to cheap raw materials and captive markets in the British Empire marked the end of England's historic maintenance of open markets as basic to economic advance. Roosevelt responded by securing gold devaluation and dollar depreciation from the Congress in January 1934. Regional protectionism and currency warfare exacerbated the Great Depression, resulting in massive unemployment and diminished living standards.

In this situation, the economist Charles Kindleberger observed: "The international economic and monetary system required leadership from a nation that had internalized a system of rules and standards of conduct that could be applied to other nations. Such a leadership role required acceptance of redundant commodities, export of investment capital, and discounting of paper. Britain performed this role in the century after 1813; the United States in the period after the Second World War." The world depression, and with it international economic warfare, followed from Britain's inability to underwrite the system and the United States' unwillingness to assume that responsibility.

On the continent of Europe, the unsuccessful response of German chancellor Heinrich Brüning to the Great Depression—namely, an austerity policy that induced massive unemployment, general deflation, and shrunken commodity prices for agriculture—opened the way for Adolf Hitler's appointment to that post in January 1933. The Führer's territorial ambitions in eastern Europe in pursuit of lebensraum and colonies in order to access cheap raw materials, and his determined pursuit of rearmament led to renewed tension in Europe.

While the Royal Navy was viewed as a roadblock to German overseas ambitions, Great Britain was in no position to check German dominion over continental Europe. Indeed, in Hitler's *Zweites Buch,* the sequel to *Mein Kampf* that remained unpublished during his lifetime, Hitler judged correctly that "a new force," namely the United States, threatened the existing balance of power. Hitler's strategy depended upon swift conquests in Europe; the success of isolationist pressures in the United States; and diversion of the United States to conflict in the Far East with Japan. Viewed in this context, the United States could either accept temporary economic cooperation with a German regime in control of Europe's manufacturing capacity while waiting for a final contest for control of the Western Hemisphere, or it could render assistance to Britain and France in order to frustrate Hitler's ambitions. This was the choice faced by Roosevelt and those who shaped Republican foreign policy.[1]

Despite the telegraphing of Nazi Germany's expansionist ambition by its march out of the Geneva Disarmament Conference and the League of Nations in October 1933, most Western diplomats were persuaded that Hitler's incessant demands were negotiable, even reasonable. Among the dissenters were Great Britain's Sir Robert Vansittart and Lord Lothian. Vansittart, a principal in Britain's foreign policy elite and an influential member of the prime minister's office, headed the American Department

(1924–28) and served subsequently as permanent undersecretary at the Foreign Office in the years 1930–37.

Vansittart subscribed to the concept of balance of power in Europe and advocated willingness to project the use of force where negotiation proved ineffective. As early as 1934, he anticipated German aggression initially toward Poland, followed by the Low Countries and France, and ultimately toward England. He reasoned that Japan would strike against British imperial interests in the Far East once England had been tied down militarily in Europe.

When State Department undersecretary William Phillips complained in September 1934 about lack of cooperation on the part of London, Vansittart countered that the United States had not been a reliable partner in international affairs despite Britain's conciliatory gestures. He was not entirely incorrect. According to Vansittart, central to the problem of unsatisfactory relations between the two nations was the sheer stupidity and self-righteousness of Congress and the American public. The United States, he claimed, conceived of the League of Nations and then committed infanticide; it convinced Britain to concede naval parity at the Washington Conference and then refused to compromise on the onerous debt obligations that came out of World War I. More recently, Roosevelt encouraged the preparations for the World Monetary and Economic Conference and then proceeded to wreck it.

Vansittart professed continued regard for the American people. "But in ageing I have lost my wind for running after the United States government. It is a futile paper chase." Indeed, "the United States government would not be a safe companion for tiger-shooting; and I for one would like a higher howdah if not a bigger and better elephant." Less metaphorically, Vansittart pointed to the "German danger" and England's inability to face warfare simultaneously in Europe and the Far East, noting the fact that Britain refused to renew its earlier alliance with Japan under pressure from the United States.

At the White House, Lord Lothian (Philip Kerr), a Liberal peer who had served as Lloyd George's private secretary at the Paris Peace Conference, in a tête-à-tête with Roosevelt raised the issue of Britain's inability to both contain Japanese expansionism in Asia and maintain a strong naval presence in the Atlantic. Britain required a concrete understanding with America or alternatively with Japan as it had done in 1904 in response to Germany's naval building program. In Lothian's words, England was "in the front line in Europe and she would not by herself be in the front line in the Far East also." As Roosevelt explained, according to Lothian, he could not make a firm commitment. Rather, if Japan broke the parities set in the Washington Naval Treaty, he would ask Congress for expanded U.S. naval construction. While the United States remained supportive of Great Britain, cooperation "would have to rest on the fundamental identity of their interests and ideals."[2]

The fundamental identity of interests and ideals, however, proved too elusive a proposition. As early as September 1934, Neville Chamberlain recorded in a memorandum that Britain could not afford to protect India, Hong Kong, and its other Far Eastern interests against Japanese expansionism in view of Roosevelt's policy of disengagement and the threat of a "fully armed and organized" Germany. The potential of war with the Hitler regime required negotiation with Japan of a nonaggression pact, which he predicated on Japan's fear of Soviet ambitions in the Far East. As for the United States, Britain could expect nothing. "When we have laid our cards on the table they shake their heads sadly and explain their regretful conviction that Congress will have nothing to do with us unless we can make an offer [in connection with the war debts] that will suit them better. Congress (and in particular the Senate) are the Mr. Jorkins [Scrooge] of American representatives." In observations further reminiscent of Dickens, British diplomats characterized Congress as often incapacitated by shallow provincials.

Unable to effect a renewal of its earlier entente with Japan or to accomplish that end with Roosevelt, who catered to domestic pressures for isolation, Britain resorted to a policy of appeasement by accepting Reichsbank president Hjalmar Schacht's neomercantilist program for a revived Germany. This development commenced with arrangements wherein Britain agreed to a partial settlement of German debts to the exclusion of other creditors as well as to bilateral trade and currency agreements. The result was much-needed hard currency for the Reich and further distancing of Great Britain from the United States. In the process, England served as Germany's main export market and its principal source of raw materials, a trade financed by London banks. The Anglo-German naval agreement of 1935 marked another critical step in accommodation of the Hitler regime, indicating England's acceptance of German naval rearmament.[3]

Unlike Great Britain, where diplomacy was shaped by a civil service elite, a congeries of powerful and diverse sectional interests determined

United States foreign policy. In the early 1930s, the president hardly enjoyed the freedom in foreign relations suggested by the term "imperial
presidency." Nor was the United States an imperial power. Defeat by
Congress of United States membership in the League of Nations; refusal
of the legislative branch to consider war-debts forgiveness; then rejection
by the Senate of membership by the United States in the International
Court of Justice in 1935 suggested, as British diplomats discerned, that
restraints in foreign affairs imposed by Congress on the chief executive
were substantial.

Isolationism was not restricted to members of the Congress. Eastern
intellectuals, including university faculty and their students, frequently
espoused pacifism or, at the least, avoidance of Old World conflicts. Western agrarians and the populace of small towns descended from German,
German-Russian, and Scandinavian immigrants also espoused pacifist
beliefs, in this instance for religious and ethnic reasons. Irish Americans
and Italian Americans in New England were not favorably disposed toward the British Empire or, for that matter, toward France.

Distaste for Europe's perennial bloodbaths was reinforced by publications such as *Fortune*'s "Arms and the Men: A Primer on Europe's Armament Makers" and Robert Wohlforth's "Armament Profiteers: 1934,"
which appeared in the *Nation*. *Merchants of Death*, by Helmuth Engel-
brecht and Frank Hanighen, and Walter Millis's *Road to War,* which attributed American involvement to a domestic recession and exaggerated
Allied propaganda and economic ties to England and France, were best
sellers marketed by the popular Book-of-the-Month Club. Peace groups
pressed the Senate for neutrality legislation in these years, among them
the Federal Council of Churches, the Women's International League for
Peace and Freedom, the National Council for the Prevention of War,
and the National Peace Council, a confederation of twenty-eight peace
groups.

Creation of the Senate Special Committee on Investigation of the
Munitions Industry, a product of the Nye-Vandenberg resolution of
March 12, 1934, reflected these sentiments. The two sponsors intended to
prove that profiteering munitions makers maneuvered the United States
into involvement in World War I. North Dakota's Gerald Nye, a man of
limited education who possessed a powerful sense of mission and self-
importance, represented a constituency made up of wheat farmers who
had emigrated from Germany and resented perceived exploitation by

eastern bankers and urban industrialists. A one-time newspaper editor and a believer in Nordic superiority, Nye was convinced that the United States had been lured into war by munitions makers and Wall Street financiers and that farmers never benefited from that conflict. In fact, the war's end marked the onset of collapsed farm prices and agrarian depression. Vandenberg, who represented a mixed industrial and farming constituency, was concerned principally with the question of excessive profits in wartime.

Roosevelt encouraged the Nye-Vandenberg investigation, which began in 1934 and ended in early 1936 and in the process lost control of the neutrality issue until the outbreak of war in Europe. Even within his entourage there was considerable opposition to involvement in Europe. Cordell Hull's State Department relied on the views of Charles Warren, an international lawyer, assistant attorney-general in the Wilson administration, and a prominent legal historian. In a paper published in *Foreign Affairs* and subsequently elaborated for the administration, Warren contended that traditional neutral rights invoked by the United States as a trading nation had involved Americans in World War I. Avoidance of participation in another major conflict necessitated a strict set of policies, including adherence to the trading regime of all belligerents, a ban on loans to warring parties, and a warning to American citizens that they traveled on the vessels of belligerents at their own risk. For all practical purposes, this would ban sale of arms to belligerents in order to stay out of war, the rationale behind Roosevelt's 1936 campaign address at Chautauqua, New York: "I have seen war. . . . I hate war."

Nye found widespread popular support for his neutrality crusade. W. T. Stone of the Foreign Policy Association and former secretary of state Frank B. Kellogg documented the wartime activities of munitions makers for the committee hearings. Father Charles Coughlin offered financial support when the Senate discontinued funding of the committee in January 1936. Nye declined. A principal speaker at a Madison Square Garden rally originated by the American Friends Service Committee and sponsored by the Emergency Peace Campaign in October 1936, Nye was joined by representatives of synagogues, churches, trade unions, and youth groups. The gathering constituted part of a mobilization involving several hundred such meetings across the nation. Speakers in New York City included Oswald Garrison Villard, former publisher of the *Nation,* Rabbi Stephen Wise, Dr. Frank Kingdon, Norman Thomas, and Joseph

Lash. A chorus of 150 was provided by the International Ladies Garment Workers Union.

Neutrality legislation of the 1930s, shaped by western anti-elitist, anti–Wall Street, anti–big business Progressive Republicans, projected a divorce of the United States from Europe's perennial conflicts. The Johnson Act in April 1934 proscribed lending to America's wartime debtors. A series of laws ensued designed to strip the Roosevelt administration of the capacity to involve the United States in a conflict outside the Western Hemisphere. Nye and the isolationists viewed the presidency itself as a force for war, a position taken subsequently by revisionist chroniclers.[4]

A collateral issue critically impacted international relations and the possibilities for peace or war: shifting patterns of international trade threatened its strangulation. The Smoot-Hawley Tariff, then Neville Chamberlain's dismantling of Britain's nineteenth-century free-trade regime, along with a host of widely utilized devices such as regional agreements, quotas, subsidies, and import and currency controls, resulted in limited access to strategic resources elsewhere and a shortage of hard currencies and gold. Hjalmar Schacht, head of the Reichsbank, followed suit for Germany, drafting a program based on self-sufficiency, bartering, and currency manipulation designed to facilitate German rearmament. Since this trade environment crippled exports by American commodities producers, Roosevelt's trade adviser and head of the Export-Import Bank, George Peek, proposed a bartering system that resembled Schacht's autarchic, corporatist economy and projected a permanent international regime based on mercantilist principles that originated in the depression environment. These, he believed, would necessarily continue with economic recovery.

Cordell Hull abhorred Peek's designs, believing that the march to self-sufficiency served as the principal cause of the Depression and fostered international tensions in Europe. Indeed, world trade volume declined by 70 percent between 1929 and 1933, United States exports by 52 percent. The solution, Hull believed with a passion, lay in unconditional most-favored-nation treatment to all and the benefits of lowered tariffs negotiated with one country extended to those nations that reciprocated, or an open trading system. Such agreements would be negotiated in the executive branch to circumvent the logrolling characteristic of tariffs formulated in the Congress to meet local interests.

Initially, Roosevelt proved reluctant to resolve the internecine dispute.

Peek, determined to force Roosevelt's hand, proposed a Foreign Trade Board and negotiated an agreement for the export of surplus raw cotton to textile producers in Germany. This arrangement proposed payment by Germany of 25 percent in dollars and 75 percent in Reichmarks, which would be used for the purchase of German goods. When Roosevelt demurred because of opposition by the Interdepartmental Trade Agreements Committee, Peek resigned his post as head of the Export-Import Bank and returned to the Republican fold, where he found considerable support.[5]

Peek, who later identified with the America First Committee, found a powerful senatorial ally in Vandenberg. The senator from Michigan advanced the proposition that national self-sufficiency was a permanent feature of the international landscape and, further, that Peek's program for accommodation to this reality by bartering raw materials for manufactures not produced in the United States made sense. From this vantage point, Hull's multilateral trade agreements program undermined the price structure of farm, factory, and office, as well as the wages of labor. Vandenberg also objected to delegation of the Senate's role in the negotiation of trade treaties to the executive branch as an abrogation of the Constitution and an unwarranted expansion of executive power, a mainstay of general Republican opposition to the Roosevelt administration.

When Maryland's Senator Millard Tydings, a Democrat, challenged the doctrine of self-sufficiency, Vandenberg countered that recapturing American prosperity through increased foreign trade was an illusion: "The old trade does not and probably will not again exist." Would Vandenberg favor a high-tariff system, Tydings pressed? According to Vandenberg, multilateral tariff agreements would open American markets to foreign competition. The United States required stiffer, not less, protection. It is interesting to note Vandenberg's failure to acknowledge that the Peek program, based on the War Industries Board structure, required a regulatory regime resembling Germany's state-managed economy.[6]

Following Landon's 1936 election defeat, Vandenberg emerged as a potential standard-bearer in the ensuing presidential contest. Yet his expectations for the future proved naïve and unhelpful to such a candidacy. Vandenberg projected a world of limited resources and closed economies at a low-level living standard. In the 1937 Neutrality Act debate, he argued that a trade embargo and prohibition of loans to all belligerents, or taking the profits out of war, could keep the United States out of another conflict. Such a position assumed that in a European arms race, Americans impacted by the Great Depression would prove willing to forego the possibility of reemployment, a doubtful proposition.

Outbreak of war in Europe in September 1939 led Roosevelt to seek revision of the 1937 Neutrality Act in order to facilitate shipment of supplies based on the principle of "cash-and-carry." Isolationists, including Republicans Nye, Vandenberg, and Borah, joined by Democrats Burton Wheeler (Montana), Homer Bone (Washington), and Bennett Champ Clark (Missouri), attempted unsuccessfully to limit the discretionary power of the presidency in the application of cash-and-carry provisions in the event of conflict. Proposed by Bernard Baruch, cash-and-carry permitted foreigners to purchase materiel including arms at their point of sale in the United States and transport such goods in their own ships. Presumably all comers were welcome; in reality, Great Britain would be the beneficiary. According to Vandenberg, "We are either all the way in or all the way out." "Chaining Mars with Rubber Bands," observed the *Literary Digest,* in an astute assessment of the attempt to keep America out of another war.[7]

While isolationists dominated both parties, constituted a majority in the Congress, and met with scant resistance by Roosevelt, who yielded to public opinion until 1939, an internationalist elite pressed for greater United States participation in world affairs. It was simply unrealistic to assume that the world's leading economy, potentially the world's dominant trading, financial, and military power, could insulate itself from international tensions. Anti-interventionism, isolationism, protectionism, unilateralism, however parsed, was a puerile exercise. The United States would be dragged into worldwide conflict as a consequence of its trade and investments and would necessarily assume a major role in shaping the global economy in the second half of the twentieth century.[8]

As early as 1934, Allen Dulles challenged isolation as a national policy: "We are inextricably tied in to world affairs." Dulles disputed the Nye-Vandenberg-Millis thesis concerning the basis for American involvement in World War I as well as the possibilities for disengagement by avoiding munitions exports. Broader considerations than trade and finance, especially the belief that German victory endangered the United States, led to United States involvement in the Great War. In the current situation, Dulles proposed cooperating with other major powers in order to check the ambitions of aggressor nations by means of an embargo.[9]

In light of his credentials, it was natural that Henry Stimson should emerge as a major spokesman for more substantial assumption of international responsibility. William Howard Taft's secretary of war and Herbert Hoover's secretary of state had been shaped by the views of Elihu Root and Theodore Roosevelt. Anchored in the law, Stimson, with Japan's invasion of Manchuria and creation of the puppet state of Manchukuo, proposed the doctrine of nonrecognition based on the Kellogg Pact and the Nine-Power Treaty. He supported passage of the Hull trade agreements legislation and regarded the doctrine of national self-sufficiency as untenable in the modern era. Clearly devoid of political ambitions—some 95 percent of Americans opposed involvement in another European conflagration—Stimson freely expressed opinions that likely echoed Roosevelt's private concerns about the rise of fascism in Europe. The former secretary of state was convinced of the inevitability of a second world war in light of Hitler's remilitarization of the Rhineland in 1936, the Spanish Civil War, and Germany's annexation of Austria (1938) and Czechoslovakia (1938–39).[10]

Stimson initially presented the case for collective action against an aggressor in a letter to the *New York Times* in reaction to Mussolini's invasion of Ethiopia. Subsequently he questioned the workability of neutrality in a modern, interdependent world: "Every war has become a potential world war." In the event, the traditional doctrine of neutrality had never meant isolation. Neutral nations had always traded with belligerents, and inevitably such trade meant involvement in warfare. There remained only one way to avoid American involvement in a worldwide conflict, namely cooperation with international efforts to prevent conflict.[11]

Between 1937 and 1939, Stimson reiterated these themes in reaction to Japanese aggression in China, criticizing particularly the supply of raw materials to Japan by Great Britain and the United States, principally petroleum and scrap iron. Neutrality legislation, he pressed, represented a policy of "moral drift" and would make even more certain involvement in a world war. By March 1939, he recognized the likelihood of an attack on Britain and France by Germany, with Italy cooperating, leaving Britain exposed to an attack in the Pacific by the Japanese. Such a development would call for "common action of the naval power of the three large democracies, including the United States." Given these circumstances, it was unwise, he added, to circumscribe the authority of the presidency, considering the chief executive's constitutional duties in the sphere of foreign affairs.

When Idaho's William E. Borah called for retention of the 1937 Neutrality Act after Hitler's invasion of Poland and the French and British declaration of war, Stimson endorsed Roosevelt's request for revision by Congress: The best chance for the United States to stay out of the European conflict was repeal of neutrality legislation, since it played into the hands of aggressor nations. International law and historical tradition, he pointed out, accommodated sale of arms to the victims of aggression. Subsequently, following the fall of France, the former secretary of state proposed compulsory military training.[12]

Conflict in Europe led Roosevelt to offer Stimson a reprise of his prior service as war secretary. Self-contained, unconcerned about opposition to his views by Vandenberg, Borah, and Republican isolationists, the one-time cavalry officer accepted at age seventy-three. A number of GOP senators balked at the nomination since it signaled Roosevelt's creation of a wartime cabinet. After service in two Republican administrations, Stimson was read out of the Republican Party, initially by the national committee in June 1940 as it gathered in Philadelphia to nominate a candidate for the presidency, then by Republican isolationists in the Senate.

According to national chairman John D. M. Hamilton, neither Stimson nor Frank Knox, who was offered the post of navy secretary upon entering the Roosevelt cabinet, was entitled to speak as a Republican. During the course of the Senate vote that confirmed Stimson's nomination (56–28), Vandenberg asserted that Stimson's views would take America into war. Robert Taft, elected to that body in 1938, joined the debate on the side of the isolationists. Interventionists, Taft enjoined, intended to educate Americans to a war policy that would embroil the nation in unending conflict and culminate in a totalitarian state like that of Germany. America's boundaries, he maintained, were limited to the Atlantic and Pacific Oceans and did not extend to the English Channel.

The GOP divided almost equally in the Senate vote on the nomination, ten voting in the affirmative, a dozen opposed. Opponents of Stimson's nomination cited a recent address in which he advocated naval convoying of U.S. vessels carrying munitions to the Allies and opening of U.S. facilities to the British fleet. Stimson's detractors were not incorrect: his was distinctly a minority viewpoint in the party, and his views, when executed, projected the United States into the European conflict. Having failed to persuade the president-elect toward international cooperation with Great Britain in the 1932–33 interregnum, Hoover's secretary of state served as point man for Roosevelt's interventionist ambitions.[13]

Relatively few Republican internationalists served in the Senate during the years preceding Pearl Harbor, notably Vermont's Warren Austin. Stimson's audience in these years was limited to those outside the party structure: eastern internationalists such as Thomas Lamont and Russell Leffingwell at Morgan & Co.; Hamilton Fish Armstrong, editor of *Foreign Affairs;* the newspaper columnists Dorothy Thompson and Walter Lippmann; Raymond Leslie Buell, head of the Foreign Policy Association, subsequently an editor of *Fortune;* and Allen and John Foster Dulles. Western internationalists included William Wesley Waymack, the Pulitzer Prize–winning editor of the *Des Moines Register and Tribune,* a Cowles publication. A majority of Americans polled in 1939 and 1940 opposed repeal of the Johnson Act, which prohibited loans to foreign nations that failed to pay their war debts (Britain and France), and favored the principle of cash-and-carry for the purchase of war materials. Such views were especially representative of the west central states. Polls also showed greater hostility toward Japan than toward Germany, and countenance of conflict with the Japanese Empire in the event of an attack on the Philippines or Hawaii.[14]

Herbert Hoover mirrored the party's ideological mainstream in foreign policy: opposition to involvement in world affairs unless explicit American interests were involved. Hoover established the groundwork for the revisionist reconstruction of the Second World War, later categorized as an example of American hegemonic imperialism. Seven years of service and observation in Europe during and after the First World War framed Hoover's views on avoidance of American entanglement beyond its borders. For the humanitarian, these strictures never varied over time or altered circumstance. Entanglement in Europe's quarrels and alliances, its class-driven mentality, and its tendency toward absolutism, totalitarianism, and periodic warfare endangered the Constitution and with it the American System. Hoover contended that American society and its economic system were unique in their emphasis on individualism, a view that dominated his outlook in the late 1930s.

In the early summer of 1939, as war clouds hovered over the Old World, Hoover surmised that bloodshed would become a reality only if the Western democracies "thought they had the full support of the United States." Effectively, he believed, the issue of war or peace rested on Roosevelt's shoulders, and world war could be avoided through "some sort of accommodation," or appeasement, of the Axis powers. "I do not believe for one moment that these democracies are in any danger of attack from Germany or Italy. . . . I am convinced it is Roosevelt's action which has stirred public opinion in France and England into the abandonment of appeasement policy and into aggressive lines."

Upon the outbreak of war in Europe in September 1939, Hoover reiterated his position: "Americans rightly are 97% against Hitler. . . . They are 97% against joining in a war." The United States, in any event, enjoyed self-sufficiency. Knox and Stimson, he maintained, served as "advance agents" of Roosevelt's intention to declare war. The nation's interests were bounded by two great oceans that protected it from the incessant turmoil reflected in Europe's perennial bloodlettings. If the Nazi regime occupied the European continent, the result would be a stalemate "for ten years at least as between the United States and Germany." Indeed, on the extreme Right such an outcome was preferable to the projection of Soviet power into eastern Europe. Japan, Hoover claimed, had been provoked by trade restrictions and other pinpricks over the years, and if left alone its military regime would collapse from internal economic pressures.[15]

The former president held court at a luncheon on February 29, 1940. Hoover demonstrated his hold on the anti-interventionists of both parties. Attendees included William Castle, Hoover's assistant secretary of state; Charles McNary, Senate minority leader; Republican senators Taft, Thomas (Idaho), Tobey (New Hampshire), and Austin (Vermont); and Democratic senators Walsh (Massachusetts) and Bailey (North Carolina). Hoover, who frequently referred to Taft as "Bob" in the process of eliciting his views, argued that the European conflict could be ended if the British dropped the condition that they would not negotiate with the Nazi regime. The result otherwise would be as follows: a Carthaginian peace with Poland permanently divided; Germany so reduced in area that it would not recover its autonomy; and European productivity declining to the extent that America would be forced to feed the continent, in other words a repetition of the post–World War I experience. Given this scenario, Hoover also proposed that tariffs and trade treaties were tertiary as an issue.[16]

An exchange between Hoover and Joseph Kennedy at the Waldorf Astoria following the German invasion of the Soviet Union is enlightening. Kennedy, recently recalled as ambassador to Britain, evaluated Churchill's tenure as precarious, perhaps due to the prime minister's decision to reject Hitler's recent peace offer made through Sweden. Britain, the Führer suggested, would retain the Empire and its fleet. In return, Germany would be afforded complete leeway in regard to a continental settlement, translated as dominance, free of British interference. According to Hoover's record, "he [Kennedy] had told the British that they had better take it" as the United States would not come to their assistance. Both assumed that United States involvement would lead to the introduction of a totalitarian state under Roosevelt and that democratic institutions required a self-contained economy.

Hoover believed that neither Britain nor Hitler could cross the Channel. Both sides possessed sufficient food and daylight air defense to continue a stalemate; night bombing would reduce cities to rubble, and the British would outlast the Germans. Kennedy doubted this last proposition on the ground that the crowded character of the island nation would induce infectious diseases. In Kennedy's estimate, American aid could not alter the inevitable result, Britain's defeat. Why then go on, Hoover inquired? Because of Churchill's stubbornness, came the reply.[17]

The fall of France and the Battle of Britain reinforced Hoover's fear that Roosevelt intended to involve the United States in the conflict. While detached from organized efforts to keep the nation out of war, such as America First or the National Council for the Prevention of War, in order to "carry more weight," Hoover associated with their membership and demonstrated a coincidence of views. "I do not object to the work of the America First Committee," he explained. "Many of them are extremists, but . . . there are even wilder extremists on the other side." His Chicago address of November 12, 1941, he explained to Robert Wood, chairman of Sears, Roebuck and a leading figure in America First, would assist in "shifting the front of opposition." Repeal of the Neutrality Act, he feared, would lead to involvement in a naval war with Germany and American expeditionary forces outside the Western Hemisphere.

The administration's proposal in early 1941 for Lend-Lease aid to England, which was desperate for material assistance, clarified the Republican Party's division on foreign policy. The legislation signaled Roosevelt's decision for direct involvement. When Robert Taft contemplated a substitute bill, the more experienced ex-president cautioned that public sympathy would sustain Roosevelt while England stood alone against Hitler's onslaught. The fight now should be waged, Hoover advised, on the basis of amendments curtailing Roosevelt's obvious preference for convoying by American naval vessels, repair of Allied ships in American ports, and "giving away our navy." Taft complied reluctantly: "War is worse," he contended, "even than a German victory."[18]

Hoover was correct in his appraisal that Lend-lease marked a turning point. With Roosevelt convinced in early 1941 that Great Britain could not overcome Hitler without United States assistance, cash-and-carry gave way to loans of war materiel in exchange for eventual repayment in kind or funds. American involvement in the war quickly extended to unneutral acts such as protection by naval vessels of convoys to England and the gradual extension of American naval power into the Atlantic.

In the process, the conservative coalition in Congress temporarily sundered. It had been forged between Republicans and southern Democrats based on common opposition to the New Deal's intrusions into the domestic economy with its social implications. But most southern whites were English in origin; westerners were largely Republican and German. And the impoverished southern economy benefited substantially from defense expenditure. Yet, one suspects that ideology and emotional attachments dominated in these years, not economic determinism.[19]

Hoover's evaluation of Roosevelt's foreign policy from late 1940 to early 1941 is summarized in memoranda and several public addresses. The Germans would not try to invade England; rather, they would try to bomb the British into submission and consequently would successfully dominate the continent of Europe and part of Africa. With the totalitarian nations in control of nearly 60 percent of the world's population, the United States would need to come to terms with the New Order. Although Americans did not desire to be dragged into the war, Roosevelt intended to order the navy to convoy vessels supplying England, engage German submarines, and dispatch an expeditionary force to northern Africa. Shortly, assisted by British propaganda, the president would provoke a German declaration of war, and a stalemate would ensue in light of Germany's command of European resources. Free speech would disappear in America, and the government would take over industry and invoke a socialized state provoking a revolution. Finally, Roosevelt's approving of supplies to the Soviets in response to Hitler's invasion meant that "Western Civilization has consecrated itself to making the world safe for Stalin."

Hoover's opposition to United States participation in the European conflict grew especially passionate with Germany's invasion of the Soviet Union in June 1941. It needs to be recalled that he had opposed recognition of the Communist state since its inception. In a statement drafted for fifteen participants, including Kennedy; Landon; the Chicago banker Charles Dawes; Robert Hutchins, president of the University of Chicago; Raymond Moley, editor of *Newsweek;* and Frank Lowden, former governor of Illinois, Hoover observed that Soviet involvement terminated the argument that the war signified a conflict between tyranny and freedom. In Hutchins's words: "We cannot join Russia in the hope of spreading democratic ideas throughout the world. There is little to choose between the domination of Europe by Nazi dictatorship or its domination by a Communistic dictatorship."

Hoover at times consoled himself with the conviction that Hitler would "defeat Russia and dispose of that infecting center of Communism" and then offer acceptable terms to Britain. In the event, "Nobody seriously believes that Hitler is now or will be in the near future in a position to threaten the independence of either this country of the Western Hemisphere." In the end, Hoover concluded, as did later revisionists, that Roosevelt provoked war with Japan and Germany, not the reverse.[20]

The time would come, Hoover felt assured, "when this war will be put into the scales of judgment," and then he would be vindicated. Both Hoover and Roosevelt waged a contest for the minds of historians as readily as for public opinion. The Hyde Park library was the original presidential repository; Hoover's arrangement of massive documentation of his views in publications and public addresses sustained his voice in the party precincts. In the interim, until academics weighed in, Hoover collaborated with J. Howard Pew in funding and encouraging the output of revisionist publishers and authors, such as Richard Current's critical biography of Henry L. Stimson, also the work of Harry Elmer Barnes, *Perpetual War for Perpetual Peace* (1953), and Charles Beard's *American Foreign Policy in the Making* (1946). Joining Joseph Pew, Sewell Avery, Robert E. Wood, Henry Regnery, and Edgar Monsanto Queeny, Hoover secured the financing of the *Pathfinder, Human Events,* the *Federalist,* and the Regnery publishing house, all founded to reverse Roosevelt's

New Deal and keep the United States out of the Second World War. The "good war" was categorized as an "unnecessary war."

Hoover's outlook typified that of a substantial majority of the GOP's elected legislators, and Robert Taft particularly emerged as his amanuensis. The two men aspired to a self-contained United States, with the New Deal and presidential authority rolled back. Aided and abetted by a coterie of Republican Party internationalists, including Stimson, Alexander Sachs, Henry Luce, and the Reid family's *New York Herald-Tribune,* Wendell Willkie conceived of an alternative scenario and contested the party's direction. Indeed, with Franklin D. Roosevelt in the White House, Hoover and Taft struggled on two political fronts in their determination to sustain the concept of limited government and insularity from the world outside the Western Hemisphere. This contest divided the GOP for a generation and more.[21]

NEITHER THE Great Depression nor the threat of a war in Europe prompted Herbert Hoover to revise his convictions. Preservation of the American System required repealing the New Deal and avoidance of Europe's affairs. The New Deal, he intoned, had "corrupted . . . liberalism for collectivism, coercion, and concentration of political power." While these views resembled those of party conservatives, the GOP's leadership determined to separate the party from the failed politician.

Hoover sought redemption nevertheless through nomination in 1940 for another residency in the White House. Unwilling to fall on its sword in defense of the Hoover administration, a condition of his candidacy, and encouraged by the election of Robert Taft to the Senate in 1938, the Republican leadership found a new champion in the crusade for minimal government and disengagement from world conflict. As the economist Alexander Sachs lectured Wendell Willkie upon his presidential nomination in 1940, the GOP had evolved into the party of the Bourbons: under its current leadership it had become "blind and unpatriotic on foreign policy and reactionary on domestic policy and devoid of contacts with [the] masses in its organizational structure." The stage was set for a bitter internecine contest. The antistatist, isolationist wing, with Taft, Hoover, and Vandenberg at the forefront, found itself challenged by a diverse group of liberal internationalists who conceded that Roosevelt's agenda would forestall a systemic economic collapse while favoring material aid to opponents of the Hitler regime in Europe.

Speakers at Lincoln Day dinners across the nation in 1937, with an eye on the 1940 presidential contest, including Hill Blackett, the National Committee's public relations director and a member of the Landon coterie; Arthur Vandenberg; John D. M. Hamilton; and Governor George Aiken of Vermont, suggested a fusion party that would formalize the congressional anti–New Deal coalition. Republicans would presumably be joined by southern anti–New Deal Democrats, including Senators Carter Glass and Harry F. Byrd (Virginia), Josiah Bailey (North Carolina), Millard Tydings (Maryland), and Bennett Clark (Missouri).[1]

Hoover balked. Parties in a democracy, he insisted in the *Atlantic Monthly*, must take a clear stand on the great issues of the day, especially in an era when individual liberty was endangered by government coercion. These views matched precisely those seeking a combination of anti–New Deal Republicans and southern Democrats led respectively by Vandenberg and Virginia's Harry Byrd. The ex-president proceeded to condemn New Deal economic planning, lump-sum appropriations by Congress that effectively delegated authority to appropriate money to the executive, intimidation of the Supreme Court, and fomenting of class antagonism. He embraced instead fiscal prudence, a return to the deflationary gold standard, repeal of the undistributed profits tax on corporations and capital gains taxes, resistance to pending wages and hours legislation, administration of relief by local voluntary agencies, and a tariff protecting labor and business from foreign competition.

Hoover protested that a new party linking conservatives of both major parties would prove unworkable and that the GOP would divide into splinter groups culminating in fascism under Roosevelt. The nation required "a party that will courageously . . . set out the affirmative alternative to the coercive direction of the New Deal." Likely the ex-president feared that southerners would veto his nomination as head of a newly created conservative party. Instead, he proposed a midterm convention for 1938 and a National Policy Committee instructed to draft an anti–New Deal agenda for Republicans. Since that agenda would be based on Wilbur and Hyde's *Hoover Policies,* published in 1937, he anticipated that he would circumvent the party leadership. A planner and organizer, Hoover summoned his usual supporters for a run at the party's 1940 nomination, including present and former governors Frank Lowden, Arthur Hyde, Wilbur Brucker, Huntley Spaulding, Alvin Fuller, and Harry Nice; former and current members of the House and Senate, among them Warren Austin, Wallace White, and Bertrand Snell; also John Bricker, Robert Moses, Otis Glenn, James Garfield, Robert Taft, Chester Rowell, and John Cowles.[2]

Despite a massive correspondence, a round of speeches and private meetings across the country, and the financing of publications heralding his presidency by supporters, Hoover gained no headway in the attempt to secure a midterm convention or a second term in office. In the end, while the National Committee agreed to a policy committee, ideological differences led to a vacuous statement of principles. Landon, Knox, and congressional leaders—including Vandenberg, McNary, and Arthur Capper of Kansas, as well as his old nemesis, Borah—balked at the idea of a Hoover-led convention dictating party policy for the 1938 and 1940 campaigns. Opponents judged the effort as a clumsy attempt to mobilize the Old Guard for a coup at the 1940 presidential convention, culminating in Hoover's nomination.[3]

While it is customary to consider presidential elections such as those of Roosevelt or Ronald Reagan as turning points in American politics, the Democratic capture of the House of Representatives in 1930 and Republican gains in the 1938 congressional election also heralded major shifts in the public mood. The 1938 contest signaled the waning of the New Deal and a Republican renaissance. After losing ground in the House and Senate in the 1930, 1932, 1934, and 1936 elections, Republicans picked up 6 seats in the Senate, and 71 in the House. More striking, the Republican congressional vote very nearly matched that of the Democratic Party, 47 percent as opposed to 48.6 percent, while the GOP made substantial gains in its traditional strongholds in New England and the Midwest, where statism was increasingly rejected by small entrepreneurs and bankers. But for the Solid South, the Republican vote would have more than matched that of the Democrats.

The 1938 result fostered internal divisions reflecting sectional diversity, not unusual as a party enlarges its representation. In the Senate, the Bourbons led by newly elected Robert Taft proved more adamant about opposing Roosevelt's domestic agenda than had McNary and party moderates. At the state level, a net shift of eleven governorships to the GOP—including election of the liberal internationalists Harold E. Stassen (Minnesota), Leverett Saltonstall (Massachusetts), and Raymond Baldwin (Connecticut)—marked the emergence of novices prepared to challenge the Old Guard. In New York, Governor Herbert H. Lehman narrowly turned back a fresh face, Thomas E. Dewey, the youthful Manhattan district attorney allied with Kenneth Simpson, a liberal who was active in local politics. Simpson, who unseated the reactionary Charles Hilles as the Manhattan party leader, openly challenged the old warhorses at a meeting of the National Committee in Washington shortly after the election.

Unable to win a seat on the executive committee—he lost out to Senator Daniel O. Hastings of Delaware, a party stalwart—Simpson proclaimed that the recent election did not constitute a mandate for conservatives connected to Hoover and the American Liberty League. The party, Simpson insisted, should follow a more liberal course. The statement, widely quoted, signaled a budding ideological division that surfaced at the 1940 convention and continued beyond. In the interim, party conservatives remained in control, led by Hamilton, Pew, and the Old Guard at the national committee level and Taft and Vandenberg in the Senate.[4]

The return to a two-party system had its roots in Roosevelt's hubris, political miscalculation, and the economic downturn in 1937–38. While the so-called "Roosevelt recession" reflected his own proclivity toward fiscal prudence, it emanated from several additional factors: the administration's concession to demands by Congress and the business community for budget balance; Federal Reserve monetary policies that tightened credit availability to tamp down presumed inflationary pressures; structural unemployment caused by industry's capacity to utilize a smaller workforce for a given amount of production; and the scaling down of an excessive inventory buildup. The result was a return to high unemployment.

Those who questioned the efficacy of governmental intervention in the economy for the purpose of recovery took heart at decade's close. The Republican Party, it appeared, stood a respectable chance of winning the White House in 1940 in light of the recent recession and the refusal of the administration to confront sit-down strikers in 1937–38, which did not suit a middle class wary of a shift in the balance of power to the union movement. Proposals by the President's Committee on Administrative Management for greater operational efficiency in the executive branch seemed to confirm the claim of excessive executive power. FDR further nourished the appearance of an imperious executive when he attempted to purge party conservatives—notably Democratic senators Walter George of Georgia, Millard Tydings of Maryland, and Ellison Smith of South Carolina, as well as John J. O'Connor, chairman of the House Rules Committee—in the 1938 Democratic primaries. Discretionary funding by Harry Hopkins, Republicans also charged, corrupted the electoral process. And reciprocal trade arrangements, according to the GOP, a high-tariff party, undermined local producers and workers.[5]

It is helpful to examine shifting political sentiment in the 1930s through the example of Everett McKinley Dirksen, the "Wizard of Ooze," since capture of the Midwest was critical to achieving an electoral majority. Dirksen symbolized the region's pragmatism both in its initial acceptance of New Deal economic subvention and his subsequent questioning of growing federal intervention. The son of German-born parents of moderate means, deeply religious, born to the Republican fold, a World War I enlistee, and engaged in the baking business, Dirksen came from a world that revolved around the small town, the American Legion, the Loyal Order of Moose, family, free enterprise, individualism, and hard work.

In the Depression years, the Illinois Republican Party found itself divided between the Chicago die-hards, the Strawn group tied to Hoover, and the downstate county chairmen who favored a liberalized party more committed to agriculture and labor than to corporate America. Dirksen, elected to Congress for the first time in 1932 with a plurality that matched Roosevelt's in his home district, deliberately distanced himself from the Hoover record. "With unemployment increasing, . . . banks popping, . . . and . . . business stagnant, what could one say," he apologized, "in behalf of Herbert Hoover and against Roosevelt?"

The congressional district he represented harbored a mixed economy based on coal mining and corn-hog and soybean production, and included the city of Peoria, a commercial-manufacturing center and railroad hub of one hundred thousand people. The "Virtuoso of the Switch," an allusion to Dirksen's contempt for party regularity, supported New Deal agricultural and social programs, including the Agricultural Adjustment Act, the National Industrial Recovery Act, social insurance legislation, the Wagner Act, and the Fair Labor Standards Act of 1938.

Yet Dirksen reflected Main Street's misgivings about the Roosevelt policies. He opposed Hull's reciprocal trade program that impinged on local corn and steel producers, and he decried federal paternalism. Like most midwesterners, he accepted the benefits bestowed by the New Deal program but deplored eastern monopolists and planners. The Illinois legislator accepted the need for a more liberal party outlook but exhibited a preference for limited government that eventually led to the conviction that executive authority exceeded constitutional norms. In time Dirksen concluded that centralized authority at the nation's capital had outlived its usefulness.[6]

Another midwestern supporter of the Roosevelt administration in its initial efforts at recovery, William Wesley Waymack, editor of the *Des Moines Register and Tribune* and a Wilsonian internationalist and a Republican, elaborated on the corn-hog belt's return to "habit, tradition, a dislike of heavy deficits, suspicion of WPA, [and] fear of Roosevelt as an enemy of business." In Iowa, though Democratic governors won office in the Roosevelt era, the legislature remained in Republican hands. The state's farm vote, Waymack noted, "is still largely registered in the Republican Party.... A certain inner 'yen' to get back to the Republican fold has continued to exist." While large urban centers such as Kansas City and St. Louis remained in the Democratic fold, the small-town bankers, merchants, and manufacturers, fearing loss of their autonomy to federal bureaucrats, turned solidly Republican.[7]

Whereas shifting tides suggested eventual return of the Grand Old Party to power, obstacles remained to majority status. Its leadership failed to address Depression remediation or reemployment in the 1930s, offering a message of self-help, community sustenance, a return to crippling deflation under the gold standard, and business confidence theory. The party needed a personality capable of mustering mass support in a world devastated by economic warfare and confronted with impending military conflict.

While polls identified Thomas E. Dewey as leading other potential 1940 presidential nominees, his viability as a candidate rested on his image as a youthful, attractive rackets-buster. Though regarded as a centrist on domestic issues, at age thirty-six in 1938 he offered neither a national program nor experience in governance or foreign affairs. Arthur Vandenberg was a more logical contender for party leadership than the ambitious New York City district attorney. The senator from Michigan, an industrial state, survived the New Deal electoral onslaught when reelected in 1934, was responsible for creation of the Federal Deposit Insurance Corporation, championed profit-sharing by employees, and pushed through liberalizing amendments to the original Social Security Act. Yet he also pursued revision of the Wagner Act on the ground of fair play to employers, criticized decisions of the National Labor Relations Board as slanted toward organized labor, and sought prohibition of sit-down strikes, positions hardly calculated to win votes in the late 1930s, when the union movement was ascendant.[8]

Typical of Vandenberg's capacity for carrying water on both shoulders, in this instance expressing concern for budget balance while shifting public expenditure to the future, was his sponsorship of the 1939 Social Security amendments. These featured the substitution of a lower rate of payroll contributions, or pay-as-you-go, undermining the original legislation's full reserve principle; and provision at the same time of generous outpayments to recipients and extension of benefits to widows and dependent children. Proponents of public expenditure as a Depression cure and socially minded liberals lauded the amendments as a cushion against poverty in old age and future economic downturns. Conservatives, on the other hand, found comfort in the conviction that a huge reserve funded by substantial payroll contributions would not be used by the executive branch as a slush fund for federal programs. In the end, future generations were left with legacy costs.[9]

Vandenberg's leadership of the continued effort to formalize ties between Senate anti–New Deal Democrats and Republicans opposed to the Roosevelt program reflected his fundamental conservatism. Virginia's Harry Byrd proposed such an arrangement at a luncheon in December 1937 attended by Vandenberg and Lewis W. Douglas, who served as budget director under Roosevelt until he resigned to protest deficit expenditure. A coalition statement was drafted at two dinner meetings held at the home of Senator Peter Gerry (Democrat, Rhode Island). Other senators in attendance included Walter George (Georgia), Josiah Bailey (North Carolina), David Walsh (Massachusetts), and Royal Copeland (New York), Democrats; and two Republicans in addition to Vandenberg, Warren Austin (Vermont), and John Townsend (Delaware). Townsend and Vandenberg drafted a statement that they hoped would be signed by twenty Democrats and ten Republicans.

The Bailey-Vandenberg manifesto addressed the complaints of conservatives who regarded excessive government intervention in the economy as an impediment to business recovery. Manifestly, they asserted, increased capital gains taxes and the undistributed profits tax of 1936 levied on large corporations curtailed investment and encouraged the resumption of a deflationary trend. The proposal also treated sit-down strikes as an invasion of property rights and emphasized states' rights. Premature distribution of the document, according to Vandenberg, undermined the undertaking. More likely, conservative Democrats lacked the stomach to take on the president while some Republicans, led by McNary and Borah in the Senate, rejected a formal venture into coalition politics. In the end, Bailey and Vandenberg issued the statement on their own.[10]

An avid student of the Constitution, Vandenberg appraised most issues on the basis of strict construction, budget balance, and potential impact on the business system. Throughout the 1930s, he led the opposition to a projected Florida Ship Canal and the Passamaquoddy power scheme, a Roosevelt favorite, on the grounds of waste. He judged Hull's reciprocal trade treaties as unconstitutional on the ground that doing so delegated Congress's power to tax to the executive branch. With Taft, he argued in 1939 against funding of additional dams for the Tennessee Valley Authority on the grounds that such expenditure would unbalance the budget and stimulate inflation. And he suggested passage of a constitutional amendment granting the item veto to the president in matters of taxation and expenditure. A xenophobe, Vandenberg endorsed the investigations of the Dies Committee, chaired by Martin Dies of Texas, in its search to root out subversive, un-American activities emanating from Moscow, a precursor of postwar McCarthyism.

While Vandenberg flirted with pursuit of the 1940 nomination, he abjured active engagement beyond securing favorite-son status with the Michigan delegation. "I have carried the flag through the lean years," he noted, and that sufficed as his contribution to society. Perhaps the decision also reflected a Gallup poll taken on November 27, 1938, which for the first time in two years indicated that the senator from Michigan no longer led Republican presidential prospects.

Though Dewey was an early front-runner and Vandenberg the most experienced, Ohio's Robert Alfonso Taft, elected to the Senate in 1938, almost immediately earned the sobriquet "Mr. Republican," and quickly emerged both as Hoover's heir and party leader. Taft led the quest for fiscal prudence, limited government, and abstention from Europe's affairs. While a flat speaking style worked to his disadvantage in the new political order and the age of radio, Taft exuded a command of detail that served him well in political campaigns and legislative combat. More quickly, too, than most he grasped the economic objectives of the Harvard economist Alvin Hansen and other New Deal economists, notably their aspirations for a permanent policy of government countercyclical expenditure as an antidote to depression.

Whereas the New Deal pursued corporate accountability through new agencies such as the Securities and Exchange Commission, Taft exuded both traditional distrust of Washington's statist solutions and middle-class abhorrence of the potential of a labor party under the Democratic banner. Destined to serve in the Senate for the remainder of his days, the Ohioan remained true to views shaped by his father, William Howard Taft—distrust of eastern capital, reliance on the commerce clause and antitrust to restrain business excess, invocation of the law to order international relations, and belief in strict construction, checks and balances, and separation of powers. Such a restricted construct of a regulatory regime was inadequate for governance in a complex economy.

Service with Herbert Hoover at the wartime Food Administration, the American Relief Administration, and the Paris Peace Conference fostered Taft's distaste for and involvement in Europe's perennial conflicts. Active on the Chief's behalf in his presidential campaigns, the then Cincinnati attorney characterized Hoover's 1934 manifesto, *The Challenge to Liberty*, as an expression of "the essential principles of American government." Both subscribed to the notion of devolution of functions to the states as a safeguard against excessive federal power.[11]

Like Hoover, aloof and hardly outgoing, a less than engaging public speaker inclined to fact-based, tract-like addresses, uncomfortable with the small talk that engaged so many politicians, and spare in friendships, Taft relied principally on his own counsel and a narrow intellectual base made up of Ohio associates. The hardships imposed by the Great Depression hardly dented Taft's personal well-being or his doctrinal consistency and preconceptions. Like the Chief, the Ohioan attributed the downturn to dislocations emanating from the Great War and its aftermath, unsound lending and speculation, cartelization leading to price maintenance, excess output of raw materials, and excess expenditure on investment as opposed to underconsumption. Remediation required renewed demand based on lower prices leading to an autonomous business recovery. Such an analysis led to the conclusion that the central government had a limited role in fostering recovery.[12]

In the years prior to his run for the Senate in 1938, Taft rejected the New Deal's approach to the Depression virtually in its entirety. While declining to serve on the American Liberty League's advisory council in 1934, he expressed complete sympathy with its objectives and willingness to cooperate in its endeavors. He regularly categorized the Roosevelt program as revolutionary and socialistic in its attempts at price raising, regulation of the private sector, inflationary policies, and tolerance of budget imbalance. The American business system, as it existed, rewarded diligence and initiative; government bureaucracy offered red tape and stifled hard work. He opposed government ownership of public utilities and the use of the tax system to redistribute income. Overall, Taft contended, government's role should be constrained to remedying abuses in the system on a case-by-case basis, "not by assuming the power . . . to regulate the details of business activity in the states."

The New Deal, Taft believed passionately, intended to substitute a government-controlled economy for private ownership and management, resulting in "complete socialism." The Social Security Act of 1935 was "extravagant" in its benefits, which were beyond the capacity of government, taxpayers, and employers, a "necessary evil" cloaked by a humanitarian gloss. Its payments, he claimed, should not be "more pleasant than relief is pleasant," since it induced sloth, discouraged enterprise, and placed government in the insurance business, incurring dangerous obligations.[13]

Taft moderated these views in the course of his 1938 Senate campaign against the Democratic incumbent Robert Bulkley. He favored a modest expansion of Social Security to include unemployment insurance as a state-administered program, minimum-wage legislation, and the right to strike. He proved an astute campaigner by tagging Bulkley unfairly as an unquestioning devotee of the president's agenda and by demonstrating a keen intellect in debates. Taft was aided by the family name and by middle-class abhorrence of Michigan governor Frank Murphy's sympathy with the sit-down strikers in their seizure of private property.[14]

A political rarity, Taft offered unvarnished elaboration of his constitutional and economic philosophy as well as his foreign-policy views. In a series of debates with Illinois representative T. V. Smith on CBS, and throughout his Senate career, the Ohioan embraced a classic view of the American System, one based on equality of opportunity, individual initiative, and "the right to conduct manufacture, commerce, agriculture, or other business on rugged individualism." Government was established, in this view, to maintain these principles, not to regulate or control business or personal activity. While recognizing the need for a social safety net in the form of unemployment insurance, relief, and old-age pensions, security had not been the nation's guiding principle. Government should create conditions conducive to opportunity and individual achievement; it was not a substitute for personal energy, initiative, and creativity.

However laudable private initiative in theory, in the contemporary economic environment, the capacity of the individual to negotiate a system dominated by large aggregates in business and finance was limited. Frustration led to hostility in the form of sit-down strikes. Antitrust, regarded by Taft as a regulatory mechanism, was substantially a puerile exercise. Yet, realistic or not, a minority in the Depression and a majority in more sanguine times could be mustered for the precepts of the American System as enunciated initially by Hoover and subsequently by Taft.

In his public debates with T. V. Smith, Taft urged that public assistance, while funded partially by the federal government, should be administered by private citizens and local charities. Social Security discouraged employment; he preferred a system based on state pensions funded by a national sales tax. While commending the Wagner Labor Relations Act with its guarantee of the right of collective bargaining, he condemned the pro-union bias of the National Labor Relations Board and held that high wages could be secured instead by tariff protection and immigration restriction. He seemed unaware that government-funded rural electrification, reforestation, new technologies, construction of airports and highways, renovation of the nation's infrastructure, and conversion of vast impoverished river systems promoted economic viability; or that the United States had become part of an international economy. In Taft's view, the Roosevelt administration's fiscal profligacy marked by excessive public expenditure and taxation stymied the potential for recovery by crippling wages, profits, and investment. It followed that Roosevelt's policies exacerbated the 1937 downturn and the Great Depression, which should have been easily reversed through continuity with the Hoover policies.[15]

In February 1939, Taft faulted the deficits projected in Roosevelt's annual budget message to the Congress. The president asserted that the recent decline in national income required public expenditure adequate to compensate for deficiencies in consumer purchasing power and private-sector investment. He distinguished between the ordinary budget and an extraordinary budget, the latter consisting of capital investments that would be amortized over a period of years. Government capital expenditure, he added, should expand or contract based on private-sector investment outlays and constituted a permanent addition to the national wealth.

Taft excoriated the president's embrace of fiscal views presented by Marriner S. Eccles, chairman of the Federal Reserve System, and several unnamed Tufts and Harvard University economists (Richard V. Gilbert, George H. Hildebrand Jr., Arthur W. Stuart, Maxine, Alan, and Paul Sweezy, Walter Salant, and Emile Depres). Taft complained that Eccles, the Federal Reserve economist Lauchlin Currie, and economists recruited by Currie to public service were engaged in a concerted effort to persuade legislators that federal fiscal stimulus could readily serve as a substitute for private-sector investment in a depression.[16]

Discussion of compensatory government expenditure in the event of a steep decline in private investment or consumption or both—in effect fiscal planning—extended back to the immediate post–World War I years, when Hoover chaired the President's (Warren Harding) Conference on Unemployment in 1921, though the commerce secretary anticipated that state governments would take up the slack. As the economy plunged in the closing years of the Hoover presidency, members of the Chicago school of economics, including Frank H. Knight, Henry C. Simons, and Jacob Viner, urged federal deficit expenditure to reverse unemployment and deflation. Financing should not rely on taxes, they advised, but rather could be accomplished through Treasury bond issues absorbed by the Federal Reserve Banks, later known as quantitative easing. As Knight observed, "The government should spend as much and tax as little as possible at a time such as this . . . up to the limit of safety." Unfortunately, during the Hoover presidency, deficiencies in revenue collections were met by instituting taxation at wartime levels, a precedent followed by Roosevelt.

The concept of compensatory fiscal policy entered Roosevelt administration circles with the accession of Eccles to the Federal Reserve System chairmanship and his recruitment of the young Harvard economist Lauchlin Currie. Beginning in the mid-1930s, Currie's views were embraced by Harry Hopkins; Leon Henderson at WPA; Isador Lubin, commissioner of labor statistics; Thomas "Tommy the Cork" Corcoran; Benjamin Cohen; William O. Douglas; and Henry Wallace.[17]

"Curried Keynes," as it was known, found the light of day in the Works Financing Act of 1939, which irked Taft. The president projected a revolving, self-liquidating public and nonpublic works program totaling $2.8 billion funded through borrowing by the Reconstruction Finance Corporation with loan expenditure recovered through tolls and fees. The complicated funding mechanism, designed to appease proponents of budget balance, would be supplemented by expansion of the borrowing power of the United States Housing Authority to the tune of $800 million.

Roosevelt's tender for a permanent revolving fund issued by agencies responsible for these programs reflected the underlying assumption that ongoing stimulus to the private sector through government capital investment was essential to an adequate level of employment. As such it was the initial step toward full-employment legislation in 1946. Currie, a clever tactician appointed presidential assistant in 1939, recruited many like-thinking economists to public service, including Harvard's Alvin Hansen, a recent convert to Keynesian-style thinking. Hansen in turn persuaded the National Resources Planning Board, successor to the original Public Works Administration, to wed compensatory spending with public planning as a continuing program for prevention of future depressions. Though the Works Financing bill went down to defeat in the Congress, signaling the end of New Deal reform, Taft and Hansen resumed their contest over the merits of public investment and planning during the course of Second World War.[18]

As opposed to the view of government as investment banker for the purpose of serving as a semi-permanent counterweight to inadequate private-sector outlay, Taft ascribed the persistence of the Great Depression to budget deficits. Whereas private debt, according to Taft, stimulated new enterprise and employment, public debt utilized for public works entailed permanent government expenditure for their maintenance, raised interest rates on private debt, and induced fears of repudiation in the event of another depression. Then too, Taft believed that the Works Financing bill represented executive usurpation of congressional authority for public expenditure through the mechanism of a revolving fund. "It is my opinion that the bill violates the letter of the Constitution as well as the spirit."[19]

Taft's analysis of debt levels was flawed. On the contrary, levels of public expenditure in the 1930s should have been higher in order to sustain a full employment economy. Annual deficits (in current prices) averaged 3.65 percent of GNP in the years 1932–40, and ranged from approxi-

Annual federal deficits and national debt as percentage of GNP, 1932–1940, in current prices (billions of dollars)

Year	GNP	Federal receipts	Federal expenditure	Deficit	Deficit as percentage of GNP	Debt as percentage of GNP
1932	58.5	2	4.7	2.7	4.6	33
1933	56	2	4.6	2.6	4.6	40
1934	65	3.1	6.7	3.6	5.5	41
1935	72.5	3.8	6.5	2.7	3.8	40
1936	82.7	4.1	8.5	4.4	5.3	41
1937	90.8	5.3	7.8	2.5	3.1	40
1938	85.2	6.2	6.8	1.6	1.4	44
1939	91.1	5.7	8.9	3.2	4.3	44
1940	100.6	5.9	9	3.1	3.9	43

Sources: U.S. Bureau of the Census, *Historical Statistics of the United States, Colonial Times to 1957* (Washington, D.C., 1960), 132–33, 139, 712, 718, 724; James D. Savage, *Balanced Budgets and American Politics* (Ithaca, N.Y., 1988), 169, 290.

mately 5.5 and 5.3 percent in 1934 and 1936—both election years when Roosevelt introduced large-scale infrastructure programs designed to induce recovery and re-employment—to a low of 1.4 percent in 1938. Gross national debt grew from 33 to 43 percent of GNP, a perfectly manageable figure. (Great Britain's debt to GNP ratio for 1932 has been estimated at 191 percent.) Deficits incurred by New Deal recovery policy could be remediated by productivity growth, increased revenue collections following economic recovery, and a resumption of international trade.

As the economist Herbert Stein observed in his classic study of New Deal expenditure, the Roosevelt administration "never produced any general theory of the fiscal policy under which [it was] working." The preponderance of thinking both in England and the United States in these years, towards which Roosevelt was inclined, stressed balanced budgets in a depression as critical to lowering interest rates for the private sector and thus stimulating investment, employment, and recovery. The theory failed to work in an environment of large-scale unemployment and decline in consumption. In order to enhance revenues and contain deficits, Hoover and Roosevelt kept taxes at near-wartime levels, which also limited recovery. Yet the squire, unlike Hoover always the pragmatist, proved willing to expand federal expenditure for recovery and relief in the current circumstances. GNP grew steadily in the 1930s, at least until the 1937–38 recession when FDR yielded to conservatives in the business and financial communities and reduced public investment. Taft's views on fiscal policy as an exercise in budget balance remained inflexible despite a depressed economy—though he proved correct in the claim that government-business collaboration and lower taxes on business would have contributed to an earlier recovery.[20]

Whereas Taft preached economic self-sufficiency and insulation, Hansen sought international economic management, creation of international economic structures for monetary equilibrium, and a lending agency designed to funnel capital investment from developed to developing economies. Both Hansen and Keynes at a meeting in London also subscribed to the view that the United States was best equipped to take the lead in provision of loan expenditure in order to foster postwar recovery. The stage was set for a contest that involved two mind-sets. Taft envisaged a United States committed to budget balance, minimal government, and self-containment. Liberal economists, Hansen in the lead, envisaged a second Great Depression on the assumption of permanent underinvestment after the war and planned for local and international governmental arrangements for a revitalized global economy.[21]

In his early Senate career, Taft voted against programs he deemed as taking the nation on the road to bankruptcy. During the Seventy-Sixth Congress, Taft voted against an increased appropriation for work relief; against the Agricultural Appropriation bill; against proposals to fund the Public Works Administration; against increased funding for the Farm Security Administration and the Bankhead-Jones Farm Tenant Act; for increased appropriations for maternal and child health, vocational rehabilitation and public health; but against the Social Security amendments bill, which passed 57 to 8. While a supporter of the United States Housing Authority, Taft voted for an amendment to reduce subsidy payments and borrowing authority; for a proposal to discontinue presidential authority to devalue the dollar; and against final passage of such authorization.[22]

Virtually from his election to the Senate, Taft contemplated a run for the presidency in 1940. Consistent to a fault, he contemplated budget balance; repeal of payroll and capital gains taxes; limitation of recent wages and hours legislation; amendment of the National Labor Relations Act to make it more equitable in its application to employers; abandonment of the WPA; and conveyance of federal administration of direct and work relief to the states.

Since isolationism required self-sufficiency, the Ohioan voted against renewal of the Trade Agreements Act, which in any event he regarded as unfair to industry. Instead, Taft favored restoration of the former Tariff Commission that supported high tariff protection for American industry, which he deemed the world's most efficient. Shortly before the Republican convention, Taft suggested an "American market" for farmers based on tariff protection, bartering, and, if necessary, export subsidies, in effect, the dumping of surplus overseas. The United States, he claimed, enjoyed natural resources sufficient to maintain a largely self-sufficient economy freed of production controls. Typically, isolationists claimed that only 5 percent of the American economy was involved in overseas trade; internationalists countered that the result was by definition a lowered standard of living for all as protectionism protected inefficient producers.[23]

Convinced that Roosevelt would involve the United States in the European war, Taft claimed limited constitutional power for the presidency in foreign affairs. Only Congress, he maintained, possessed the power to raise an army, fund a navy, or "act in the field covered by the Neutrality Act, involving the embargo of shipments abroad, restraint of American ships, . . . or loaning of money, or credit to foreign nations." He opposed the entry of American ships into war zones and the Thomas amendment authorizing the president to discriminate among belligerents under cash-and-carry provisions. Further, from Taft's vantage point, their alliance with Communist Russia belied the claim by the Allies that they led a group of democracies in challenging Hitler's ambitions. Germany and Italy, in the event, represented no threat to the United States.

Like most isolationists in Congress, Taft voted for army and navy appropriations, limited however to defense, not for overseas adventures. He opposed the institution of economic sanctions. A war to preserve democracy, he maintained, was a contradiction in terms. United States intervention in 1917 led to the destruction of more democracies than it preserved. To ensure neutrality, he favored prohibition of arms shipments to all belligerents, thus reducing the likelihood of American involvement in war; further, the president should not be empowered to impose sanctions on aggressor nations.[24]

As the 1940 Republican convention approached, Hoover, hopeful of an opportunity to exorcise the Roosevelt agenda, domestic and foreign, pursued his own ambitions for the nomination rather than combine forces with a more popular candidate, namely Taft or Dewey, for a contest with the Democratic Party's presidential nominee. Taft was an unequivocal representative of the Hoover policies, domestic retrenchment and insulation from Europe's affairs. Dewey gave no indication of an internationalist viewpoint but showed strength with party moderates and a newly elected coterie of youthful GOP governors who were more receptive to advanced ideas. Vandenberg was perennially unavailable. Another obstacle to a clear selection of a presidential nominee surfaced, namely growing dissatisfaction among eastern internationalists with extreme neutrality in the face of German aspirations to control the Eurasian landmass. This latter group, however, lacked a candidate. Stimson was unavailable, given his age and association with Roosevelt's foreign policy. The door opened for a liberal internationalist dark horse.

THE REPUBLICAN PARTY divided sharply in anticipation of Roosevelt's pursuit of an unprecedented third term in 1940. A coalition of GOP internationalists favored a candidate who backed a policy of material assistance to the Allies despite the possibility that it might well lead to direct involvement in the conflict. Isolationists, who also anticipated possible involvement of the United States in a second Great War, aspired to limit the president's authority in foreign affairs.

Herbert Hoover, first out of the gate in another quest for redemption, pursuing the party's presidential nomination described himself as engaged in "a battle against the forces of evil," translated as Roosevelt's interventionist foreign policy. Following Landon's 1936 defeat, Hoover designed a strategy to induce the party to adopt a platform suited to his outlook: opposition to interventionism overseas; defense of his presidency as having resolved the economic and banking crises of the early 1930s only to be reversed by the Roosevelt policies; return to the gold standard as a mechanism for restraining government intervention in the economy; economic self-sufficiency sustained by a high-tariff regime; budget balance; and reliance on the states for management of social programs in the economic crisis.

Preparation for a return bout between Hoover and FDR was undertaken by the Republican Circles, an informal group with a membership estimated by Hoover at some eighty-five thousand. Substantial funding was provided by Sewell Avery, the anti-union president of Montgomery Ward and a supporter of the Crusaders, an antistatist business group; W. K. Kellogg of Battle Creek; and Henry Robinson, a California financier and Hoover adviser. The Circles also consisted of a hodgepodge of old political associates, former politicians such as New Jersey's H. Alexander Smith and Walter Edge, participants in Belgian relief, informal advisers associated with his presidential administration, and lawyers and businessmen of substance who opposed Roosevelt's monetary and fiscal policies. Included as well, at least informally, were journalist-supporters such as Boake Carter; David Lawrence; Ashmun Brown; Paul Block, proprietor of several newspapers; and Agnes and Eugene Meyer, owners of the *Washington Post*.

Constitutional Publications, funded by wealthy supporters, financed the distribution of the Hoover message though the publication of his speeches and his writings. William Starr Myers assembled for this undertaking *The True Republican Effort, 1929–1933*, a defense of the Hoover presidency. The Republican Program Committee, chaired by Glenn Frank, former chancellor of the University of Wisconsin and a Hoover supporter, drafted the guiding principles for foreign and domestic policy with the intention that they would be adopted by the National Committee.

The Frank Committee proposed that the United States should stay out of the war in Europe on the grounds that the "economic system of free enterprise [and] . . . our political system of representative self-government" would not survive participation. On the domestic front, the Frank Committee condemned excessive government expenditure and taxation, growth of the national debt, the Social Security reserve fund, and provision for social welfare at the national level. It challenged Alvin Hansen's stagnation theory and the argument that the nation's industrial plant was built. Business recovery and reemployment, it also predicted, would be based on emergence of new industries emanating from technological advances. These and other recommendations served as a platform for a Hoover run at the presidency.

The Rocky Mountain and Pacific Coast states served as the geographical bedrock of Hoover's venture, with California's substantial convention delegation critical to his early plans. Influential supporters of Thomas E. Dewey, especially William Knowland, publisher of the *Oakland Tribune*, checkmated Hoover's effort to capture the California delegation and turned to the youthful New Yorker when it became apparent that he also had wide appeal in the Mountain states. As a result, the ex-president's strategy shifted to engineering a convention stalemate based on uninstructed delegations.[1]

According to polling by Princeton's Opinion Research Corporation in May 1940, shortly before the GOP convention, Roosevelt was calculated to win a third term in contests with Dewey (52 to 48 percent), Vandenberg (53 to 47 percent), and Taft (58 to 42 percent). When Republicans were canvassed to name their preferred candidate, 62 percent opted for Dewey, 14 percent for Vandenberg, and 13 percent for Taft. Wendell Willkie, favored by 5 percent of those polled, drew his support largely from the Middle Atlantic states and the business community. While he made a "good showing," the pollster noted, Willkie was an unknown beyond the East Coast, hence unlikely to head off Dewey.

Dewey's early appeal rested on his youth, a reputation for attacking graft and corruption in government, and his comparative liberalism. In response to the tutelage of Lewis W. Douglas, Roosevelt's budget director, he took a liberal internationalist view of the importance of world trade. He did not demand a return of relief to the states, and he insisted on labor's right to collective bargaining. Dewey as a result offered a better chance for the GOP than Hoover or Taft to siphon off those who customarily voted Democratic, including lower-class voters and the middle-income or swing group.[2]

When Harrison Spangler, member for Iowa on the Republican National Committee, warned Hoover that "a certain group of extreme internationalists centered in the lower part of New York are . . . bringing all pressure possible to stampede the convention for Willkie," Hoover and his supporters decided to checkmate the utility magnate by publicizing Willkie's lifelong ties to the Democratic Party including support for Roosevelt in the 1932 campaign. A convention deadlock could be further secured by convincing a reluctant Vandenberg to take on Dewey. With Willkie and Dewey stymied, the party would presumably turn to Hoover.[3]

As the Philadelphia convention approached, the Republican leadership became increasingly apprehensive, equating Dewey's youth with inexperience and with a tendency toward independence. Doubts increased exponentially with Germany's invasion of the Low Countries and the fall of France. It was one matter to indict and convict Lucky Luciano, quite another to cope with Adolf Hitler. The thirty-eight-year-old New York rackets-buster possessed no direct experience in foreign affairs, yet with Europe in turmoil he would need to contest for the nation's highest office against the occupant of the White House. Always capable of rising to the occasion, Roosevelt's acerbic interior secretary, Harold Ickes, quipped that Dewey had thrown his diaper into the ring.[4]

Dewey's early delegate lead withered after the convention's first ballot. On the critical question of foreign policy, the district attorney's pronouncements seemed vapid and contradictory. American crisis diplomacy, in his view, consisted of upholding the Monroe Doctrine and avoiding the dispatch of soldiers to Europe. As Hitler's armies paraded across Europe virtually unopposed and the British army faced annihilation on the beaches of Dunkirk, Dewey stood firmly on the principle of no entangling alliances and of nonrecognition of the Soviet Union. At his most belligerent, he called for a two-ocean navy.

When it became evident that he could not muster a majority at the Philadelphia enclave without an alliance, the district attorney turned to the perennial reluctant bride to join forces. On the morning of June 25, New Hampshire senator Styles Bridges approached Arthur Vandenberg with a message from Dewey. "He wants you to take the vice presidency with him, and he says if you will, you can write your own ticket." In the resulting exchange, each proved unwilling to serve as bridesmaid in such an arrangement.

Vandenberg was not impressed. Since he was a sitting senator, he countered, he would have more influence on the Senate floor than presiding over that body as vice president. Vandenberg proposed instead that he should be at the top of the ticket, assuring Dewey that he would serve only one term as president, leaving the door open for the vice president's succession. "Also tell him," Vandenberg recorded, "that if this is too much for him to swallow . . . I'll make him a sporting proposition. I'll meet him at 11 o'clock and flip a coin to see which end of the ticket we each take." Dewey failed to reply until Willkie's nomination became imminent. According to Vandenberg, the New Yorker's frantic telephone calls to "stop Willkie" came too late. As was his habit at conventions, the senator from Michigan simply refused to pick up the phone. In the event, the "insulist" who believed in economic self-containment preferred Taft.

With Dewey's support dwindling, he put in a last-minute call to Hoover in search of an endorsement. Hoover refused on the grounds that it would constitute a violation of his neutrality pledge to the other candidates. Indeed, he had maneuvered for a stalemate. Bolstered by the support of John L. Lewis, DuPont economist Edmund E. Lincoln, and some, not all, of his old associates, the ex-president likely anticipated that the convention would turn to him.[5]

Secure in his command of domestic affairs and constitutional issues, Robert Taft served as the right wing's last best hope, yet he failed to collect a majority of delegates. Observers noted his dour public persona and unwillingness to recognize a tectonic shift in world affairs. Self-contained and advised largely by a chorus of yes-men, Taft's final pre-convention address at St. Louis—in search of midwestern and Mountain states delegates—preached detachment from a world at war. Taft offered support of a military and naval buildup, limited, however, to hemispheric defense. He also insisted on budget balance and complete avoidance of foreign entanglement.

Whereas most of Taft's advisers confined their disagreement with the candidate on foreign affairs to private exchanges, Richard Scandrett, a Wall Street attorney involved in previous Republican presidential campaigns, attempted to dissuade Taft from saying what he feared he would say at St. Louis. Since Munich, Scandrett was persuaded that Hitler had visions of world conquest; that most Americans underestimated German military capacity; and that American interests would be in jeopardy should Germany defeat the Allies, then a distinct possibility. Whereas most Republicans isolationists did not hesitate to express their views openly, Scandrett advised Taft not to get himself out on a limb. The admonition went unheeded.

Though he never openly endorsed America First, Taft encouraged its formation and views. After all, a majority of that organization's central committee consisted of Republicans. And his wife, Martha, herself a political activist and avid campaigner who knew her husband's opinions well, spoke frequently across the nation on behalf of the anti-interventionist group headed by Robert Wood of Sears, Roebuck, a one-time Roosevelt supporter. In the interim, Taft contended privately that "I do not believe that victory for either side would seriously endanger our position. I hope the president's hands are going to be tied." At St. Louis, he asserted openly: "There is a good deal more danger from the New Deal circle in Washington than . . . from any activities by the communists or the Nazi bund." He rejected any financial or naval support for the Allies, notwithstanding the fact that all but the United Kingdom were in the process of being overrun by the Wehrmacht. In the event, "Our going to war would be more likely to destroy American democracy than to destroy German dictatorship."

Representative A. Willis Robertson of Virginia, a Taft supporter, observed hopefully that Taft did not suggest at St. Louis that the United States could trade just as readily with a victorious Germany as with a victorious British Empire. In fact, that was Taft's conclusion, namely that the

United States would have no difficulty in establishing trade relationships with a Nazi-dominated Europe. As midwestern public opinion began to shift toward unlimited aid to Britain, the door opened to an internationalist candidate at Philadelphia.[6]

Wendell Willkie's entry on the political stage visited turmoil in the Republican Party at least until his sudden demise in 1944. He followed in the footsteps of Newton D. Baker, Woodrow Wilson's secretary of war. Though liberal internationalism of the 1930s conjures an image of eastern financiers and their legal factotums, elitist New England prep schools and universities, the Council of Foreign Relations, and the Foreign Policy Association, hegemony does not surface as its principal rationale. Baker and Willkie did not equate open markets with dominance, but rather with universal prosperity and the prevention of international conflict. As Baker put the issue, "There were two halves to the Wilson thesis: one was genuine cooperation among nations; and the other was an atmosphere of economic liberalism." So defined, Wilsonianism in the late 1930s dominated the editorial views of the influential *New York Times* and *Herald Tribune* as well as highly regarded regional papers such as the *Louisville Courier-Journal,* Joseph Pulitzer's *St. Louis Post-Dispatch,* Henry Haskell's *Kansas City Star,* George Fort Milton's *Chattanooga Times,* and the Cowles-owned *Des Moines Register and Tribune,* edited by William Wesley Waymack.[7]

In his physical stature and his personal and public persona, Willkie could not have been more unlike Taft and Hoover. A bear of a man, passionate, often intemperate and impulsive, endowed with considerable appetite for food, drink, and women, adaptable and open to views suited to changing times, the Hoosier utilities magnate challenged the party establishment with abandon. In the end, he forfeited his political life and his personal well-being, dying of a heart attack at the early age of fifty-two. "His faults, like his virtues, were on a big scale," the *Financial Times* later noted. Turner Catledge of the *New York Times* observed that Willkie was "the most disorderly man I ever knew," offering that he would not have made a good president.

Yet Willkie stands as one of the most fascinating and important political figures in twentieth-century American history, for in these brief years he accomplished several major ends. As provocateur, like Henry Stimson, the Hoosier supported Roosevelt's successful interventionist policies, helping to save Europe from the Nazi yoke. By pointing to the disintegration of the British Empire and publishing *One World,* he opened the American electorate to acceptance of the need for the United States to play a major role in shaping a postwar order; and while personally ostracized by the GOP's isolationist wing, he suggested to international-minded Republicans that such an ordered world required bipartisanship in American foreign policy, with Warren Austin and ultimately Arthur Vandenberg offering that leadership.

Born in Elwood, Indiana, to Herman and Henrietta Willkie, law partners in that small industrial community, Lewis Wendell—the given names later reversed by an army clerk—was remembered as an unkempt, brash, and relatively unsophisticated youth, characteristics that did not disappear with adulthood. After attending the University of Indiana, Willkie taught civics briefly at the Coffeyville, Kansas, secondary school, then attended law school at Bloomington, Indiana, and joined his parents' law practice. After service in the field artillery in France during World War I, Willkie moved on to Mather, Nesbit & Willkie in Akron, representing large railroads and industrial, banking, and utility interests in northern Ohio. In 1929, Willkie joined the firm of Weadock & Willkie in New York, whose principal client was the Commonwealth & Southern Corporation. Willkie became president of the utility on January 24, 1933 at age forty.[8]

Willkie's worldview reflected both the internationalist weltanschauung of Newton Baker as well as his mentor's critique of the New Deal's animus toward business, which crystallized in the struggle to preserve the territorial integrity of Commonwealth & Southern (C&S) from unfair competition by a government-subsidized entity, the Tennessee Valley Authority (TVA). A registered Democrat, Willkie served as a delegate to the 1924 Democratic Party convention, where he supported Baker's dogged but unsuccessful campaign to win over the platform committee to endorsement of United States membership in the League of Nations. He supported Baker again for the presidential nomination at the party's 1932 Chicago convention. When Roosevelt won the contest, Willkie voted for the New York governor in the campaign against Hoover. An ardent internationalist, Willkie condemned Hoover's willingness to sign the Smoot-Hawley Tariff and then Roosevelt's wrecking in 1933 of the World Monetary and Economic Conference.

Until the signing of the Munich Agreement and the sale of C&S subsidiaries to the TVA, Willkie was preoccupied with protecting Commonwealth and Southern from David Lillienthal and the public-power

Progressives. That struggle confirmed Willkie's conviction that the president and the TVA head were committed to the expropriation of private property, or the "socialization of industry." This supposition was reinforced with passage of the Public Utilities Holding Company (Wheeler-Rayburn) Act of 1935. Title I of the statute, known widely as the "death sentence," authorized the Securities and Exchange Commission "to simplify holding-company structures and eliminate uneconomic systems," by limitation of their operations.[9]

The TVA, created on May 18, 1933, afforded broad scope for regional planning through reforestation, navigation, flood control, and social rehabilitation in one of the nation's most impoverished regions. Designed to be emulated in the Columbia River Valley and elsewhere, it embodied the planners' belief that the Great Depression reflected deep structural problems. Economic distortions between prosperous, highly developed regions and raw-materials producers living on the edge required federal melioration through public investment in underdeveloped areas of the United States, a view represented by Alvin Hansen.

The statute provided that state-chartered public agencies in the TVA's service area should receive preference in the purchase and sale of power, though power could also be sold to private utilities for resale. The three-member board further declared its intent to provide service to the entire drainage area and beyond, to large municipalities as readily as to farms and smaller communities. This task was entrusted to the youthful David E. Lilienthal, an avid public-power Progressive who with Roosevelt regarded the private utilities' holding companies as parasitical "tapeworms sucking the nourishment out of the operating companies." C&S, like several other holding companies formed in the 1920s that survived the Depression, did not fit this image. Rather, they served the capital, managerial, and technological requirements of integrated, complex networks.

Since the TVA initially found itself confronted with inadequate sources of power, Lilienthal negotiated with Willkie for the purchase of additional capacity in the C&S-dominated territory until completion of Norris Dam. With the opening of the Norris facility in 1936, preference in sales of TVA-generated power at the bus bars was given to municipally owned operating companies. Willkie insisted on an extension of the original contract, which stipulated that the TVA would refrain from competition with C&S in its service area. Lilienthal refused.

Alexander Sachs, a Lehman Corporation executive with access to the White House, proposed a compromise in the form of a southeastern power pool that blended public and private investment on the British model with oversight by the Federal Power Commission. Public-power advocates charged with rural electrification and Nebraska's Senator George Norris countered that a joint public-private enterprise was subject to capture by private utilities. Originally interested in the notion of a public-private enterprise, Roosevelt backed off. Since C&S could not compete with a federally subsidized entity, Willkie determined to extract the best price he could from Lillienthal for the C&S properties located in TVA's territory.[10]

As a result of the C&S-TVA dispute, the Hoosier Democrat emerged as a leading exponent of the view that government interference in legitimate business constituted an impediment to free enterprise and recovery from the Depression. Beginning in 1934, Willkie associated with Democratic Party opponents of the New Deal, among them Bainbridge Colby, the Liberty League group, Jeffersonian Democrats, and Raymond Moley, editor of *Today.* An exchange between the president and Willkie at the White House in November 1937 exacerbated the situation, with each man uncompromising and determined to pursue his agenda.

In time, Willkie aired his views in publications such as the *New York Times Magazine.* Since electric power, he contended, constituted the principal catalyst for contemporary economic development, politicians coveted government ownership of generation and distribution. The result, in his view, would be bureaucratic management of all industry. As a lifelong Democrat, Willkie wrote an old friend in December 1937, he "sincerely believed that the least government was the best and that government subsidy and competition, even to the extent of creating tariff walls, was politically deleterious. I am entirely opposed to what government is doing."

Willkie's conversion to the Republican fold was gradual. Despite registration as a Democrat, he joined with Ernest Weir of Weirton Steel, Lammot du Pont, Robert Lund, Colby Chester, and Lewis W. Brown of Johns Manville, all anti–New Deal industrialists, for a dinner at the Metropolitan Club in April 1936, evidently designed to muster support for Landon. At the same time, Willkie remained in contact with Moley, who also crossed the political divide when he endorsed Landon for the presidency.[11]

The coincidence of the sale of C&S properties to the TVA and the agreements negotiated by Chamberlain and Hitler at the Munich Conference turned Willkie's attention to foreign affairs and domestic politics. He was out of a job, in his words, and in search of a new line of work. A liaison with Irita van Doren, book editor of the liberal internationalist *New York Herald-Tribune,* and his association with Helen and Ogden Reid, owners of the *Tribune,* and a cluster of journalists employed by Henry Luce, publisher of *Time, Life,* and *Fortune,* broadened the utility executive's horizon in foreign affairs. Willkie was introduced to Claire Booth Luce, Russell Davenport, and Raymond Leslie Buell. Important outliers included the journalists Walter Lippmann and Dorothy Thompson.

Increasingly confident and tutored by Irita van Doren and Russell Davenport, Willkie published a series of articles and letters to the editor outlining his views on public policy. He attributed the Depression's depth and persistence to federal obstruction of business investment and free enterprise leading inevitably to a socialized economy. Thus far, little in Willkie's assessment of domestic policy differentiated the utilities executive from Taft or Vandenberg.[12]

Early Willkie supporters spanned the ideological spectrum: from Russell Davenport, a liberal on social issues and an interventionist; to Raymond Moley, who was mentored by Charles Beard in his graduate years at Columbia University and had become an anti–New Deal isolationist espousing the notion that an economically self-sufficient United States had no business engaging in another European war. Willkie supporters also included the Du Ponts, opponents of the Roosevelt administration but anxious for Great Britain's survival; Thomas Lamont and Russell Leffingwell of J. P. Morgan & Co.; and Lewis W. Douglas, founder of the New York–based Century Group, committed to reversal of American isolationism.

Willkie's political ambitions surfaced in late 1939, when he let it be known that, with C&S bought out by the government, he was available for a new line of employment, namely politics. Willkie conceded his interest in a two-and-one-half hour chat with Benjamin Cohen, counsel to the National Power Policy Committee, which was charged with defending public utility control legislation. (The two held frequent exchanges during these years in connection with the implications of the Public Utilities Holding Company Act.) The substance of their exchange, Willkie undoubtedly knew, would surely reach Roosevelt's ears. When the conversation veered to the coming presidential contest, Willkie suggested his preference for Arthur Vandenberg as Republican nominee, yet he was distressed by Vandenberg's position on neutrality and the tariff. Then again, he might support Cordell Hull for the presidency, the likely Democratic nominee in the event Roosevelt declined to run for a third term.

When Cohen teased Willkie concerning rumors circulating in the press that he himself was a candidate, the Hoosier demurred. Cohen reported to the president that, according to Willkie, supporters "offered to put up money (several hundred thousand) to finance him and get him delegates." Initially, Willkie demurred since "he could not imagine himself making the equivocating statements which a candidate must make." Then again, if a telegram informed him that he "had been nominated for president on a platform that embodied principles with which he agreed," he could not refuse. In January 1940, Willkie formally announced his affiliation with the Republican Party. In March, following a successful address at the Commonwealth Club of San Francisco, Willkie and Russell Davenport, his key aide, decided on a run for the main prize.[13]

"We the People," an extensive piece published in *Fortune* in April, elaborated on Willkie's domestic policies and touched on foreign economic policy through support of the Hull trade program and military aid to Finland. Though regarded as skeptical of isolationism, Willkie displayed caution on the subject of assistance to the Allies until the Nazi forces swept through the Low Countries and into France in May 1940. At Akron on May 28, he asked for all-out aid for France and England as the first line of defense for the United States. "We don't want to get into any war if we can possibly help it," Willkie cautioned, yet he managed to differentiate his views from those of Taft.[14]

On the morning of June 27, 1940, Pierre du Pont was informed that with Dewey fading, Taft and Willkie would contest for the nomination at Philadelphia: "Wendell Willkie appears definitely beaten." "For the past twenty-four hours Mr. Hoover has spread every possible poison against the Willkie candidacy." When Hoover failed to impress the party faithful with his convention address, Robert Taft emerged as the legatee of the Great Engineer. Yet Du Pont's source, like so many observers, concluded that Taft, an "able, conscientious, sincere man," was unlikely to defeat

The GOP Senate leadership gathers before the party's 1940 convention, which nominated Wendell Willkie. *Left to right:* Charles McNary (Oregon), Senate minority leader, public-power advocate, early New Deal supporter, and, by this date, an isolationist; Arthur Vandenberg (Michigan), shadow secretary of state, an "insulist" who trusted to economic self-sufficiency, later a mediator between the party's nationalist and internationalist wings; Warren Austin (Vermont), soon identified as a Willkie internationalist and strong advocate of U.S. membership in the United Nations; and Robert A. Taft (Ohio), "Mr. Republican," isolationist, advocate of a balanced budget, stridently in favor of limited powers for the central government, and, at war's end, opposed to American funding of international organizations. (AP Images)

Roosevelt. As for Hoover: "It is agreed by the closest observers at Philadelphia that he would do anything in the world to get the nomination for himself. Failing that, he does not want Willkie to have it."

Willkie proved to be the beneficiary of the convention stalemate engineered in part by Hoover. The Hoosier internationalist won the nomination when Michigan and Pennsylvania dropped favorite-son candidacies. While Vandenberg, Michigan's initial choice, belatedly indicated his preference for Taft, the eastern industrial states, largely internationalist in viewpoint, voted for Willkie. In the end, Taft's hold on the southern delegations and portions of the Midwest proved to be insufficient to block Willkie's victory on the sixth ballot at Convention Hall, a vote no doubt influenced by the capitulation of France to Hitler days earlier. The battle within the party between the isolationists and the internationalists was under way.[15]

It is virtually axiomatic that business competence does not necessarily translate into political success. This was true of Wendell Willkie's leadership of the Republican Party in the remaining short span of his life. While a stunning one-man show at Commonwealth and Southern, Willkie failed to carry along congressional Republicans, who viewed him as an interloper. Support of Roosevelt's foreign policies alienated party isolationists, who were in a majority. He went considerably beyond the party's perfunctory ties to the African American in his advocacy of civil rights. Though admired by his adversaries, including Lillienthal and Benjamin Cohen, who crafted the Public Utilities Holding Company Act, they remained Roosevelt Democrats. His Republican admirers, Ogden and Helen Reid and the Luce *Time-Life-Fortune* coterie upon whom he relied for advice on intraparty decisions were internationalists who operated at the periphery of the GOP's power structure. The Republican Party of Taft and Hoover remained insular, antistatist, and, ultimately, in control.

There were vital personality differences between Willkie and Roosevelt that helped to determine the outcome in 1940. The squire of Hyde Park was an experienced and astute politician who kept dissenters such as Bernard Baruch close to his vest and even co-opted their ideas. Diversity of opinion was tolerated and losing causes often abandoned, no matter how worthy of pursuit. Willkie's 1940 campaign, by way of contrast, was poorly organized, exhausting, and unstructured, whereas Roosevelt's was limited and controlled.

Several early major decisions illustrate Willkie's methods. The choice of Charles McNary as a running mate is open to question. While those around him, especially Ogden and Helen Reid, touted McNary's appeal in the Pacific Northwest, where his support of public power enjoyed wide approval, and in the agricultural Midwest, outsiders who knew the senator best noted that he was indolent and frail. Willkie plunged ahead and persuaded the Senate's minority leader to serve as his running mate. McNary's value as a campaigner was debatable, and Willkie seldom consulted him.[16]

The replacement of John D. M. Hamilton as party chairman by the House minority leader Joseph Martin, at the behest of the Reids, Russell

Davenport, and Alf Landon, also appears to have been less than completely thought out. Hamilton was a reactionary, an isolationist, and a principal in the excommunication of Knox and Stimson from the party following their acceptance of cabinet positions in a Democratic administration bent on aid to the Allies. He was tied to Hoover and the Pews and shared their deep-seated antistatist mentality and determination to repeal the social legislation of the 1930s. Nevertheless, the handsome and dapper Hamilton, well connected in political and moneyed circles, replenished the party's coffers following the failed 1936 campaign. He was an experienced and effective organizer and strongly associated with congressional Republicans in shaping anti–New Deal strategy as opposed to Willkie's advisers, often described as a collection of "boy scouts" (Oren Root's Willkie Clubs) and resented by the party regulars. Yet, this amateur group was responsible for getting a political outsider to the altar, and Willkie distrusted the party regulars.

Hamilton subsequently furnished interviewers with detailed memoranda that described the nominee as a bull in a china shop who was willing to offend Joe Pew and the party regulars, including Ohio's Governor John W. Bricker. Indeed, Joseph Martin, as Hamilton predicted, devoted too little time managing what became a disorganized campaign, and Willkie accorded too little attention to the local party functionaries who swarmed like a bunch of unwelcome locusts about his campaign train. That said, Willkie as presidential candidate and then party leader devoted his energy and last years to a task of enormous dimensions: convincing the Republican Party, anchored in the past, that the United States needed to engage with the modern era by accepting the New Deal's social reforms within a framework of limited government and to assume a role in world affairs it could no longer shun.[17]

A meeting with Hoover in the course of a lengthy vacation at the Broadmoor in Colorado Springs prior to Labor Day illustrates Willkie's insouciance in the world of politics. Indeed, there was no possibility of a meeting of the minds between the two on America's response to Britain's potential demise or rumors of a settlement with the Hitler regime. Yet, typically, consciously or not, Willkie proved less than gracious in his encounters with the party's Old Guard, Hoover included. A recent convert to the church, so to speak, he showed contempt for its stodgy antediluvian elders.

Willkie was exhausted by the prenomination maneuvers and clearly required a respite. Yet, being a workaholic, he decided to confer with the party's elders, notably Hoover. Quite accidentally, it developed, the president's son Elliott Roosevelt checked into the Broadmoor en route to a fishing vacation in Wyoming at the very time Hoover arrived accompanied by his son Allan. When Willkie invited Elliott Roosevelt to dinner with Hoover, the ex-president objected. Willkie: "Why not, why not?" He intended to deal with issues in the campaign, not personalities. (Hoover and FDR loathed one another.) When the invitation to Elliott changed to a brief discussion in Willkie's room with Hoover present, the ex-president absented himself until Roosevelt departed. Several days later, Willkie dismissed Hoover's influence before a group of reporters. This proved to be a precursor of Willkie's habit of ignoring the regulars, resulting in their diminishing support.[18]

In the course of the presidential contest, Willkie affirmed the social programs legislated during the 1930s, supported organized labor, and presented a major statement on the status of the Negro. While it was common in the 1930s for GOP principals to court the Negro vote, it was uncommon to openly express views as strongly as those put forward by Willkie at Chicago on September 13. He committed, if elected, to terminate Jim Crow policies in the federal bureaucracy, including separation of the races and discrimination in hiring; as well as in the administration of relief; and to helping to find "creative work for the Negro." He condemned lynching and, in contrast to Roosevelt, pledged to seek passage of "legislation to curb this evil."[19]

Initially, Willkie's foreign-policy statements were ambivalent. He hedged when offering support for "some form of selective service," which was passed in mid-September as the Burke-Wadsworth Selective Service Act, despite considerable Republican opposition. In the Senate, Taft and Vandenberg opposed. Taft was convinced that a volunteer army would suffice, proposing to Willkie that "there should be a declaration that we are opposed to the draft unless it is absolutely necessary." There is no evidence of a reply. In the House, an amendment by the isolationist Hamilton Fish of New York limiting the number of draftees and imposing a sixty-day delay won the support of 140 Republican votes, with 22 opposed. The statute also limited military service by draftees to the confines of the Western Hemisphere. Harold Ickes's observation proved incisive: It was evident that the party would not follow Willkie's foreign policy, if elected, with Hiram Johnson chairman of the Senate Foreign Relations

Committee and Hamilton Fish heading the House committee. Both were committed isolationists.[20]

Willkie also supported measures designed to maintain Great Britain's war effort including tacitly, if not openly, the destroyer-bases agreement. This was the work largely of William Allen White, chairman of the Committee to Defend America by Aiding the Allies, who served as an intermediary between Roosevelt and Willkie after the party conventions. As result of White's intervention, upon Roosevelt's announcement of the deal on September 3, Willkie, Martin, and McNary remained silent.

As the candidate of the Republican Party, Willkie was torn, nevertheless, in one direction by internationalist supporters and in another by the party regulars, most of whom were isolationists. Thus Grenville Clark, a founder of the World War I Military Training Camps Association (the "Plattsburg movement"), member of the interventionist Century Group, and coauthor of the Burke-Wadsworth bill, distressed by Willkie's recent speeches, expressed a growing receptivity to Roosevelt's third-term bid. As Clark wrote Lewis Douglas, head of Democrats for Willkie, he had become keenly disappointed with Willkie's recent utterances on foreign policy which "changed his tack completely" by suggesting that possible Nazi conquest of Britain and its empire should not take the country into war.

The most passionate missive to Willkie along these lines emanated from the powerful pen of the *Herald-Tribune* journalist Dorothy Thompson, an international columnist expelled from Hitlerite Germany after writing a series of dispatches critical of that regime and its potential for evil. A keen student of history and observer of current affairs in central and eastern Europe, she warned the candidate shortly after his nomination of a world revolution encompassing divergent classes of society and have-not nations led by tyrants desperate for resources—impacted by abrupt scientific and technological change. Germany's advantage, she explained, was informed by a quick grasp of new technologies and their application to the waging of scientific war, while Britain remained tethered to the ways of its commercial and financial classes. Germany's weakness, on the other hand, was based on the notion of its biological superiority, resulting in a lack of the concept of world integration.[21]

Interestingly, Willkie subsequently expressed regret for pressing Roosevelt to pledge that he would not send American boys to die in another European war. Willkie's immediate position on direct involvement, however, seems tactical, even insincere. Both contestants knew better despite firm pledges of abstention. The fact remains, however, that in 1940 Americans of entirely or partial German, Italian, and Irish origin, who were hardly enamored of the British, constituted a powerful voting bloc totaling some 8.7 million as opposed to those of English origin, who numbered some 1.8 million. "I am convinced," Hoover observed, "that if Mr. Willkie would take a clear stand that he was going to keep us out of war, he could carry the whole of the Western states on this issue." With Roosevelt's lead uncertain and a majority of Americans opposed to a replay of United States involvement in the Great War, the GOP candidate pledged on September 16: "Except for the protection of this beloved land of ours, I shall, if you elect me president of the United States, never send an American soldier boy to fight in the shambles of European trenches."[22]

As the campaign wore on and the Luftwaffe attempted to bomb Britain into submission, joined by submarines that sunk a massive amount of British shipping, Willkie pursued Roosevelt like a terrier. The president, he claimed, was responsible for the coming of the war and the lack of American preparedness for its defense; worse still, he was scheming to involve the United States in another war on foreign soil. "Willkie Demands Roosevelt Tell If He Plans War," asserted a *New York Times* headline. "If elected," the Republican nominee pledged, he would "put the question of entrance into the war . . . up to the people." In St. Louis, Missouri, a pivotal electoral state with a substantial population of German origin, Willkie declaimed: "Is it that we should send an expeditionary force over there? Is it that we should join again in a foreign war?" "I believe if you re-elect the third-term candidate they [our boys] will be sent. We cannot and we must not undertake to maintain by arms the peace of Europe." Hoover, satisfied, was willing to appear jointly with California's Senator Hiram Johnson, an aging isolationist, in a speech in support of Willkie.

As the campaign drew to an end, with Willkie closing the gap in polls, Roosevelt responded. At Madison Square Garden, he pointed to the opposition to rearmament of Vandenberg, Taft, Hoover, and the Republicans in Congress generally, coining the catchphrase "Martin, Barton, and Fish" to connote Republican isolationism. At Boston, in an appeal to Irish-Catholic voters, the squire pledged: "I have said this before, but I shall say it again and again and again. Your boys are not going to be sent into any foreign wars." Willkie later rued the decision to press Roosevelt into an impossible claim.

Willkie waged a strenuous campaign, tallying 22.3 million votes as opposed to Landon's 16.7 million and Hoover's 15.7 million, but it was insufficient to overcome 27.2 million for Roosevelt. A combination of ten Deep South states and some half dozen of the nation's largest cities and their surrounding areas proved sufficient to ensure a Democratic presidency. The Republican National Committee outspent its Democratic counterpart by $14 million to $12 million, but the party required a substantial number of rural midwestern states to counteract labor and the minorities in urban areas, groups that were substantial beneficiaries of the New Deal. Roosevelt might not have defeated Willkie but for the widespread conviction that the commander in chief enjoyed greater experience in dealing with an international crisis.

Broken down by region, the results in New England proved disappointing for the Republicans. In 1932 and 1936, the region had been a party mainstay. Willkie fared well in Massachusetts, though he lost ground elsewhere as a consequence of his support for England and Roosevelt's union strength. Roosevelt barely carried the mid-Atlantic states with a plurality of only 600,000 votes. As usual, Republican strength centered in the Midwest, where Willkie received 50.2 percent of the vote. He carried Indiana and Michigan, winning the support of farmers and small-town businessmen and bankers who feared involvement in the war and opposed Hull's trade policies. Roosevelt prevailed in the Mountain states and the Pacific Northwest, an area liberal in outlook and supportive of public power and other New Deal programs. Comparison of the presidential tally with that of the senatorial and congressional vote showed no substantial difference, though gubernatorial candidates fared somewhat better than Willkie, winning some 49.2 percent of the total vote as opposed to his 47.5 percent.

The Roosevelt vote showed a notable difference in social composition to Willkie's. Roosevelt appealed to a majority of skilled and unskilled labor, union members, residents in the larger urban areas, Catholics, Jews, and the foreign-born. African Americans returned to the Democratic fold after a brief flirtation with the GOP in 1938. While the war in Europe probably determined the result, there is no doubt that Depression legislation such as the WPA, Social Security, and the creation of the Federal Housing Administration also affected the outcome.

Willkie's support depended on those of more substantial income, those who did not receive direct government benefits or belong to unions, such as managerial and white-collar workers, residents of small towns, farmers, Protestants, and the native-born. These groups looked for efficiency and economy in government, fiscal prudence, and better relations between business and government and between labor and capital; opposed a third term; feared excessive executive authority; and viewed Willkie as better equipped to bring a return to prosperity.[23]

The closeness of the election, suggesting the possibility that the Republicans might return to majority status in the near future, may well have exacerbated the divisions between Willkie Clubs and the party regulars, between the candidate and the Old Guard, between the internationalists and isolationists. Willkie did not suffer at the hands of Republican voters on the grounds of party irregularity. Yet, the Hoover-Taft wing of the party determined to restore ideological constancy in the face of his advocacy of a liberalized agenda on the domestic and foreign fronts.

W ILLKIE'S 1940 CAMPAIGN for the presidency and his subsequent persistence as party spokesman who pressed the issue
of active participation by the United States in world affairs,
however unwelcome by the party stalwarts, compelled the reconsider-
ation of Republican foreign policy categorized as "insulism" by Michigan's Arthur Vandenberg. In 1941, Roosevelt and Willkie joined in an
effort to maneuver America into participation in another European conflict. In the brief spell culminating with Willkie's death in 1944, Vandenberg, effectively the GOP's shadow secretary of state, gradually in collaboration with Vermont's Senator Warren Austin—whose views replicated
those of Willkie in foreign affairs—moved the party away from isolationism in the direction of active engagement in a cooperative international
effort to prevent another such conflict.

Even before the June 1941 invasion of the Soviet Union, it appeared
that either the world economy would be controlled by a mercantilist
German empire, or alternatively, the United States would promote a relatively open exchange of goods and investment based on the dollar in
place of the pound sterling as the dominant medium of exchange. It became apparent in these years that Great Britain, exhausted by the 1914–18
conflict and rearmament, would prove unable to dominate world trade
and finance. Since the inception of the industrial era, it has been the
function of a powerful leader in the world economy to utilize its economic power to manage trade liberalization, offer monetary stability,
and promote investment. As further explained by Immanuel Wallerstein,
the United States also encouraged multiparty elections, human rights,
moderate decolonization, and free movement of capital. Responding to
domestic pressures, however, the hegemon benefited by advancing its
own economic interests. Thus the Atlantic Charter inferred a partnership

between Britain and America and terminated with American advantage at Bretton Woods.[1]

The belief that the United States could do business with the Hitler regime—propounded by the insular group led by Hoover, Taft, and Vandenberg—ignored both geopolitics and economics. Hitler's strategy, based on the so-called Heartland theory, sought German industrial self-sufficiency through control of international sources of raw materials. Rooted in the works of the British geographer Halford Mackinder, Heartland theory was popular in Weimar and disseminated in the United States. According to Mackinder, he who controls the Eurasian landmass dominates the world. Reconfigured for Hitler by Karl Haushofer, a geographer, retired military officer, and academician, and Rudolf Hess, Haushofer's acolyte and eventually Hitler's deputy führer, Heartland theory held as follows: domination over the Caucasus, the Urals, and the steppes of Central Asia would circumvent the naval superiority of the British Empire. Haushofer advised Hitler while he was a Munich rabble-rouser and subsequently when he was incarcerated in the Weimar years to the effect that acquisition of land and resources were vital for lebensraum and German imperial development. Whereas Haushofer urged alliance with the Soviet Union, Hitler turned instead to German conquest and colonization.[1]

German leadership anticipated that Berlin would serve as the center of a vast economic regime designed to support the Nazi economy. Such a scheme dictated extermination of tens of millions of people in central and eastern Europe and securing needed foodstuffs produced by the German colonizers. This end would be accomplished in collaboration with Japan, which had similar raw-material requirements in the Far East. Since Britain lacked the wherewithal to block these ambitions, an alliance of the island nation with United States was required to withstand domination by Germany in Europe and Africa and the Japanese Empire in Asia.

On January 9, 1941, Hitler forecast that defeat of Russia would be followed by a "battle of the continents," meaning the German Empire opposed by Britain and the United States. Hitler understood that the American economy, by far the world's largest when put to full utilization of resources and combined with that of the British Empire, stood in his way. Indeed, by 1944, the United States produced some 40 percent of the world's armaments. Hitler had modeled his empire on the conquest of the North American continent by the United States as well as on European colonization of Africa and Australia. And his imperial ambitions depended on blitzkrieg, or swift conquests and mobilization of the resources of the conquered territories.

Republican foreign policy needs to be evaluated in this light and as a response to Roosevelt's approach to Depression causation and the coming of the Second World War. Both Hitler and Roosevelt believed that the economic collapse and accompanying massive unemployment ultimately required a worldwide response. That of Hitler depended on rearmament and reemployment induced by statist policies, direct control of resources, extermination of the Jews and subject peoples, and centralized economic management by the Nazi regime. Roosevelt, once the Hull-Peek controversy was settled in favor of the trade agreements program, ascribed the Depression to the collapse of the open trading regime that preceded the First World War. He rejected autarchy, protectionism, and, along with Willkie, colonialism. His policy of economic nationalism in the early 1930s is best understood as "intranationalism," or the conviction that immediate recovery required temporary insulation from world tides. Long-term recovery necessitated the reversal of Britain's imperial trading system, its colonialism, and the consequent strangulation of international trade and investment, a point established in his negotiations with Churchill leading to the Atlantic Charter.[2]

Roosevelt was not inclined to play a major role in Europe until the fall of France, when Hitler's imperial ambitions bordered on realization. The United States faced the likelihood of a cartelized and mercantilist trading system controlled out of Berlin. That FDR would tolerate a German empire tied to imperial Japan controlling the world's resources is doubtful. Once he abandoned neutrality with cash-and-carry, Lend-Lease, assorted naval operations in the Atlantic, and aid to Britain, the stage was set for a struggle within the Republican Party, one that lasted through the war.

The internationalists, a minority in the party—most prominently Stimson, Knox, Willkie, and other members of the party elite—supported Roosevelt's foreign policy. They were opposed by Hoover, Taft, and Vandenberg, the old isolationists and party reactionaries who were untroubled by the likelihood of German economic hegemony. The party lead-

Roosevelt (joined by sons Elliott and FDR Jr.) and Churchill conferred at Placentia Bay off Newfoundland in August 1941, their first meeting. They drafted the Atlantic Charter, a statement of principles for a postwar world. These included "the right of all peoples to choose the form of government under which they will live," "freedom from fear and want," and equal access to trade and raw materials.

ership feared instead Roosevelt's capacity as president to steer the nation into the European conflict and presidential dictatorship, and doubted Great Britain's ability on its own to reverse the Reich's domination of much of the European landmass. "There is no real division upon the cardinal question of arms and munitions for the defense of Britain and the methods of financing them when her resources are exhausted, even to the extent of gifts," Hoover conceded during the Lend-Lease debate in early 1941. On the other hand, he abhorred the congressional delegation of unlimited authority to an unrestrained presidency to purchase and supply arms to belligerents on the ground that "it financially underwrites wars," making the United States effectively a participant in the European conflict.

Hoover insisted that Britain's resources in the United States should be liquidated to finance acquisition of war materiel before the United States afforded financial aid. He also deplored the absence of congressional restrictions on the use of the navy for convoying, and opposed the opening of American ports for repair of belligerent (meaning British) ships. Equally undesirable in his view was the likelihood that the president would give Britain naval vessels, airplanes, and military equipment. Roosevelt's unfettered power to aid Britain short of war, Hoover complained, constituted a formula for involving the United States in another of Europe's perennial conflicts.[3]

With Hoover no longer a serious presidential contender and constrained to the role of party oracle and behind-the-scenes mentor, Robert Taft took the initiative on several fronts. He attempted to limit Roosevelt's maritime adventures and supply of weaponry and naval vessels to Britain; opposed unbalanced budgets used to finance rearmament; sought to prevent or at the least limit Lend-Lease; opposed the centralizing economic tendencies of the modern economy with its implications for overhead economic management; and worked to dispatch Wendell Willkie as a nascent party power.

Taft never modified his views on the critical issues of his time. Before the outbreak of war in Europe, he advised total disengagement by the United States: "I do not believe that victory for either side would seriously endanger our position." The fall of France did not alter this outlook, which was legalistic, nationalistic, and indifferent to the outcome. He voted for repeal of the arms embargo, Taft explained, because international law recognized the right of belligerents to purchase armaments from neutrals. The Ohioan rejected the argument that a British defeat would jeopardize American security, since the Atlantic Ocean and a large navy were sufficient to ensure United States interests. He opposed the transfer of fifty destroyers to Britain on the ground that it would weaken American defenses. Without congressional consent, a presidential transfer would reduce "to scraps of paper in truly Hitler fashion several treaties which are clearly binding on our government."[4]

Passage of Lend-Lease, Taft argued, would inevitably involve the United States in a worldwide war. Concurrently, the financing of preparedness and assistance to Britain threatened budget balance on a massive scale far beyond Roosevelt's projections, leading to inflation and another depression. Roosevelt, Taft held, rationalized excessive expenditure as a stimulus to business and employment; instead it would induce national bankruptcy.[5]

Taft's struggle to purify the Republican Party of Wendell Willkie's interventionist views depended on stalemate in Europe, since England could not conceivably invade the continent. Accordingly, he feared Roosevelt's intention—propounded by Henry Stimson and Frank Knox, Republican apostates—to deliberately create a situation in the Atlantic that provoked direct conflict with Germany. In an address delivered in his hometown of Cincinnati on May 17, 1941, in opposition to Roosevelt's decision to authorize United States convoying of merchant ships carrying munitions for the defense of Great Britain, Taft held:

1. Britain controlled the seas, and convoying British shipping carrying munitions would antagonize the German regime and so was tantamount to American involvement in the war. Taft was not incorrect. Convoying, Lend-Lease, occupation of Iceland, the Roosevelt-Churchill proclamation of an Atlantic Charter, and covert cooperation between the two nations on military strategy effectively made the United States an undeclared belligerent.

2. Direct entry of the United States into the European conflict would require massive expenditure, which would drain the United States economically, lead to insolvency, and result in substantial loss of lives in an extraordinary effort to land troops on the continent. Yet, "we could not be sure that we could finally be able to crush Germany."

3. Assuming the successful defeat of Germany, "we will have to maintain a police force in Germany and throughout Europe." The unavoidable result would be an American Empire.

4. Europe needed to work out its own salvation.

5. Intervention by the United States would result in the destruction of democracy through the granting of unlimited powers to the president.

6. Taft rejected the argument that the defeat of Britain would lead to an attack on the United States by the Axis powers. The contention that the preservation of the British fleet was necessary to the defense of America was "a misrepresentation of fact." The United States possessed the resources to defend itself since the Atlantic and Pacific Oceans constituted an impenetrable barrier.

7. Alliance with Britain was a strategic error since that nation, given its interests and position, was bound to interfere on the Continent.

8. Taft rejected Willkie's contention "that we are wholly dependent on foreign trade" on the grounds that the United States was virtually self-sufficient. Total exports amounted to 5 percent of national income. Nor

was strangulation of foreign trade a factor in the Great Depression. He had no problem with German investment and economic penetration in South America, which simply replicated that of the British.

9. It did not matter whether Germany or England won the contest in Europe. Both would be impoverished at its end.[6]

"One of the best fellows in the world," Taft's uncle Horace called his nephew, but "dead wrong on our foreign policy." According to Taft's biographer, "he consistently underestimated German power." Indeed, while well informed on domestic policy, Robert Taft was disinterested in foreign affairs and indifferent to the moral implications of the European struggle.[7]

"I feel very strongly that Hitler's defeat is not vital to us," Taft wrote his good friend and political advisor Richard B. Scandrett in January 1941. Following a dinner in June with the senator, Scandrett summed up: "Our differences of opinion really boiled down to your conviction that the United States would not be in serious jeopardy if England were defeated," although Taft's position, Scandrett conceded, differed from that of Charles Lindbergh, who "had less revulsion in respect to the Nazi creed than you have." Scandrett elaborated his own position: "The important issue in this isolationist against internationalist controversy . . . is as to what constitutes a necessary defense for the United States. I think we are in great danger if we don't get into the war quickly and you think we are in great danger if we do."[8]

An exchange with Colby Chester, president of General Foods Corporation, in June 1942 illustrates Taft's fear of an omnicompetent state and his belief in the need for insularity. The corporate executive and liberal internationalist proposed that the GOP remained a minority party unable to curb Roosevelt's statist policies because it missed the two most pressing issues of the previous decade, provision of social insurance and the need for international security. Chester cited surveys by the Opinion Research Corporation that demonstrated that the Roosevelt administration had met the need "to protect ourselves against the aggression of the dictators," and argued further that Willkie would have won in 1940 by a narrow majority but for the Republican Party's association with opposition to preparedness. According to Chester, the GOP needed to move to the center and win over the marginal vote. Thus, while 63 percent of Republican voters polled in June 1940 favored one year's military training for able-bodied males, in September, Republicans in the House voted against conscription 112 to 52. While a majority of voters supported Lend-Lease and Neutrality Act revision, a substantial majority of House Republicans opposed.

Taft's reply is instructive. Polls taken considerably before the next congressional election in November 1942, he maintained, had scant current validity. The Republican Party, he replied, had not missed the two great challenges of the previous decade. It had not opposed social insurance; rather, it had opposed the New Deal's excesses and suffered weak party leadership, meaning, of course, the compromises offered by Landon and Willkie in 1936 and 1940. As for "missing the boat on international security," Taft conceded nothing. "Mr. Willkie presented an international policy exactly similar to that of Mr. Roosevelt." Republicans should have opposed conscription and taken a clear position against involvement in war. The fundamental fallacy of Chester's memorandum, according to Taft, was its contention that the Republican Party need follow public opinion. Rather, the party should commit to principles based on the Constitution without compromise while accommodating to modern conditions. His principal fear for the Republicans, he related, was Wendell Willkie's capacity to divide the party at war's end.[9]

Election of a number of former isolationists in the 1942 congressional contest signaled that prewar opposition to involvement with Europe carried no political liability. The isolationists neither offered a mea culpa nor conceded a substantial degree of American participation in the postwar world. As Taft later framed the issue, initially "I was opposed to entering the war because I did not believe that aggression in Europe was so dangerous so as to threaten our own safety." This was particularly true once Germany invaded Russia. The American century, he also insisted to the end of his days, should be based exclusively on the principle of moral leadership.[10]

Following American entry into the war, old isolationists and the internationalists in the Congress contested the level of American aid to Europe, the issue of postwar reimbursement by recipients of economic and material assistance, and the nature of commitments to an international organization resembling the League of Nations. Prewar isolationists—among them McNary, Nye, Vandenberg, James Davis of Pennsylvania, Robert La Follette Jr., Hiram Johnson, Henrik Shipstead, and Arthur Capper—dominated the minority party's representation on the Senate Foreign Relations Committee and stood ready to block postwar agreements unless limited to their nationalist premises. They sought to limit Lend-Lease and were critical of British and Soviet management of United States aid. Led by Vandenberg, they sought greater congressional involvement in negotiation of reciprocal trade agreements when extension of the Hull program came up for renewal, and extended reciprocity legislation for only two years.

Recalling the unwillingness of the United States—with the GOP in the lead—to join the League of Nations following the First World War, Roosevelt and Hull moved cautiously with regard to involvement in a postwar organization. In the Senate, Tom Connally, chairman of the Senate Foreign Relations Committee, set up a special subcommittee for consideration of postwar resolutions. Vandenberg emerged as a bridge between Senate Republicans and the administration and between isolationists and internationalists in the GOP. He noted that he was positioned "somewhere between the international extremists, who contemplate the new modeling of the world in all the global consequences the term implies, and national extremists who can still think exclusively in pre–Pearl Harbor terms." An informal arrangement with Taft left Vandenberg in charge of shaping Republican foreign policy for the next presidential campaign. Both renounced any intention to secure the party's 1944 nomination in part to find a compromise candidate who could block Willkie's ambition in that direction.[11]

With few exceptions, accounts of this era center on involvement of the United States in the Second World War and the postwar arrangements. Yet, the nation's future was also shaped substantially with the defeat in 1943 of proposals formulated in the executive branch by the National Resources Planning Board (NRPB). In this instance, the GOP, led by Taft, who allied with southern Democrats, checkmated the Roosevelt administration's attempt to implement state-centered economic planning and a comprehensive welfare system following the war's conclusion. The Senate countered by creating a Special Committee on Post-War Economic Planning, its role being to ensure legislative participation in the international settlement and a return to a market economy as expeditiously as possible.[12]

The NRPB plan for peacetime planning presented by the president was intended to avoid repetition of the recession that followed the First World War and to ensure a full-employment economy. The NRPB originated, under Title II of the National Industrial Recovery Act of June 1933, as the National Planning Board. It was funded by public-works monies and guided by a board of three volunteers: FDR's uncle Frederic A. Delano, a city and regional planner, who chaired; and two distinguished academicians, the University of Chicago political scientist Charles E. Merriam and the Columbia University economist Wesley Clair Mitchell.

Merriam's influence on the National Planning Board reflected his summary chapter of *Recent Social Trends,* a study initiated by the Hoover administration. There he observed that contemporary advances in international trade and investment, sanitation, communication, transportation, and industry required attention at all levels of government. Administrative agencies staffed by trained professionals and the advance of research would facilitate government replication of the business model. This would serve as a basis for the next stage of development, an agency geared to remediation of the business cycle.[13]

The National Resources Committee (NRC), successor to the National Planning Board, enlarged its brief to include studies of population, consumption, industrial location, output, and other factors that impacted the business cycle. In the process, Merriam envisioned the need for government economic planning, as "business cannot protect itself effectively against the business cycle hazard." This task was assigned to the NRC's Industrial Committee. In view of the growing strength of the congressional conservative coalition in the late 1930s, questions about the renewal of the NRC became entangled with opposition to executive reorganization, and the agency was very nearly aborted by the Congress. It was rescued by the president as the National Resources Planning Board in 1939 and domiciled in the Executive Office of the President, yet it depended on annual funding by a hostile Congress averse to the concept of planning.

Relying on a paper, "Price Flexibility and the Full Employment of Resources," by the Harvard economist Alvin Hansen, a consultant and frequent adviser, the newly formed NRPB adopted his views as the bedrock of its future agenda: government investment or countercyclical expenditure when the private sector failed to sustain a full-employment economy. Hansen's work appealed to Marriner Eccles at the Federal Reserve and to Lauchlin Currie, Leon Henderson, and Harry Dexter White and won over a generation of young economists lodged in the Roosevelt administration.[14]

The NRPB adopted Hansen's formula for a full-employment economy including public-works expenditure financed by deficit spending, income redistribution through tax revision, and expanded social insurance. At their meetings with Roosevelt, they projected studies of relief and unemployment; an industrial-economic study accompanied by programs of action; study of defense problems including a shelf of public projects to head off a postwar recession; and estimates of national income required to absorb the labor supply into an economy based partly on business expansion, partly on net government contributions. In order to assist in future funding of public works through the Federal Reserve, Hansen was appointed special economic adviser to the Federal Reserve's Board of Governors in 1941. These and other reports designed to forestall a postwar depression saw the light of day as *National Resources Development Report for 1943, Part I. Post War Plan and Program,* accompanied by *Security, Work, and Relief Policies.* Congress, with Taft in the lead, responded by withdrawing funding for the agency in 1943.[15]

Hansen's views were predicated on the assumption that the deep recession following the First World War would be repeated and that economic downdrafts did not automatically self-correct. The economist foresaw an additional burden following the current conflict: absorption of millions of defense workers and war veterans into productive civilian life. In its publications directed by John Kenneth Galbraith, *After Defense—What?*—of which more than one hundred thousand copies were distributed—and in Hansen's *After the War—Full Employment,* a considerable level of unemployment was assumed requiring government investment in multipurpose regional programs resembling the TVA. Though modified on an annual basis at a level sufficient to assure full employment, these would be long-range infrastructure projects for integrated transport, industrial location, the national electric grid, urban redevelopment, public-health programs, and hospital, educational, and recreational facilities—all funded by temporary reliance on deficit spending. Such expenditure would be coordinated with government loans, banking control, labor and wage regulations, and price management.[16]

According to Hansen, a full-employment postwar program necessitated the creation of a central planning agency in tandem with a fiscal authority designed to coordinate federal investment with long-term projects and the business cycle. While lodged in the Executive Office of the President and capable of timing investments, such an agency would be responsible to the House and Senate, which would provide expenditure within authorized guidelines. Such an authority was never created, and fiscal policy remained part of the political process.

Hansen's proposals for a full-employment economy and increased levels of national income following the war included social provision for health, nutrition and medical care, education, youth employment, recreation, library services, and minimum security including loss of normal income, insurance against unemployment, illness and accident, and loss of the family breadwinner. The drafting of specific proposals became the responsibility of a Columbia University economist, Eveline Burns.

Security, Work and Relief Policies, submitted by the president to Congress in March 1943, represented Burns's projection of a desirable social insurance program intended to mitigate downward cyclical fluctuation and meet society's social obligations. Burns had taken her doctorate at the London School of Economics, and her findings resembled the recent *Beveridge Report,* which served as the foundation of Great Britain's postwar welfare state. A highly regarded scholar of German and British social-welfare systems, Burns participated in the National Consumers League, a group of reformist women attorneys and social scientists, and served as a major contributor to the New Deal Social Security program.[17]

The Burns report assumed a postwar program geared to income maintenance, including access to public work at prevailing wages for employables unable to find work in the private sector; comprehensive guarantees against the hazards of accident, disease, and old age; and assurance of a minimum living standard. Unemployment insurance would be extended to twenty-six weeks and, like Social Security, federalized with coverage extended to domestics and agricultural labor. Social insurance would reach those unable to work, the blind, the disabled, and dependent children. Youths would benefit from apprenticeships or financial aid for higher education. Health services would reach mothers and dependent children and cover nutrition and disease prevention.

The results of the 1942 congressional election sealed the fate of reforms directed toward planning and a welfare state. Moreover, there is no evidence that a majority of Americans favored European-style social guarantees or an industrial policy. Considerably before Roosevelt transmitted the NRPB report to Congress in May 1943, both James Byrnes, an astute political manager during his Senate service and currently head of the Office of Economic Stabilization, and Corrington Gill, a longtime aide to the socially minded Harry Hopkins, urged the president not to wage a fight with a hostile Congress on the continuation of the NRPB or its proposed agenda. Privately, Roosevelt offered concessions to the archconservative Virginia Democrat Carter Glass. To no avail. Burns was attacked in the Congress as author of an "American Beveridge Plan," and the NRPB was killed in conference.

In theory, the NRPB agenda, based on Merriam's point of view, called for decentralized management through regional planning at the state and local level. It would have developed and utilized the sort of expertise at the state level envisioned in Hoover's New Economic Era of the 1920s. Nevertheless, Taft bridled and led the Republican opposition, categorizing Burns as a "socialist disciple of Harold Laski." Instead Taft preferred a society rooted in "individual initiative and reward for hard work and ability" and anticipated "full employment through private enterprise and no other way."[18]

In a series of addresses in response to Hansen's and the NRPB's plans for a postwar America, Taft rejected the notion of government assumption of responsibility for full employment and a welfare state. "Mr. Republican" recapitulated Hoover's doctrine of limited government: resort to the private sector for full employment and self-reliance, turning to the states and local organizations for sustenance when in need.

Taft's political philosophy rested on the separation of powers. He conceded to the president broad authority as commander in chief in wartime, notably the management of military strategy and defense, but he objected to the gradual accretion of power to the executive at the expense of the legislative branch. Congress, he argued, needed to reverse its tendency to grant unnecessary authority over the domestic economy to executive agencies such as the NRPB, a perfect example of the usurpation of power by an unelected bureaucracy. Had Hansen, he wanted to know, testified before a congressional committee? Had the legislative branch granted authority to the president for creation of an authority to draft an agenda represented as a domestic Atlantic Charter and an economic Bill of Rights?

Taft contrasted excessive economic controls over the individual under Roosevelt to the voluntarism that had characterized organization for the First World War. "We are a self-organizing nation," Taft insisted, and once Americans were offered a sensible reason for self-denial and the need for cooperation, they would comply. Currently "the Price Administration is full of professors and theorists with hardly a practical businessman in the crowd. . . . I would like to see a Congress that does not accept blindly every idea thrust upon the president by some professor of economics." This appeared especially true of Hansen's economics.

Post-War Plan and Program, also released by the NRPB in 1943, suggested the possibility of joint federal-private management of corporations essential to national defense, embracing aluminum, magnesium, basic metals, synthetic rubber, and aircraft production. Mixed public-private ownership also would be utilized for urban redevelopment, housing, and electric power, with the degree of government ownership determined by the public interest. Earlier, in June 1942, Hansen, according to the *Chicago Journal of Commerce,* predicted before a group of bankers and business executives that Congress in the future would need to surrender the power to tax except within broad limits. The economist apparently meant that an agency within the executive branch should be given some latitude in the use of fiscal power similar to the Fed's use of monetary policy to counter short-term fluctuations in the cycle. When he added that social reforms would be delegated to the administration, which would later retain its wartime authority, Taft condemned the planners as contemplating "socialization of the United States after the war."

A conciliatory reply by Hansen referred Taft to enclosures from the liberal newspaper *P.M.,* which he claimed corrected a "misimpression" by a prejudiced reporter. The economist also dispatched an article published in *Fortune* in which the "Prophet of the New Economics" explained the peacetime need for a bank of public works available in periods of slack to sustain a full-employment economy. His nonpartisan program found an increasingly favorable response in New York, Philadelphia, and Cincinnati among businessmen and bankers in light of the widely accepted forecast of a postwar depression.[19]

Unconvinced, Taft, Vandenberg, and other legislators, both Democratic and Republican, created an alternative to the NRPB, the Senate Special Committee on Post-War Economic Planning, a subcommittee of the Senate Finance Committee, both of which were chaired by Georgia's Walter George. According to the Vandenberg Diary, "I think this may be the most important committee in the history of the Senate." With its mission defined as responsibility for shaping postwar national policy, the so-called George Committee represented Congress's determination to retain authority over postwar fiscal and economic policy rather than cede virtual control in these areas to the executive branch. Yet Congress was not equipped to rationalize fiscal policy in the face of political pressures. While Hansen and Keynes proposed fiscal restraint in a boom and compensating expenditure in a recession, political pressures and immediate requirements determined public expenditure as opposed to rationalization of the cycle.[20]

"Mr. Republican" suffered no significant opposition in the Grand Old Party following Wendell Willkie's fatal heart attack in 1944. Taft's message was simple and constant: balance the budget; limit central authority in order to preserve traditional freedoms; and rely on free enterprise to prevent a postwar depression. There is no mention of monetary policy in Taft's correspondence beyond a return to gold and the removal of authority granted to the president by the Thomas Amendment for currency depreciation. Fiscal policy was defined as a balanced budget. Nor is there evidence of recognition on Taft's part that Willkie, whom he regarded as an outlier, pulled in substantially more votes than Hoover or Landon, or that the party fared well in the 1940 campaign under Willkie's centrist domestic and international philosophy. Indeed, Taft preferred that the Republican Party retain minority status rather than veer from fundamental principles.

8 | CHALLENGING ISOLATION: THE PROVOCATEUR, THE PATRICIAN, AND THE MEDIATOR

A T THE OUTSET, Wendell Willkie's decision to engage the Republican Party on the issue of foreign policy met with a rebuff. A substantial number of Republican legislators at the national level were isolationist—or later termed nationalists—and remained so even after America's involvement in the Second World War. This group included Taft, Vandenberg, who later accommodated his views to political necessity and America's postwar role, and Charles McNary, Willkie's 1940 running mate and Senate minority leader. In addition, the legislative branch included many alumni of America First including Gerald Nye, Hiram Johnson, Karl Mundt, and the Wisconsin Progressive Robert La Follette Jr., who served on the Senate Foreign Relations Committee.

Willkie was regarded as an outsider by the GOP leadership, including his chosen party chairman, Joe Martin, an isolationist who opposed the prewar draft and Lend-Lease. According to Martin, while Willkie would have his say in party councils, "Members of Congress and Republican governors would be looked to for advice." Even this observation overstated the chairman's receptivity to the party's youthful liberal internationalist governors such as Leverett Saltonstall (Massachusetts), Raymond Baldwin (Connecticut), Earl Warren (California), and Harold Stassen (Minnesota), who were aligned with Willkie internationalism at the Mackinac Island Conference of 1943, which considered American membership in an organ for preservation of the postwar peace.[1]

Willkie's internationalism has been ascribed to the influence of some prominent Republicans such as Henry Luce and his writers, notably Russell Davenport; Wall Street bankers, particularly Morgan & Co.'s Thomas Lamont and Russell Leffingwell; and the Reid family's *New York Herald Tribune,* notably the newspaper's book editor, Irita Van Doren. His openness to their ideas led to a willingness to challenge outdated notions of America's role in the world. Regarded as argumentative and thin-skinned, Willkie was an overachiever who rose in the business universe through ambition, hard work, and extraordinary personal will. Unfortunately, he was too erratic, too undisciplined, and too willing to engage in personal combat to assume national leadership.

However flawed in temperament, Willkie managed over time to pressure the Grand Old Party toward a greater awareness of a world impacted by depression, war, globalization, the emergence of nonwhite societies, and the responsibilities of America as the major player in the international economy. The Republican Party, he also insisted, "arose from the people's urge to build a strong national government to offset the disruptive, weakening influence of states' rights doctrine." This view, founded in his consciousness of its origins as a party of emancipation and civil rights, waited for acceptance by a later generation.[2]

The Morgan & Co. partners were astute observers of Willkie's capacities and shortcomings. Thomas Lamont cautioned that the independence and contempt demonstrated toward the party regulars by Oren Root's Willkie Clubs, and by the candidate personally during and after the 1940 presidential campaign, would prove damaging to his future political ambitions. Wary of Willkie's attempt at re-creating the Wilsonian vision of a world shaped by American institutions, Russell Leffingwell preached instead some degree of disengagement. German ambitions in Eurasia needed to be checked, he reasoned, but Germany itself need not be destroyed: "My notion is . . . to stop the Germans, to defeat them, and then to leave them and the continental Europeans to work out their own salvation. . . . And I don't think we have to rebuild Europe." Leffingwell cautioned that the United States should avoid veering between "the extreme of isolationism to the extreme of Messianic delusion." Like Willkie, on the other hand, he believed that, in the current setting, America needed to defend itself, the British Empire, Russia, and China against German ambitions for world dominion, lest it, too, become a servile state existing on Germany's terms.[3]

Willkie expressed willingness to undertake another run for the presidency in 1944, if nominated by the party, with the proviso that the party abandon its narrow nationalism, which included rejection of Hull's doctrine of open trade. This required initial support for Britain in its contest against the Nazi regime through all-out aid, particularly by providing naval vessels and other armaments, and by keeping the sea lanes open. If Hitler won, he maintained with critical insight, "America will shortly find herself, either because of trade or defense, on a totalitarian basis as it would not be able to exist otherwise against a totalitarian Europe."[4]

By early 1941, with Roosevelt determined to afford substantial aid to Britain in the form of Lend-Lease and to enlist such Republican support as he could muster, Willkie was invited to the White House for a pre-inaugural private dinner. The former combatants sat in the president's study until after midnight, according to James Roosevelt, "and at regular intervals great bursts of laughter from the two congenial men could be heard coming from behind the closed door." The journalist Roscoe Drummond cautioned, however, that while Willkie had moments of admiration and respect for Roosevelt, "there were deep philosophical differences between the two[,] and I always felt that Willkie considered that it was necessary to be on his guard in his relations with Roosevelt."

At a dinner hosted by Irita Van Doren, the *New York Herald Tribune* book review editor, on January 15, 1941, Willkie elaborated on his newfound differences with the business community and his decision to support United States aid to Britain. A small group attended: the *Tribune* columnist Joseph Alsop, who reported Willkie's observations to Roosevelt; Robert Kintner, Alsop's colleague; Harold Guinzburg, a founder of Viking Press; and Guinzburg's wife, the columnist Dorothy Thompson. The occasion emanated from a suggestion made on New Year's Day by Alsop and Guinzburg that Willkie undertake a trip to Britain to determine its needs, hopefully undercutting Republican isolationist criticism of aid to London. Willkie had made that visit in early January.

Addressing the small gathering, Willkie categorized the Republican Party leadership of Taft, Landon, Vandenberg, Dewey, and Joe Martin as nationalist, with Hoover "the brains of the isolationist movement today." He described the business community as restive under what it regarded as New Deal economic interference. Most businessmen, he believed, were convinced that the war could be brought to a close if the United States exerted sufficient pressure to that end inasmuch as they "could do more profitable business with Europe than ever before," with Nazi unification.

A few days earlier, upon learning that both Hoover and Landon planned to announce their opposition to Roosevelt's proposal for Lend-Lease to Britain, Willkie had stated on January 12, 1941: "I have examined the so-called 'Lend-Lease' bill in the light of the current emergency, and I have personally come to the conclusion that, with modification, it should be passed." He proposed a time limit of two years, requiring the

Following a trip to beleaguered London, Wendell Willkie conveyed his observations to Secretary of State Cordell Hull and the president. A few days later, in testimony before the Senate Foreign Relations Committee, he endorsed Lend-Lease to the dismay of Republican isolationists. Willkie proceeded to support the balance of Roosevelt's agenda for all-out aid to Britain. (AP Images)

measure's renewal. His recent trip to England and endorsement of Lend-Lease meant, for all practical purposes, that Willkie joined Stimson and Knox in exile from the Grand Old Party as a consequence of informal membership in Roosevelt's war cabinet. This became evident when he testified before congressional committees regarding his visit to Britain.[5]

Willkie received a cool welcome in February from the members of the Senate Foreign Relations Committee, where isolationists dominated. The notion of a loyal opposition was unacceptable in the eyes of Willkie's fellow Republicans, who evidently inferred that the party's 1940 presidential nominee had joined the enemy with his trip to London and by hobnobbing with FDR. Earlier, Vandenberg, a member of the committee, had indicated that he regarded a United States guarantee of a negotiated peace in Europe preferable to American involvement in the war. In the interim, he argued, the American public would not support "all-out aid to Great Britain." He would endorse aid to Britain on the condition that "we do not become a co-belligerent" and provided that the United States would refrain from stripping its own defenses.[6]

The debate between Roosevelt and Arthur Vandenberg over aid to Britain prior to the introduction of Lend-Lease (H.R. 1776) reflected another consideration in the senator's view: the pending introduction of socialism under Ernest Bevin in England after the war promised a welfare state and the nationalization of key industries in the island nation. Vandenberg fumed: "Are we to fight for that, too?" Antistatist Republicans suspected that various provisions found in H.R. 1776, as originally presented by the administration, signaled duplication of the Bevin program by New Dealers.[7]

In his opening statement before the Senate Foreign Relations Committee, Willkie suggested that the American people and their representatives had not yet grasped the implications of a German victory in Europe: Africa, Southeast Asia, and ultimately the Atlantic Ocean and Latin America would come under the control of the totalitarian powers. "Great nations cannot isolate themselves," he said. The United States would need to respond with equally centralized domestic controls and would eventually be drawn into a war that it would need to fight on its own.

Vandenberg opened the questioning. Did Willkie believe that all-out aid to Britain would lead to American conflict with Germany? Did he favor direct involvement should it appear that Britain would collapse? He was not a member of Congress, Willkie parried, but then responded that he contemplated no need for United States involvement in the present circumstances, reflecting his awareness that a substantial majority of the American public favored Lend-Lease but opposed entry into the European war.

When isolationist Democrats—Bennett Champ Clark (Missouri), Guy Gillette (Iowa), and Robert Reynolds (North Carolina)—pressed Willkie along similar lines with respect to convoying and the dispatch of destroyers to England, they too received evasive replies. He favored all-out aid but was unwilling to predict the future, and he opposed direct United States involvement in the European conflict.

On March 8, 1941, H.R. 1776 passed the Senate by a vote of 62 to 33. The House of Representatives voted along party lines: 135 Republicans, including minority leader Joe Martin, opposed Lend-Lease aid to Britain. The final act made no provision for the nationalization of industry;

convoying of Lend-Lease aid by United States naval vessels was prohibited; and American vessels were enjoined from entering combat zones. Of twenty-two senators representing the Midwest, fourteen voted against Lend-Lease, eleven of this number Republican. Other Republican opponents of Lend-Lease included four in the Northeast, a reflection of the anti-British feelings of voters of Irish and Italian heritage, and three in the Far West, where there was more concern with Japan than Europe. Support for Lend-Lease, further broken down, was strongest in urban-industrial areas of New England, the southern states, and Ohio, areas proximate to Europe; opposition was centered largely in agrarian America. Vandenberg was distressed. "If America 'cracks up,' " he recorded in his diary, "you can put your finger on this precise moment when the crime was committed."

Lend-Lease, Vandenberg believed, destroyed traditional American foreign policy, placed the nation in the midst of power politics, and committed the United States to "nothing short of full participation in the war if that be necessary to a British victory. . . . We have said to Hitler, Mussolini and Japan: We are at undeclared war on you." Involvement would lead to the expenditure of billions, dollar devaluation, and ultimately totalitarianism. As for the situation at hand, the United States would need to provide convoys to protect the goods it shipped to England, and the president, as commander in chief, could order the navy to do as he pleased. "At that . . . instant we are in the war up to our necks." "All of our protests may be futile," Hoover agreed, "but the day will come when there will be retribution. . . . It is vital that men like yourself have stood steadfast." Vandenberg "had the feeling, as the result of the ballot was announced, that I was witnessing the suicide of the Republic."

Conceding privately that he had lost the fight for insulation from Europe's turmoil, Vandenberg gradually shifted gears. He rationalized aid to London in the expectation that it would facilitate a stalemate between Britain and Germany, leading to termination of their conflict. Sympathetic with the views of America First, Vandenberg was persuaded—likely by Charles Lindbergh's estimates—that Germany could not be defeated. Hitler and Churchill, he concluded, would ultimately be compelled to reach a negotiated peace lest chaos and mutual exhaustion result in a Communist takeover of Europe. Vandenberg's concerns typified those of the isolationists: German military could not be overcome except by a costly invasion of the European landmass; the United States was made impregnable by the Atlantic and Pacific Oceans; and British interests were at the bottom of interventionist pressures.[8]

In time, Vandenberg expressed willingness to see the United States guarantee a negotiated European peace as a means of avoiding involvement in war. His opposition to arming merchant vessels or sending them into combat zones softened. He voted for Lend-Lease appropriations since Congress and the president acted strictly within the Constitution. There came a time, he ventured, when one must concede the issue to the legislative majority or democracy cannot function.[9]

Confronted by the depth of isolationist sentiment in the GOP, Willkie initially offered support for Roosevelt's interventionist program in a context of national unity, provided American aid was limited to the provision of arms and supplies for England against the Nazi onslaught. In time he embraced convoying, repeal of the Neutrality Act, and other measures that signaled growing American belligerence. Undoubtedly, both Willkie and Roosevelt anticipated eventual direct involvement.

In the process, Willkie gained support among internationalist Republicans in the Senate, notably Vermont's Warren Austin, a patrician and an attorney whose practice initially focused on economic investment and development in China. Appointed to the Senate in 1931, Austin won reelection until his designation as ambassador to the newly created United Nations after the Second World War. While an opponent of Roosevelt's domestic policies, the two politicians maintained a cordial relationship. Highly regarded by his colleagues and by Charles McNary, minority leader in the Senate, Austin served as acting leader during McNary's frequent absences until ousted from that post by the isolationists in 1943.

The rift between Austin and the isolationists began with his support of Roosevelt's interventionist policies on Britain's behalf, particularly after the fall of France, when it appeared that the president intended to maneuver the nation into involvement in the European conflict. Austin voted for repeal of the arms embargo on the grounds that it favored the Axis by depriving Britain and France of their defense requirements, and for legislation reviving the draft, Lend-Lease, and approval of Henry Stimson as secretary of war. All of these measures were opposed by a majority of his Republican colleagues. Deliberative in nature, Austin hesitated to alienate isolationist Republicans in the Senate given his role as deputy minority leader.

Prior to Pearl Harbor, Austin in his service as senior Republican member of the Military Affairs Committee treated as unrealistic the concept of neutrality by a democracy in the face of the Nazi regime. Only one or the other type of regime would survive. He considered an "introvert" foreign policy based on the protection afforded by the Atlantic Ocean as dangerous, since an Axis victory in Europe would expose American shores to invasion more readily than the reverse. Defeat of Britain would give Germany command of that nation's shipping and control of the seas, cutting off strategic commodities required by the United States. The resulting negotiations would not be with the Germans, Austin concluded, but with the Nazis. Fundamentally, Austin feared the end of democracy and with it those institutions sheltered by democracies, "justice, morality, and spiritual development."

In his deliberate maneuvers over several years, Austin provided the legal basis for American involvement in the rebirth of a confederation of nations to preserve the peace. More impulsive, Willkie served in the role of provocateur by moving a minority of the party toward acceptance of America's role in the world transformed by a major shift in economic power.

In the process, Willkie won the support of columnists such as Arthur Krock, Walter Lippmann, Dorothy Thompson, and Joe Alsop, as well as the internationalist press, including the Luce publications *Time, Life,* and *Fortune;* the *New York Times* and *Herald Tribune;* the *Chicago Daily News, Kansas City Star,* Pulitzer's *St. Louis Post Dispatch* and the *Minneapolis Star and Tribune* and *Des Moines Register and Tribune,* both owned by the Cowles brothers; and Lewis Douglas, an ardent warhawk in the critical years 1940–41.

In these years, a popular majority composed largely of those with German roots in the Midwest and of Irish background in New England was persuaded by the arguments of America First and similar antiwar and anti-involvement groups nurtured by antagonism to the British Empire. The claim was made that Germany was militarily invincible, German ambitions were legitimate, and American involvement in the defeat of the Hitler regime was sought essentially by international bankers and an eastern Jewish elite that dominated the press, finance, and the Roosevelt entourage.

In response to an article published by Charles Lindbergh, Willkie, more openly aggressive than Roosevelt on the issue of supplying Britain with war materials, urged the United States to give Britain "the ships in our docks, the ships in our coastwise trade—until it hurts." Germany's victory would give the United States two alternatives: trade on the terms of the totalitarian powers or self-containment and inevitable bankruptcy. "The capital of the world of tomorrow," he predicted, "will be either Berlin or Washington. I prefer Washington."

At its core, the pre–Pearl Harbor debate between Willkie as Roosevelt's surrogate and Lindbergh on the other represented a rerun of Vansittart's geopolitical evaluation some years earlier. Vansittart envisaged an inevitable conflict between Britain and the United States on the one hand and an alliance of Germany and Japan on the other. Whereas the Lindbergh-Hoover-Taft-Vandenberg axis was given to the conviction that the Nazi regime could not be defeated on military grounds, Willkie attempted to persuade the party's internationalist minority to support Roosevelt's decision to ally with Britain.

Lindbergh's argument, at bottom, while rooted in anti-Semitism, racist theory, and admiration of the Hitler regime, argued the hopelessness of an American attempt to outgun the economic machine forged in Berlin and its military might, especially air power. This was a fiction. German recovery, despite exceptional state intervention, was irregular and for the most part sluggish in the 1930s and did not match that of the United States. Both economies recovered from the Depression's depth in 1932, but whether measured in GNP, average annual growth, output per man-hour, or real wages, American economic advancement far exceeded that of Germany in the interwar era.

In the process, Willkie took on the isolationist wing of the party. At Madison Square Garden, New York, in May he challenged the doctrine that London was likely to fall, that aid to Britain would denude the United States of its own defenses, and that German production was capable of surpassing that of England and the United States. "Give to her destroyers," he urged at the very time Hoover proclaimed in a radio address that the nation was unprepared for involvement in Europe, and that Germany's economic and military strength required a lengthy American buildup and consequently a debilitating decade of conflict. Hoover contended further that Congress should vote on the underlying issue: "Shall we declare war on Germany or Italy or Japan?" Indeed, as Grenville Clark, the Wall Street attorney and adviser to Willkie, put it, the only practical means of aiding England was to provide convoys; and the convoying of merchant vessels led to the conclusion that, effectively, the United States was at war with the Hitler regime.[10]

Willkie entered into a direct confrontation with the party powers, one he lost in a series of encounters that continued up to his death on the eve of the 1944 presidential election. In September 1941, he announced his intention to either rid the GOP of its isolationist legislators or to form a new coalition based on internationalist foreign policies and a return to liberal domestic policies. Further, according to the columnist Jay Hayden, Willkie assembled a "proscribed list" that totaled 202 members of the House of Representatives: 133 Republicans including Minority Leader Joe Martin, 65 Democrats, and 4 Progressives who very nearly defeated the Army Selective Service Extension bill.[11]

With American entry into the war, Willkie continued to tackle the isolationists, beginning with the Republican National Committee gathering of April 20, 1942. Customarily these meetings were routine and had little effect on party doctrine. Party ideology and programmatic matters are decided by the congressional leadership. The Chicago conclave proved to be an exception, with Taft and Willkie contesting the extent of future participation of the United States in international affairs.

Willkie desired a declaration on postwar policy that pledged that with the conflict's end, the United States would undertake "reasonable international responsibilities" including support of "free institutions and a free way of life." In an interview and a subsequent statement, he insisted that the party repudiate isolationism, advocate full participation by the nation in world affairs, and support in the coming primaries the candidates who endorsed these principles. Taft viewed the resolution introduced by Willkie's supporters as endangering those in Congress who had opposed war preparations and involvement in the conflict. Taft countered with a resolution that made no mention of postwar policy. In its place, he emphasized elimination of waste and unnecessary wartime expenditure; equitable distribution of the war's burdens; control of prices, wages, and profits; and curtailment of strikes and other interference with war production.

The internationalist press concluded that Willkie "buried isolationism once and for all" in the Republican Party and "made the Hearst-McCormick-Patterson [isolationist] press a group without a party." According to Taft, the Willkie statement was rendered innocuous when his supporters agreed to a vague resolution that endorsed "understanding, comity, and cooperation among the nations of the world." Indeed, such a stance reflected no greater commitment to a postwar international body for preservation of the peace than followed the First World War. Anticipating the 1942 primaries, Taft summed up: "We are heading for a direct fight for control of the party machinery. . . . It would be fatal to the future of the party if Willkie and [Henry] Luce and Dorothy Thompson, together with the wealthy crowd in the east, succeed in their aim."[12]

Despite an effort by Willkie to terminate the careers of isolationist congressmen in the 1942 election, most retained their seats. A statement issued in February hinted at his willingness to cross party lines: "The party that should prevail is the party that selects candidates who understand . . . that both during the war and after the war America must forever abandon isolationism." The survival of freedom, he added, was inconsistent with narrow nationalism and restricted trade.

Working in tandem with Willkie, Roosevelt suggested a White House luncheon devoted to supporting candidates inclined to their views, "some Democrats, some Republicans." Willkie replied from the West Coast: "As you know, I am exceedingly hopeful that all traces of isolationism can be washed out of both the Republican and Democratic parties." Future political debate, he hoped, would be confined to a "framework of the recognition of America's necessary position in world affairs and of world leadership."[13]

Willkie and Roosevelt lost the contest. The result was foreshadowed as early as the April Illinois primary, when C. Wayland Brooks, a prewar isolationist endorsed by Robert "Bertie" McCormick's *Chicago Tribune,* won the senatorial nomination over a supporter of the administration's foreign policy. Brooks then won reelection in November. Hamilton Fish (who represented Dutchess County, New York, the president's residence), the most vocal and insistent isolationist in the House, opposed by Willkie and the president, also won the party's nomination and reelection.[14]

During the period leading up to the 1942 congressional campaign, Willkie also engaged in a contest with Dewey for the New York gubernatorial nomination—widely considered a step toward the party's 1944 presidential preference and an opportunity to shape its postwar policy. According to *Time,* a Luce publication that shared Willkie's views, "The Republican Party must now make up its mind to represent either its old bosses—the Hoover, Martin, Pew, Grundy, Landon crowd, or the people who believe in Willkie's leadership." Willkie was convinced that Hoover was the éminence grise behind Dewey, in the expectation that he could influence Dewey's presidency. He concluded further that Dewey "represents, perhaps unconsciously, those forces in the Republican Party and in the country, which may, when this war ends, cause a repetition of the destructive attitude that kept America out of the League of Nations in 1919 and 1920." Led to understand that Dewey commanded the allegiance of the county leaders and other state politicos, Willkie withdrew from the contest on the eve of the state party convention. According to a Willkie informant, the county leaders declared Willkie to be "through in the Republican Party." Told that the ordinary Republican voter favored Willkie, the New York politicians responded that he was no longer a Republican and was "more New Dealish than Roosevelt."[15]

Another sharp-edged contest developed at the National Committee meeting in St. Louis in December 1942, following Joe Martin's decision to give up the party chairmanship. Conservatives and former isolationists presented the name of Werner Schroeder of Illinois, anointed by the *Chicago Tribune* and supported largely by midwestern and southern representatives. A deadlock between Schroeder and Willkie's nominee resulted in a compromise selection of Harrison Spangler as Martin's successor.

"Nobody here," the *Chicago Tribune* crowed, "has any thought that Harrison Spangler will be found among the Willkie backers in 1944." Spangler, an Iowa committee member who had supported Hoover since the 1930s, was an old-line regular committed to patching up ideological differences. Hoover judged the result as a defeat for Willkie, who "fell into a complete trap" with the claim that he had managed the strategy responsible for Spangler's victory from the outset. It appeared that a small but powerful isolationist group centered in the Midwest had managed a rejection of Willkie's internationalism and progressivism. Willkie instead claimed a victory when, in a surprise move, the national committee at Taft's urging reaffirmed a resolution passed at the April 20 meeting, commended both by Taft and Willkie, pledging cooperation among the nations of the world. This left open the critical issue of the degree of United States involvement in a successor to the League of Nations.[16]

Meanwhile, Willkie lost traction with the Republican members of Congress, where the specifics of a postwar international organization to ensure the peace would require Senate consent. He was inclined to badger GOP legislators in his occasional visits to Washington, where, in the

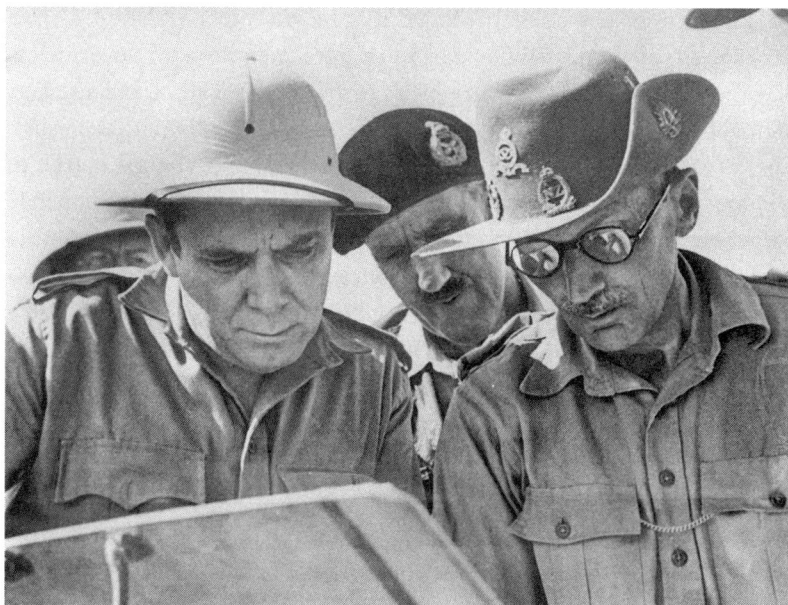

Despite Wendell Willkie's popularity with a large segment of the Republican Party and his ability to amass more votes at the polls by far in 1940 than had Landon and Hoover before him, the GOP leadership opted for a narrower constituency than Willkie commanded. His commitment to United States involvement in the postwar settlements and international structures prompted his overseas trips and the publication of his best-selling *One World*. As provocateur, he urged freedom for colonial peoples and the end of imperialism as well as his party's adoption of a civil rights agenda locally and acceptance of the role of organized labor in government and the economy. (AP Images)

event, most considered him too tied to the Roosevelt policies. He also earned resentment by endorsing internationalist-minded Democrats in the run-up to the 1942 congressional election. Willkie defended his reasoning to Henry Luce: a very conservative element of the party favored reversion to a high-tariff system and strict nationalism. A Republican congressman from Nebraska summarized Willkie's standing in the party accurately: "I find that you have a great deal of support from the grass roots but not from the professional politicians."[17]

With the 1942 election widely interpreted as a victory for the isolationists, rumors circulated that a movement had taken shape for the ouster of Warren Austin, regarded as a Willkie internationalist, who had served as McNary's deputy minority leader in the Senate since 1935. Initially, in

December, McNary publicly denied that he and other isolationists had considered ousting Austin as part of an agreement. Austin nevertheless was thrown out in mid-January by, as he put it, a "cabal" of isolationists, actually the Republican caucus, based on the specious claim that no such post existed. Austin attributed McNary's reversal to a visceral hatred of Willkie, who, he claimed, had publicly held the isolationists responsible for smearing "the face of the Republican Party." Concurrently, upon the death of a Republican member of the Foreign Relations Committee, Austin's application for membership was rejected by the party's Committee on Committees in favor of James Davis of Pennsylvania. The Foreign Relations Committee of the Senate consequently consisted of the following Republicans: Hiram Johnson, Capper, La Follette Jr., Vandenberg, White, Shipstead, Nye, and Davis. All but White were isolationists.[18]

Austin's return to favor on the eve of the Mackinac Island Conference, eventuating in a collaborative effort with Vandenberg, signaled a turning point. The decision to reverse course and welcome Austin once again into the fold began with McNary's designation of the senator for membership in the powerful George Committee. (Republican members also included Vandenberg, Taft, and McNary.) The committee, headed by the conservative Democrat Walter George of Georgia, had been created by a Senate resolution providing for a postwar return to a peacetime economy by taking the government out of business.

In his role as chairman of the National Committee, Spangler, eager to avoid disharmony in the party, organized the Republican Postwar Advisory Council to meet in early September 1943 at Mackinac Island, Michigan, to coordinate the party's position on postwar policy for the 1944 presidential contest. In order to tilt the result toward the nationalists, he included only elected officials selected from the House, the Senate, and National Committee. Republican governors were also invited. This disqualified Willkie and the internationalist cohort organized in Chicago by Deneen Watson, the Republican Postwar Policy Association. Spangler evidently felt compelled, however, to include Austin as one of five senators at Mackinac—with Vandenberg, Taft, McNary, and Albert Hawkes of New Jersey—as he was highly regarded and had been involved since 1942 in consultations with Hull on postwar policy.

Released from a sense of obligation to the isolationists by the termination of his service as deputy leader to McNary, Austin had come out into the open as a strong proponent of United States membership in a United Nations capable of preventing a future world war. Indeed, when Spangler requested that Austin withdraw as principal speaker at a conference sponsored by the Watson group in New York City, Austin refused to comply. The internationalist group, he observed, "have presented views similar to mine and [are] ready to fight for them." "Palaver of an America Firster," Austin noted on Spangler's lengthy appeal.[19]

The vague commitment to American participation in a postwar international organization offered by the National Committee and contemplated by Vandenberg would no longer suffice, in Austin's view. He was going to Mackinac Island as a party member, he informed a supporter, to establish American leadership to secure the peace after the war. "This means that the Republican Party must advocate some sort of world organization including a political body, a judicial body and a military power to maintain security, promulgate the law and administer it." Selection of a nationalist candidate in 1944 would lead to "a considerable group of us Senators who will openly support a Democrat who is not an Isolationist rather than an Isolationist Republican."

Concurrently, in light of the unwillingness of the United States—with the GOP in the lead—to join the League of Nations following the First World War, both Roosevelt and Cordell Hull proved cautious regarding the nature of involvement in a postwar organization, opening the way to a bipartisan approach to the issue. In the Senate, Tom Connally (Democrat, Texas), chairman of the Foreign Relations Committee, set up a special subcommittee for the consideration of postwar resolutions. Vandenberg served as a bridge between Senate Republicans and the administration as well as between party isolationists and internationalists. Privately, he conferred with Hull on foreign policy. Determined to protect the Senate's constitutional prerogatives, he won support in Congress for a report on the continued appropriation for Lend-Lease, which stipulated that it did not bind the Senate to postwar terms such as tariff reduction pledged in the Atlantic Charter without that body's consent.[20]

Publication of Willkie's *One World,* which sold several million copies in the United States and worldwide, prodded the Republican Party toward acceptance of America's role in a postwar organization. The record of Willkie's voyage around the globe exuded naiveté in its appraisal of China and Russian communism and in its judgments of Stalin and

Chiang Kai-shek. Yet, it also challenged American innocence about the world beyond its borders and sought to stymie the noninterventionists who might be tempted to maintain their views in the postwar era.

As the Mackinac Island Conference approached, Vandenberg was compelled to offer his own plan as a result of bipartisan support for a Senate resolution known as B2H2, submitted in March by Democrats Carl Hatch (New Mexico) and Lister Hill (Alabama), and two Republicans, Joseph Ball (Minnesota) and Harold Burton (Ohio). The Ball-Burton resolution proposed that the United Nations include machinery for settlement of disputes and employ a military force to "suppress by immediate use of such force any future attempt at military aggression by any nation." Such an arrangement required ceding of a degree of sovereignty to a supranational entity.

While some former anti-interventionists assumed a more extreme stand, Taft acknowledged the desirability of establishing a postwar structure for the maintenance of peace. But he preferred limited surrender of American sovereignty and an organic approach to the creation of an international arrangement for the prevention of aggression. For all practical purposes, the details of Taft's gradualist approach required careful calibration of the sovereignty issue over a period of years. Postwar resolutions as well as talk of "international machinery with power," according to Taft, must by nature be general and ineffective until satisfactory peacetime arrangements were concluded. A successful peace program required creation of a series of conditions: defeat and disarmament of the Axis powers; provision of an army, navy, and air force sufficient to assure the nation of an adequate defense; initial relief and reconstruction followed by a policy of noninterference by the Unites States in the affairs of other nations; the drawing of boundaries to assure satisfactory national economic conditions and access to necessary raw materials; resolution with the Soviets of the problems of eastern Europe and with London of the question of empire; and creation of a system of international law governing the relations of sovereign nations enforced by education and voluntarism. Accomplishment of these ends would lead in time to creation of an international organization.

According to Taft, an "Association of Nations" would be the product of "sovereign nations" agreeing to settle disputes by arbitration and judicial decision. "It would further be supported by covenants to join in the use of force against any nation determined to be an aggressor by the deci-

sion of some international tribunal." Favoring instead a "cooperative" arrangement that implied some surrender of sovereignty were Austin and
a substantial number of the party's recently elected younger governors,
newcomers to political office who were not bound by the party's previous
association with isolationism, and who were currently members of the
Republican Postwar Advisory Council appointed by Spangler.[21]

In late June, Vandenberg proposed to Austin, the informal leader
of the internationalists, cosponsorship of a Senate resolution designed
to secure "safe ground" between the proponents of B2H2 and the anti-
interventionists. Austin declined, sensing that such a venture would not
go much beyond pursuit of a military victory and a meaningless commitment to "cooperation by sovereign nations" after the conclusion of
hostilities. Indeed, Vandenberg's proposed resolution differed fundamentally from that of the internationalists. In his words: It asserted the permanent sovereignty of the United States; demanded that "all of America's
decisions in this respect shall be made by due constitutional process";
and insisted on "faithful recognition of American interests."

Vandenberg turned to the more compliant Wallace White of Maine.
The Vandenberg-White resolution reflected readiness to avoid the post-
Versailles debacle while asserting the authority of the Senate under the
treaty-making power. Congress, in their words, favored United States
participation in "postwar cooperation" between "sovereign nations" to
prevent aggression and "peace with justice in a free world," in a framework limited by "due constitutional process and with faithful recognition
of American responsibilities and American interests."

Dissatisfied with the Vandenberg-White effort, Austin resolved to
draft an alternative, minority proposal. As he explained to White, despite
the risk of losing support in the Midwest, "the fears of controversy ought
not to further postpone action which will indicate without question, that
the United States can be counted on to participate not merely . . . 'as a
sovereign nation' but in a new way involving surrender of enough sovereignty to a world organization to establish guarantees of peace and security." Pressured by internationalist-minded governors, particularly Earl
Warren of California and Raymond Baldwin of Connecticut, Vandenberg compromised with Austin.[22]

Hoover hoped alternatively that the Mackinac Island Conference
would endorse suggestions for a postwar agenda delineated in the *Problems with Lasting Peace* (1942), published in collaboration with a for-

mer diplomat, Hugh Gibson. Based in part on his negative experience at the World War I peace conferences and their subsequent failure, the ex-president suggested a transitional period after the current war lasting several years in which commissions would provide for the government of nations created by the dissolution of empires; the settlement of economic problems such as trade and intergovernmental debts; the determination of national boundaries; and the "building of international machinery to preserve peace." This arrangement presumably would allow sufficient time for deliberation by the American people in order to "protect our interests"—in the process affording an opportunity, he hoped, for Willkie internationalism to subside and for the current fervor to dismember Germany to evaporate.

The Hoover proposals were conveyed to the Mackinac group through the offices of Ohio governor John Bricker, a conservative also inclined toward isolationism and the ex-president's choice for the party's 1944 nomination. Informed by an apologetic Taft that the conference committee on foreign affairs had opted for the endorsement of Warren Austin's internationalist views, which represented those of Willkie, Hoover decided that he had nevertheless shaped the conference deliberations and its concluding statement.[23]

The Mackinac Island Conference foreign-policy group, chaired by Vandenberg, began its work with a draft by New Jersey congressman Charles Eaton. The Eaton draft—its operative phrase borrowed from the Vandenberg-White resolution and from Vandenberg's June 29 proposal to Austin—provided for "postwar cooperation" among sovereign nations, including the United States, to prevent military aggression and to establish "permanent peace in a free world." "Following hours of fighting," Austin recalled, and the threat of a minority report, he secured a substantive change in the wording. "The weasel-worded proposition," as he put it, read: "responsible participation by the United States in postwar cooperation . . . with organized justice."

The final Declaration on foreign policy, authored by Austin, substituted the words "cooperative organization" in its description of the proposed United Nations, wording that appealed to the internationalists. It read as follows: "Responsible participation by the United States in postwar cooperative organization among sovereign nations to prevent military aggression and to attain permanent peace with organized justice in a free world." A hedge for the benefit of the party's isolationists, the so-called Federal group led by Taft presumably served as a constraint on executive agreements in the making of peace. In the event of a conflict between foreign and domestic policies, "the United States of America should adhere to the policy which will preserve its constitutionalism as expressed in the Declaration of Independence, the Constitution itself, and the Bill of Rights. . . . Constitutionalism should be adhered to in determining the substance of our policies and shall be followed in . . . making international agreements."

Precisely what degree of sovereignty, if any, would be conceded to an international organization for peace was scarcely a matter of universal agreement. Though Vandenberg did not commit himself to an exact definition, Austin viewed the new terminology as forecasting "extension of the exercise of sovereignty rather than the limitation of sovereignty," a position he elaborated before the American Bar Association the following year. Vandenberg believed that the GOP could not survive a repetition of the blame assigned, fairly or not, to its post–World War I record. Yet he hesitated to explain the Mackinac Declaration beyond reaffirming its language, hoping to prevent the party from being torn apart by ideological differences. Then again, as Governor Arthur Langlie of Washington put the issue: "All I can say is that it [the Resolution] is an elastic, and an elastic can stretch both ways."[24]

Despite its limitations, the Mackinac Declaration offered the potential for a bipartisan foreign policy. It weakened the isolationist remnant and the powerful Federal group. "It's men like you," Willkie congratulated Austin, "who are going to put the Republican Party on the right track, particularly in the field of international relations." Austin mustered the support of a younger generation of governors, many the product of the 1942 midterm election, less bound to the Washington Old Guard— legislators and the National Committee—and representative of newer, more popular trends. This younger cohort—Dewey, Bourke Hickenlooper (Iowa), Earl Warren (California), Sumner Sewall (Maine), Raymond Baldwin (Connecticut), Leverett Saltonstall (Massachusetts), Andrew Schoeppel (Kansas), and Dwight Griswold (Nebraska), to name a few—shaped the conference and distanced the party from its past. Also signaling change was the emergence of Dewey as a serious, youthful, centrist presidential candidate widely viewed as inclined to bridge disparate elements of the party and sufficiently mature to challenge Roosevelt in his likely quest for a fourth term.[25]

The Mackinac Declaration on domestic policy, largely Taft's work, pledged to take the government out of competition with private enterprise; sought to terminate emergency powers accorded the administration for wartime rationing and price-fixing; and reproached the National Resources Planning Board for reckless spending and proposing socialism. It committed the party to the "Federal system," meaning states' rights, as opposed to bureaucratic expansion under the New Deal, which presumably threatened fascism. The party offered workers "fair and equitable laws" and endorsed their right to "bargain collectively through agents of [their] own free choice."[26]

H ENRY STIMSON paved the way for Willkie internationalism when, as secretary of state, he questioned Hoover's guarded response to Japan's incursions into Manchuria. Willkie's untimely death in October 1944 stilled his critique of Republican Party ideology as shaped by Hoover, Landon, and Nye. By that time, his internationalist views had already been taken up by Warren Austin of Vermont and, by way of Austin, John Foster Dulles, Dewey's foreign policy adviser. Yet until the end, he challenged isolationism as an outsider by dint of his forceful personality and insistence that the balance of humanity could no longer be colonized by Europe or ignored by the United States.

Willkie's world outlook was more closely aligned with the Republican Party rank-and-file than with those of the party leadership. His willingness to risk political suicide facilitated Roosevelt's interventionist policies in the prelude to war. And he afforded cover for a group of young liberal-internationalist Republican governors and senators after 1942. While he did not hold office, he was an important outlier, like Lincoln and Theodore Roosevelt, who failed to persuade the Republican Party to fully adopt his advanced views.

As the Second World War began to favor the Allies, the party's leadership, looking to forge a compromise among its competing factions, focused on Dewey as a possible choice for the 1944 presidential nomination. The contest began informally when the governor of New York surprised the press at the Mackinac Island gathering by suggesting a postwar alliance between the United States and Great Britain for the prevention of future conflicts. While only one of many such proposals for American postwar cooperation, it signaled the end of Dewey's flirtation with the isolationists and his availability as a candidate for the presidency. Though leading Willkie in the polls, Dewey pledged to fill the balance of his four-year term and refused to formally declare his candidacy, likely on the assumption that Roosevelt would easily win again if the war lasted through 1944.

Precisely what motivated Willkie to announce his candidacy in late September 1943 in the face of opposition by the party organization—which regarded him as too close to Roosevelt—and polls showing Dewey in the lead among Republican voters is a matter of conjecture. He had little support in the party's congressional delegation, which he studiously ignored or occasionally berated as unreformed in its views. A poll among 208 House Republicans showed 89 votes for Dewey, while even Douglas MacArthur and Bricker bested Willkie, who managed only 6 supporters. A survey of the National Committee showed a similar result.

Businessmen who had formerly financed Willkie's candidacy, believing that his war on the TVA made him one of their own, now regarded him as a pro-labor New Dealer. On the other hand, he had come into the 1940 convention as an underdog and evidently believed that he could once again muster the party's rank-and-file through a revival of the Willkie Clubs. He also enjoyed a favorable reputation among the younger Progressive governors, though several entertained their own ambitions for the presidency. Polling results aside, according to Turner Catledge of the *New York Times,* the stop-Willkie movement needed to run its course before the party could get down to a choice for the 1944 contest. In the interim, Dewey bided his time. He was young enough to wait out both Willkie and Roosevelt.[1]

When interviewed by the *New York Times* on September 21, 1943, Willkie took the position that he would appear on the Republican ticket only if the party adopted a liberal platform that included protection of minorities, efficient administration, and encouragement of free enterprise. Troubling to his former business supporters was his distinction between private enterprise, which he regarded as "self-centered," and free enterprise, which embraced "workers on the assembly line," competition, and lower prices. He embraced social protections that resembled those proposed by the National Resources Planning Board including guarantees against unemployment, want in old age, injury, and incapacity. Still more disturbing to conservatives was his assertion that the Republican Party, which had become "corrupted by vested interests," desperately required rejuvenation as a liberal force for change.

By embracing several of the New Deal's domestic programs, Willkie's views spurred an ideological contest with the party's conservative wing.

Taft had recently joined with southern Democrats when they interred the NRPB proposals for a welfare state and an industrial policy on the European model. Corporate heads were repelled by Willkie's sympathy for the rise of industrial unionism, the restraints imposed by the Fair Labor Standards Act, pro-labor decisions rendered by the National Labor Relations Board, wartime strikes and wage demands, and the growing political input of organized labor.[2]

As early as 1940, the Pew group centered in Pennsylvania and Sun Oil rejected the posture taken in the candidate's Pittsburgh speech and his failure to protest strikes by organized labor in defense industries. When Willkie pledged support during the campaign for "a free, strong labor, earning a decent wage, working fair hours, under the right kind of working conditions," the Pews, who had financed the National Committee since the Landon effort, refused further funding until the interloper was banished from the party. Willkie's continued and insistent support for labor fueled further corporate opposition, which included that of Alfred P. Sloan of General Motors, Ernest Weir of Weirton Steel (the party's 1940 finance chairman}, and Edgar Monsanto Queeny.[3]

The challenge to a Willkie candidacy commenced with the "Battle of St. Louis" in the early autumn of 1943. A bellwether state in presidential elections, Missouri was strongly isolationist and the home of a substantial population of German origin. The members of the state party's 1940 delegation to the national convention, led by Queeny, chairman of the board of Monsanto Chemical and supporter of Willkie's 1940 candidacy, raised three issues: the nature of his worldview; limitations on the executive branch and the central government; and the growth of unionism as opposed to the prerogatives of management.

As a bitter-end opponent of Roosevelt's policies, Queeny gave the Willkie 1940 campaign half of his time, collecting only a partial salary from his firm. Blunt and open in his views, he expressed disapproval of Willkie's stance on domestic and foreign policy issues soon thereafter. The Monsanto head, along with the Du Ponts and the Pews, identified themselves as self-made men who had built substantial firms by innovation and acquisition. Queeny had inherited a successful chemical company founded by his father, a pharmacist, built on a German patent for saccharin and other basic products. He added more complex chemical output, weathered the Great Depression without cutting employment, and built a highly profitable enterprise.

In his *The Spirit of Enterprise,* published in 1943, Queeny asserted that a free-enterprise economy would better serve the people than a powerful centralized bureaucracy. He condemned the large eastern urban centers as hotbeds of communism led by New Dealers and academicians, presumably the Kerenskys of the coming revolution. Similarly inclined, Joe Pew regretted "the ever-growing peril of our great cities and their influence over rural America." He advocated abolition of the Securities and Exchange Commission and the National Labor Relations Board; downward revision of the income tax; and repeal of the capital gains tax.[4]

Such views were hardly exceptional in the corporate world, which resented the regulations and centralized controls occasioned by the war effort. The claim that investment uncertainty had resulted from the New Deal policies of the late 1930s was widespread. Nearly 50 percent of Republican funding in the 1940 campaign came from bankers, brokers, and manufacturers as opposed to 10 percent for the Democrats. Three thousand industrial leaders, Queeny and J. Howard Pew among them, attended a meeting of the Congress of American Industry in December 1939, its keynote the liberation of American enterprise by confinement of government to strict constitutional limits.

Like Vandenberg, Queeny and Pew considered themselves to be students of the Constitution and the writings of the Founding Fathers and so homed in on limited government and decentralization of executive power. The group condemned unfair implementation of the Wagner Act and the National Labor Relations Act. They did not oppose labor organizations as long as they were local or company unions, and they regarded national unions, which in their view had taken over the Democratic Party, as no less exemplars of concentrated power than corporate monopolies. They were fierce competitors and favored stiff enforcement of antitrust legislation.

In wartime, Pew and Queeny deplored Willkie's and Henry Wallace's vision of extending the New Deal and American largesse to Europe or the underdeveloped world. Pew was wary of aid to Britain after the war on the grounds that it was socialistic and a potential competitor. He did not envision an American Empire, but rather a competitive United States quite capable of outproducing foreigners. "The troubles we have gotten into," he claimed at war's end, emanated from "cartels, quotas, trade agreements, [and] group bargaining." Pew, Taft, and Queeny preferred Douglas MacArthur and Ohio's Governor John Bricker, a stand-in for

Taft who declined to run in 1944. With Hoover, they regarded Willkie as a visionary who planned to steer their party toward New Deal interventionist policies at home and overseas. A decentralist and admirer of fading rural and small-town values, Pew regarded Willkie as a mouthpiece for international bankers and New York's liberal Republican press. Taft believed that "if Willkie were elected we would simply have another New Deal, perhaps more difficult to combat than the Roosevelt New Deal today."[5]

In a series of letters that bristled with claims of betrayal, Queeny accused Willkie of ingratitude to those who supported him, pointing to the $96,000 he himself had spent on the 1940 campaign. He challenged Willkie's "importuning for funds for the relief of foreigners . . . including the relief of Stalin"; his 1942 crusade against three Missouri Republican isolationists, notably Representative Dewey Short, an adviser to the America First Committee; his indulgence of labor unions and their leaders, who hampered the war effort through strikes, production delays, and imposition of union rules; his critique at a Red Cross dinner in St. Louis of the Smith-Connally Act, which limited wartime strikes; his failure to assume leadership in securing the demise of the WPA, CCC, and NYA; and, generally, his acquiescence in Roosevelt's domestic policies. "You see too much of the Park Avenue intelligentsia, who think of humanity and America in terms of stinking subways and Union Square. This is America!"[6]

The confrontation between these two strong-willed combatants led to an ultimatum dispatched to Willkie on September 1, 1943, by the members of Missouri delegation to the 1940 convention. Did Willkie embrace the idea of United States membership in a supranational state? Did he believe in free trade without restrictions to protect the American standard of living? Did he believe in a world monetary system and an economic system based on One World? Did he favor the free movement of peoples, including Asians, who might overrun the United States and flood the country with alien ideas? Willkie was asked to define what he meant by a liberal platform as the basis for the party's 1944 presidential quest and to affirm support for the nominee if it developed that he was not the party's choice. When Willkie offered to meet off-the-record with the inquisitors, the Missouri delegation insisted on a public appearance. Willkie appeared at the Kiel Municipal Auditorium, St. Louis, on October 15.[7]

In the interim, utilizing the Missouri delegation as a vehicle for his views, Queeny began coordinating with Hoover to forestall a second Willkie candidacy and cleanse his views from the party. "How I wish the leadership of the country were in your hands," Queeny confided to Hoover. "There is nothing I would be unwilling to sacrifice if this could be so." Like Vandenberg, both decided on General Douglas MacArthur for the presidency. When it became evident that MacArthur was unavailable, Queeny and Hoover settled on the conservative, colorless governor of Ohio, John Bricker.

In December 1942, Queeny dispatched a proposed book manuscript to Hoover for criticism. Hoover offered several suggestions—notably emphasis on Roosevelt's currency devaluation in early 1934, "one-sided tariff agreements," the deficit, and the likely cost of New Deal postwar plans. Details took shape at a discussion at the Waldorf Towers, Hoover's New York residence. These deliberations, based on the ex-president's Freedom House file—the group founded in New York to further Willkie's internationalist ideals—served as the source of the questions put to Willkie on October 1 by the Missouri delegation.[8]

Questions began with a textual analysis of his utterances and an examination of his "sponsors." The language of *One World* failed to dispel their suspicion that Willkie favored a "world state" under the rubric of a United Nations. As a founder and director of Freedom House, according to the material provided by Hoover, Willkie was a member of a group that "long prior to Pearl Harbor" campaigned for American intervention in the European war. According to Queeny, a number of this cohort, including Russell Davenport and Gardner Cowles, publisher of *Look,* currently favored creation of a "supranational state" along the lines of Clarence Streit's *Union Now,* its largest benefactors Henry Luce and Thomas Lamont, Willkie's backers.

Queeny subsequently elaborated on these queries, which he had drafted. He defined a liberal party platform as "freedom from government restraint," which he attributed to Thomas Jefferson, the Declaration of Independence, the Bill of Rights, and the Constitution as opposed to the current vogue that pursued constant increase of government authority. The result of the contemporary approach to liberalism would be a totalitarian state along the lines favored by the *New Republic* and its writers, including the economists Stuart Chase and George Soule, defined by

Queeny as socialistic planners who supported Willkie and Roosevelt. Finally, Queeny expressed appreciation of the Dies Committee's work and offered Willkie the opportunity to explain away his extremist positions and associations.[9]

In his October appearance in St. Louis, the party's 1940 presidential standard-bearer noted his Republican bona fides. While he criticized the Roosevelt administration's failure to prepare the nation for conflict—actually, the GOP led the opposition to preparedness—and FDR's overlong stay in office, he explained that the Republican Party could not win in 1944 as a coalition of "negative groups." It required a national policy that afforded protection of those in want through expanded social insurance. It required a world based on cooperation and open trade, as well as business-government cooperation to moderate the economic cycle by eliminating fluctuations in capital expenditures. He endorsed a "wise labor policy" designed to secure adequate economic and social protection "through collective strength" and urged direct participation of organized labor in government. "I do not mean just by the appointment of a labor representative as Secretary of Labor. I mean that . . . labor's representatives shall help determine government's fiscal, domestic and international policies."[10]

Willkie characterized as "punitive" the Smith-Connally Act, a precursor of Taft-Hartley, passed in May over Roosevelt's veto. It won the support of southern Democrats, along with Republicans representing an alliance of Texas petroleum producers eager to keep the unions out and midwestern manufacturers ambitious to curb the growing power of industrial unions that emerged under protective New Deal labor legislation and prospered under wartime conditions. Wartime coal strikes by John L. Lewis's United Mine Workers union, widely viewed as unpatriotic, played into the hands of anti-union corporate heads.

Designed to limit strikes in defense industries, Smith-Connally also attempted to curtail labor support rendered Roosevelt in the 1936 and 1940 campaigns by prohibiting union contributions to political campaigns. Sidney Hillman of the Amalgamated Clothing Workers Union and the CIO's Phillip Murray parried by creating the CIO Political Action Committee, signaling labor's intention to circumvent these restraints. Considering the developing contest between manufacturers and organized labor, Willkie's support for unions, according to corporate heads, took him out of the running for the 1944 nomination. At St. Louis, Willkie in turn described the corporate leaders who dominated the National Committee as a political "liability."[11]

An exchange between Alfred P. Sloan of General Motors and Willkie a year earlier further illustrates the divide between the corporate supporters of the Republican Party and Willkie. According to an internal memorandum brought to Sloan's attention, Willkie told the Los Angeles Industrial Council that anti-unionism at North American Aviation typified the attitude of its owner, General Motors. When Sloan complained, Willkie replied: "I did . . . say to businessmen and to the labor leaders that the right of men employed in modern industrial plants to organize was indispensable." Those who failed to recognize this principle, in Willkie's view, were destined "to live in a world gone forever." As for North American Aviation, it was obdurate and unfair to the union. His entire life, Willkie reminded Sloan, had been dedicated to the preservation of free enterprise. The system was endangered by the "cowardice and self-seeking of some of the representatives of the enterprise system."[12]

Gradually, Landon, Hoover, and much of the party leadership converged on a stop-Willkie movement, viewing Dewey as a compromise candidate based on his strong showing in the 1942 New York gubernatorial campaign. Vandenberg and Taft removed themselves from the picture for 1944; MacArthur, still in uniform, could not campaign for office; and Bricker, who was colorless and intellectually limited, was considered unelectable.

The denouement occurred in Wisconsin in the spring of 1944. Like Missouri, Wisconsin was a bellwether state with a large German American population and a history of support for isolationist Republicans. Willkie was particularly concerned that Robert La Follette intended to shift his ties from the Progressive Party to the Republicans, making him the third-ranking member of the Senate Foreign Relations Committee. As the two more senior Republicans, Hiram Johnson and Arthur Capper, were aged and infirm, Willkie feared a committee led by La Follette, an anti-interventionist and a leading opponent of United States membership in the League of Nations, the World Court, and Lend-Lease. Willkie believed that given this scenario, La Follette would be empowered to block postwar agreements, while a malleable Dewey would be controlled by the isolationists.

After taking six of eleven delegates in the New Hampshire primary with the assistance of Sherman Adams, Willkie decided to enter the Wisconsin primary in March 1944. This proved a questionable gamble. His advisers preferred a campaign on the two coasts, where he was viewed more favorably. Further, Americans of German and Polish descent in the Midwest were concerned about Stalin's ambitions in eastern and central Europe. Polish voters regarded Willkie as naïve on the question of Russian imperialism, according to the publisher of *Novy Swiat.* Further, as Michaela Hoenecke Moore explains: "A strong countercurrent of opinion saw Nazism as a departure from mainstream German culture.... Parts of American elites and wider sections of the public struggled intellectually to keep the Germans in the fold of a common civilization for reasons of ethnic identification." Equally important, there remained a considerable legacy of dislike for Woodrow Wilson and the Carthaginian peace imposed on Germany after the First Great War. Willkie in this environment was nevertheless unwilling to support a United Nations declaration opposing dismemberment of Germany. Instead, in an essay in the *New York Times Magazine,* he urged restraint by Republicans in judging Stalin's intentions in eastern Europe.

The tendency to defy political convention and his advisers, Willkie's strength, worked to his disadvantage in his pursuit of the 1944 nomination. A survey of "prominent Republicans" by the *Madison Capital Times* showed that "the Old Guard . . . would rather see Roosevelt win a fourth term than see Willkie win the nomination." Since Dewey had won Wisconsin in the 1940 primary, Willkie decided that overcoming these obstacles in the 1944 primary would demonstrate his election potential. He took the gamble and lost, running behind Dewey, Stassen, and MacArthur. Shortly after, he withdrew his candidacy.[13]

Willkie's last effort at liberalizing his adopted party took place in the form of a series of articles, summarized as a proposed platform for the benefit of the resolutions committee at the 1944 Chicago convention. Several newspapers oriented toward liberal internationalism published the pieces, entitled "An American Program." In the domestic arena, Willkie argued that a strong national government was required to counteract the disruptive nature of states' rights doctrine. In foreign affairs, he urged a departure from the party's association with the high tariffs of the 1920s and adoption instead of a liberal foreign policy based on downward tariff revision; arrangements for international currency stabilization and exchange; abandonment of nationalistic allusions to "sovereignty" in party statements; and investment in undeveloped countries since "the day of economic imperialism is over."

With respect to foreign affairs, the platform committee genuflected to both wings of the party, tilting, in Willkie's view, toward the nationalists. The platform supported international cooperation while rejecting membership in a world state. It pledged "responsible participation by the United States in postwar cooperative organization among sovereign nations" as well as "collaboration with the United Nations." "Cooperation," "collaboration," "participation," "sovereign nations," resembled the Mackinac Island agreement's hedges and the Missouri delegation's insistence on preservation of American independence of action in a postwar environment.

Willkie feared that Senate control of foreign policy by the nationalists would be assured through that body's veto over any international agreements reached by the executive branch. In the platform committee's words: "We shall sustain the Constitution of the United States in the attainment of our international aims." Consequently, "Any treaty or agreement to attain such aims made . . . with any other nation or association of nations shall be made only with the advice and consent of the Senate." Such a requirement imposed on executive agreements would cripple the reciprocal trade agreements program and more. As the editorial page of the *Washington Post* suggested, "a small dissident bloc of Senators, representing no more than one-twelfth of our population . . . [could] nullify an exchange stabilization compact such as agreed upon by the representatives of 44 nations at Bretton Woods."

There were problems for the party leadership, currently Vandenberg and Austin, with Willkie's critique of its foreign-policy plank, given their desire to maintain both the Midwest and the eastern internationalist wing under one umbrella. At the same time, there were contradictions in Willkie's piece entitled "Federal Power and States Rights." He condemned the Roosevelt administration's "abuses of vast authority" and its reliance on personal government. "The solution lies in a weakened central government," according to Willkie, with administration of many federal functions at the local level. Yet in an earlier article, as in St. Louis, he noted the necessity for a strong national government that in the current industrial environment should prevent "disruption of the economic and social structure" by divergent interests. Assertion of states' rights, he claimed in a summary of his views dispatched to Chicago, could not be permitted to obstruct the federal government in the performance of its function. The party platform emphasized, on the other hand, avoidance of federalization of government activities so that "our schools and cities shall be free."

Allied with Walter White of the National Association for the Advancement of Colored People in these years, Willkie claimed that "the Constitution did not provide for first and second class citizens." Blacks were entitled to the same housing and educational facilities as whites, according to Willkie, and the platform should also support federal legislation to eliminate the poll tax and make lynching a federal crime. The platform, in this instance, resembled Willkie's proposals, pledging antilynching legislation; a congressional investigation of discrimination against Negroes in the armed forces; establishment of a permanent Fair Employment Practice Commission at the federal level; and a proposed constitutional amendment abolishing the poll tax in federal elections.

The need for social insurance, Willkie admonished, could not be separated from the nature of the modern economic system. He proposed Republican support for the Wagner-Murray-Dingell bill, which provided for a unified system of social insurance, including old-age benefits, federal provision for unemployment and disability insurance, maternity benefits, insurance for members of the armed forces and agricultural labor, and a national scheme for medical care. The platform proposed extension of old-age insurance to those not covered; otherwise it offered vague statements on "strengthening" existing social programs and an injunction against "socialized medicine."

The "economy of demobilization," currently the subject of a major debate in the Congress, reflected concern for the absorption of returning veterans and war-industry workers in the peacetime economy. Willkie rejected as a move backward the argument by party conservatives for a return to free enterprise. Instead, at the inception of a postwar depression that was widely anticipated, Willkie proposed that government should fund major countercyclical projects executed by private contract. The platform emphasized reliance on the private sector and "the initiative of civic groups" for reemployment.

Willkie also proposed reversal of the GOP's image as an anti-union party. Workers in modern industry needed "to control for themselves the circumstances which dictate their working lives," he admonished. The 1944 platform should recognize the legitimacy of the Federal Wages and Hours Law and the machinery for its enforcement, the wartime National Labor Board. Compulsory social insurance should be broadened in scope and an annual wage assured to those engaged in seasonal work. At the same time, labor unions should be obliged to account for their funds and expenditures. Finally, as he held in the "Battle of St. Louis," Willkie suggested that organized labor be represented in the cabinet and, like other economic groups, participate in the shaping of government policies. The platform accepted the purposes of the National Labor Relations Act, the Wage and Hour Act, and similar New Deal legislation.[14]

In a postmortem labeled "Cowardice in Chicago," Willkie charged the party with adoption of a program beset with compromises tailored to a Dewey campaign. Willkie was miffed. "For the first time in history," he complained, "the latest Republican candidate for President was not invited to be a delegate-at-large from his home state of New York." Unlike Hoover, he had not been selected to address the convention; he was not invited to participate in the proceedings; and he lacked direct input into the platform. Instead, when "Mr. Spangler very kindly offered to provide me with a ticket to sit on the platform so that I could listen to the proceedings," Willkie recalled, he declined and denounced the Platform Committee's position on foreign policy as a waffle. Confronted by "ex-isolationists rechristened nationalists," the committee and the convention by unanimous vote proposed that every postwar agreement for international collaboration would require a two-thirds vote in the Senate. "It is interesting to note," Willkie warned, "that the emasculation of the treaty [the League of Nation's covenant] began with a proviso by the Foreign Affairs Committee, of which the present Republican plank is reminiscent." Willkie's assumption that the Senate would surrender its right to approve the creation of an international structure without assertion of its authority to approve by a two-thirds vote seems unreasonable. He also found objectionable, in this instance with reason, the promise that multilateral trade agreements should be subject to Senate approval, since in reality they would be eviscerated by logrolling along the lines of the what had happened with the Smoot-Hawley Tariff.

Willkie's dissatisfaction with the platform; his distrust of Dewey as a candidate in the belief that he was inclined to accommodate all sections of the party including the nationalists; and rumors of undisclosed visits with Roosevelt at the White House all fed conjecture concerning his endorsement of Dewey before the election. There was speculation whether after the 1944 election, as Roosevelt proposed, he would join with FDR in a party realignment embracing liberals and internationalists of both parties. With the South opposed to Roosevelt's social programs and the Midwest to Willkie's internationalism, such a new coalition, Roosevelt anticipated, would exclude the reactionaries of both parties. Whether such a coalition could have been realized at this time, or would prove desirable, remains open to conjecture.

In the event, a letter to Governor Leverett Saltonstall of Massachusetts, written when Willkie was hospitalized just before his death, suggested that he sought the survival of the Republican Party with "ideals we can rebuild" despite his dissatisfaction with the tenor of the Dewey campaign. In the end, a lengthy, handwritten, passionate letter from Henry Luce urging Willkie to "take a leading part in the common task," namely the demolition of Roosevelt's New Deal and support of Dewey as the party's choice, appears to have borne no fruit. As for Willkie and Roosevelt, while there were unrecorded private meetings between the two designed to forge a new party based on liberal principles during the summer of 1944, the negotiations ended when Willkie died in October.

Willkie's discontents with the 1944 party platform seem overdone. A considerable portion of the document shows his imprint. The platform's endorsement of a successor international structure to the League of Nations and the conceptualization of its wording, which escaped Willkie, represented the work of a Willkie internationalist, Warren Austin. The platform also took an advanced position on the issue of African American rights, particularly advocacy of the Fair Employment Practice Act; of an amendment to the Constitution outlawing the poll tax; and of an equal rights amendment for men and women. In foreign affairs, no nation was prepared to surrender its sovereignty.[15]

In the end, Vandenberg, with the cooperation of Austin and John Foster Dulles in tandem with Cordell Hull, forged a foreign policy that overcame the Midwest's penchant for nationalism, at least in connection with establishment of a United Nations structure after the war. Yet, Willkie failed to convince the party leadership to assume an advanced position with regard to international economics. None of the party's leaders approached monetary policy beyond the procyclical policies offered by the Federal Reserve in the 1920s. None of the GOP leadership displayed substantial support for the Bretton Woods proceedings that led to the creation of the World Bank and the International Monetary Fund. Nor does there seem to have been awareness of the implications of an integrated world economy in which America created some 50 percent of the gross national product worldwide and represented the main source of consumption in the world marketplace.

A s THE 1944 Republican convention opened in Chicago, Turner
Catledge of the *New York Times* confronted Vandenberg: Willkie, he had heard, nursed strong reservations about the platform's stance on foreign policy. Vandenberg hedged, and Catledge pressed:
Willkie was disappointed, and Walter Edge of New Jersey, joined by other
Republican governors, planned to lead a fight on the convention floor for
a foreign policy plank that "says what it means and means what it says."
Vandenberg snapped: "They'd better leave well enough alone. . . . If they
insist on opening the foreign policy question on the convention floor
they may get an out-and-out isolationist, or nationalist, plank that would
curl your hair." Beneath the surface, nationalism survived Pearl Harbor
and flourished in the Midwest in opposition to the convictions of the internationalists concentrated on the Eastern Seaboard.[1]

Officially, Vandenberg sat on the Foreign Relations Committee and on
the Republican Party's steering committee. Informally, he assumed the
responsibilities of shadow secretary of state. While working in tandem
with Vermont's Warren Austin, who represented the internationalists,
and with John Foster Dulles, Dewey's emissary, Vandenberg also conferred frequently with Hull at the State Department on the content of
postwar agreements negotiated by the administration. Interchanges with
Hull reflected Vandenberg's insistence on a "just peace" as the foundation of a successful international organization to keep the peace; on protection of the Senate's prerogatives in foreign policy; and on bridging the
gap between the nationalists and the internationalists in his party.

Precisely what compelled the senator from Michigan to make the
long, cautious trek from his opposition to Lend-Lease and repeal of the
Neutrality Act to the pivotal address he made before the Senate on January 10, 1945, is open to discussion. Gabriel Kolko, in his provocative
and seminal study of the years 1943–45, avers that Vandenberg, wary of

Soviet postwar intentions in eastern Europe, especially Poland, contemplated a new international structure as an instrument of American policy in order to protect capitalism and its national interests from the Left and from Russia. While there is evidence that Vandenberg and Senate conservatives feared for the future of capitalism, the source they most suspected was near at hand, namely Roosevelt. As for Russia, Vandenberg proposed an American guarantee against renewed German aggression.[2]

As early as June 1942, Vandenberg expressed concern regarding the belated declaration of war by the United States on Bulgaria and Romania at the behest of Russian foreign minister Molotov. He judged that it was "part of a series of demands . . . as the price of her continued belligerence" and a step toward annexation as well of Latvia, Estonia, and Lithuania. While Vandenberg recognized Russia's sacrifice in the war, he also noted that "Moscow has always been a shrewd trader—for Moscow. . . . It will be horribly interesting to check the final results, one day, against June 4, 1942." In his opinion, the "four freedoms" had become a "scrap of paper." Subsequent evidence of Soviet ambitions in the direction of Poland exacerbated the situation, with Vandenberg suggesting that perhaps Soviet imperialism might not justify American participation in a world organization after the war in the absence of a just peace.[3]

Warren Austin was equally distressed. "Russia has made . . . clear," he noted in June 1942, "her purpose to demand property, territory, and sovereignty over such areas as Estonia, Latvia, a part of Poland, and other Balkan states. The idea marches with seven-league boots." Whereas Austin never tied this issue to United States membership in a successor to the League of Nations, which functioned on the principles of international law, Vandenberg questioned American participation in a postwar vehicle in the absence of justice for smaller nations, considering Stalin's territorial ambitions in eastern Europe and those of Winston Churchill for retention of the British Empire. Both were potent figures, he noted, with undefined ambitions, and under these circumstances "we must prepare ourselves to accept a larger degree of international responsibility."

According to Vandenberg, despite the fact that the average American had been an isolationist before the war, most favored reasonable participation in a postwar security system. But war's end also would present an awkward reality to the typical American, "at least west of the Allegheny Mountains." "He is a middle-of-the-roader," neither isolationist nor internationalist, Vandenberg noted, desirous of a realistic peace, the end of aggression, and governing the postwar world through justice rather than force. Yet, at the same time, it was unwise before the war was won to foster discord among the Allied powers.

Vandenberg's shifting positions on a postwar structure for maintenance of the peace appear to have been resolved in a proposal to Cordell Hull in March 1943 in which the Senate would advise that it supported a "United Nations to create a world in which military aggression shall be permanently curbed; in which justice rather than force shall prevail; and in which self-governing people shall be free to work out their own destinies in the closest, practical cooperation with each other." Yet he was not prepared to antagonize Stalin, he explained to the editor of the *Detroit Polish Daily News.* "It is probably wise that these boundary questions have been postponed to the days of subsequent peace (although this has its grave dangers) because continued Russian cooperation with the United Nations is absolutely indispensable to the victory itself."[4]

Vandenberg raised another concern in a magazine article published in 1943: "Why Not Deal the Congress In?" While conceding that strategic considerations in wartime limited consultation by the executive with legislators, he insisted on greater regard for congressional powers with respect to postwar policy, notably in connection with Lend-Lease, renewal of trade agreements, and American participation in the United Nations Relief and Rehabilitation Administration. Wary also of postwar commitments by the Roosevelt administration to Russia and Great Britain, the senator insisted on winning the war against Germany and consideration of the nature of the peace before binding the Senate to geopolitical and trade commitments. In a Senate speech on the extension of Lend-Lease, he explained that his position "lies somewhere between the international extremists, who contemplate the new modeling of the world in all the global consequences the term implies, and national extremists who can still think exclusively in pre–Pearl Harbor terms."[5]

Vandenberg's intention to limit American involvement in another European war likely explains his rejection of the Ball-Burton resolution, which called for American participation in an international police force commanded by a supranational structure: "It could be acceptable under certain conditions and highly unacceptable under others. For example, if the ultimate Russian boundaries extinguish Latvia, Lithuania, Estonia, Eastern Poland, etc. it would be very questionable whether American soldiers could appropriately be included in an 'international police force' to patrol such boundaries." He was determined to find a middle ground between the extreme points of view in the creation of an international structure to prevent recurrence of aggression while preserving American interests, just as Stalin and Churchill intended to do. He also took a middle ground on international relations in the 1944 campaign, his objective being the termination of the New Deal. The "'last roundup' for the American way of life" required avoidance of a foreign policy that might sunder the Republican Party.[6]

During the winter and early spring months of 1943–44, Vandenberg committed considerable time and energy—in collaboration with John Hamilton and General Robert Wood of Sears, Roebuck & Co., who had served as head of America First—to securing the party's presidential nomination for Douglas MacArthur. The enterprise continued into early April based on the hope that Dewey's victory in Wisconsin simply reflected an aversion by primary voters there to Willkie as nominee. In the interim, Vandenberg decided the time had come to organize a meeting of the group that had fashioned the Mackinac Declaration in order to frame a foreign-policy plank for the 1944 platform. When assembly of such a large, geographically dispersed group in wartime proved tactically impossible and the MacArthur episode fell through, Vandenberg turned for advice to Austin and John Foster Dulles, Dewey's agent in foreign-policy matters.[7]

Austin shaped the critical phrases in the party's 1944 platform that laid the foundation for an international cooperative organization. Dewey referred foreign-policy issues to Dulles, who agreed to retain the key phrase authored by Austin in the Mackinac Declaration pledging American commitment to a postwar cooperative structure for the maintenance of peace. Austin added another determining phrase to the platform's foreign-policy plank: "Such organization should develop effective cooperative means to direct peace forces to prevent or repel military aggression." When Dewey doubted the need for such "elaboration" and Dulles questioned the implications of the word "direct," Vandenberg explained: Though "Austin's fetish," it was "sound" and retained on the basis of need for a unanimous report. Dulles, Dewey, and Taft concurred.[8]

With the National Committee dominated by nationalists and headed by an isolationist, Austin concluded that its real sentiment was covered over by "a pretense of at least non-isolationism." He also needed to take note of a group founded in Chicago, the Republican Nationalist Revival

Committee, committed to a reprise of the prewar isolationist movement. The Nationalists originated in late 1943 as a response to Deneen Watson's internationalist Republican Postwar Policy Association with which Austin was affiliated. The Chicago group, anchored in America First, opposed postwar involvement in an international body dedicated to preservation of the peace. Indeed, this served as the prime issue in the 1944 Illinois senatorial contest, where an effort was made to defeat the incumbent Scott Lucas, a supporter of Roosevelt's foreign policy. The group, hopeful of influencing the presidential race, condemned the Mackinac Charter, "internationalism in all its forms," and involvement with the British Empire and Russia. While internationalist groups also existed in the Midwest, notably Watson's and a cohort organized by William Wesley Waymack, a Wilsonian Republican and editor of the *Des Moines Register and Tribune,* nationalism remained a force in the nation's heartland and was deeply entrenched in the Republican Party.[9]

Though relations between Vandenberg and Austin remained cordial on the surface, the senator from Michigan was more inclined than the Vermonter to accommodate the Midwest's nationalist sentiments. "I have been struggling for an agreement on basic ideas with Senator Austin of Vermont," Vandenberg confided in a lengthy letter to Dewey in mid-May, explaining that Austin was a member of the "Eastern internationalist school of thought." While willing to pledge the party to international cooperation to prevent military aggression, Vandenberg wanted to affirm "that we intend to protect and conserve the *legitimate* self-interest of the United States." This pledge was necessary, he held, "to save our situation in the Middle West," which required an unequivocal commitment to unimpaired sovereignty. In a postscript, Vandenberg also contended that a new "league of nations" would not survive in the absence of a "just peace."[10]

In an address before the Section on International and Comparative Law of the American Bar Association on April 28, 1944, Austin offered a legal elucidation of the nature of sovereignty as it relates to international comity. He observed that the Moscow Declaration and the Connally Resolution recognized the principle of the sovereign equality of all member nations in an international organization formed for preserving the peace. External sovereignty delegated to such an instrumentality did not entail the loss of internal sovereignty. Over the course of its history, the United States had entered into a host of arrangements such as the Pan American Union, the Wheat Advisory Committee, the Congress of the Postal Union, and similar cooperative ventures without the loss of sovereignty. Rather, such arrangements marked its extension. The nationalist argument challenging the legality of a cooperative organization for the preservation of the peace lacked realism, defied precedent, and represented a "naked assertion."

Austin summed up: adoption by the House of the Fulbright Resolution, by the Senate of the Connally Resolution, and by the National Committee of the Mackinac Declaration "evidence[s] the faith of our people in the feasibility of a cooperative organization in which each nation can legally condition its sovereignty without in any material degree impairing . . . its internal sovereignty." Such an organization would in fact "guarantee such freedom and independence by the application of justice" by a judicial tribunal created for that purpose. Austin was not naïve in this respect. The development of laws and precedent ensuring peace would require time. "The foundation of the New World ought to be a brief code of international law, in which the difference between right and wrong will be the spirit of the law." In the interim, he regretted, "we are obliged to rely upon force as the sanction for security and peace."[11]

While Vandenberg, Dulles, and Austin managed general approval for a successor organization to the League, gaining acceptance for open markets proved more challenging. The DuPont economist Edmund E. Lincoln protested Dewey's association with eastern internationalists such as John Foster Dulles and the "foreign trade fanatics." Senate approval of the Hull trade program depended on Democratic votes. Senate Republicans voted almost unanimously against the original Trade Agreements Act in 1934 and on the occasion of subsequent renewals in 1937 and 1940. The 1943 renewal finally gathered majority support among Republican senators, but barely, by a vote of 18 to 14. Even then, an amendment by Senator John Danaher, Connecticut Republican and an isolationist who led the group that ousted Austin as deputy party leader, would have authorized Congress by joint resolution to renounce all trade agreements within six months after the war's conclusion. Twenty-five GOP senators, a majority, voted their approval. Realistically, congressional participation in such agreements would have resulted in logrolling and a return to the high-tariff regime featured in the Smoot-Hawley Tariff.[12]

The domestic portion of the party's 1944 platform, shaped largely by Taft, pledged American farmers, workers, and industry a protective tariff. In addition, the platform promised that reciprocal trade agreements reached by the State Department would be subject to congressional approval with an eye to protecting the American market from foreign competition. Hoover took the argument further in his address to the convention. He condemned the "Degeneration of Freedom in the United States" in the course of the past decade. The New Deal, he claimed, "has followed the tactics of European revolutions. . . . They seek to destroy every safeguard of personal liberty and justice. Their method was to create centralized government. . . . [The New Deal] put shackles on our farmers . . . [o]n honest labor unions, on the freedom of workmen, on honest business enterprise." Hoover deplored the suspension of the Constitution in wartime and the support of Communists and fellow travelers offered by the current regime in Washington.

Dewey's presidential quest began with a pledge of continuity with Hull's postwar policies, particularly the creation of a system of "general international cooperation"—subject to the exercise of "sovereign rights" and "self-government." He focused on Roosevelt's mismanagement of diplomacy and war production. Indeed, Roosevelt did not excel in management. Unlike his challenger, Roosevelt tolerated dissent and internal bickering and was not given to the strict top-down supervision favored by Dewey. The challenger also pledged a return to private enterprise, relief from overregulation and high taxation, and a return to states' rights. And he questioned the projected domination of the postwar United Nations by the Four Powers—namely the United States, the Soviet Union, Great Britain, and China—at the expense of smaller nations, a claim intended to appeal to the Polish vote.

The delicate question of whether the American delegate at the international organization could commit the United States to a police action by "peace forces," in the event the United Nations decided to check aggression, presented difficulties. In mid-July, Vandenberg turned to Austin to decide on a definition of "peace forces" so that the principals in the campaign could offer the same definition if questioned. As a point of departure, Vandenberg suggested: "By 'peace forces' we mean whatever force, whether economic or military, is necessary to keep the peace whenever an emergency exists." Austin informed Dulles that "peace forces" had been his suggestion and explained that the concept was grounded in common law. It was intended as an extension of the role of "peace officer" or conservator of the peace. Austin explained in greater detail to

Vandenberg that the phrase was central to the plank on war and peace since it dealt with the initial step toward a just peace, namely, security. He maintained that the term "peace forces" included all that was required to maintain peace and order. Accordingly, it included "the moral power of international tribunals administering justice" as well as commercial sanctions such as embargoes. Then again: "If the threat should indicate that military action is required, then military force would be also comprehended in the term." Substitution of the term "military forces" for "peace forces" would have limited its application.

Dulles proposed that "peace forces" be defined more broadly to embrace the mustering of the moral force of public opinion by a world organization to prevent aggression. Austin and Vandenberg agreed.[13]

The veto power also occasioned an exchange of views. These remained unresolved for some time in light of the implications for the small nations. At a press conference, when asked about the ongoing Dumbarton Oaks proceedings, Dewey posited that military prowess did not justify the Big Four's right to dominate a proposed world organization. Hull promptly requested a meeting in Washington. Dulles was dispatched in Dewey's stead, and an agreement was reached to keep discussion of the successor to the League of Nations out of the campaign.[14]

Dulles and Austin discussed the issue of a veto power for the Big Four privately. Dulles's views on a revised League of Nations reflected his distaste for the postwar reparations imposed on Germany and the ineffectiveness of the old League. These observations were reflected in Dulles's publication of the "Six Pillars of Peace," shaped during his service as chairman of the Commission to Study the Bases of a Just and Durable Peace. Established by the Federal Council of Churches in America in 1940, the committee sought to outline a peace that avoided the Carthaginian nature of the Versailles agreements. In early 1943, the group issued the "Six Pillars of Peace," in which Dulles urged United States participation in an international alliance to preserve peace based on the United Nations; agreements for control of financial and economic acts of governments that impacted the international economy; autonomy for subject peoples; armaments control; and religious and individual liberty. Dulles's work was based on moral law as "controlling in world affairs . . . and that the United States had been assigned a special role in the establishment and maintenance of world peace." The transition from Christian morality to awareness of the realities of power politics evidently occurred at the San Francisco conference.[15]

Critiquing an article published by Austin in *Foreign Affairs*, Dulles assumed that the "big powers" would likely want a veto "over any direction aimed at them, and if this is the case I doubt whether there can be any absolute right to direct the forces of other and smaller nations." In a crisis, the newly created international organization would need to organize world opinion, resulting in voluntary commitments "to take concurrent action under the centralizing direction of the general organization." Effectively, any political organization worked through voluntary cooperation. Austin agreed. While progress toward security assumed the council's power to "direct," the veto power "is probably necessary at the present state of development of public opinion."

Fundamentally, Dulles was dissatisfied with the Dumbarton Oaks framework negotiated between August and October 1944. He wanted revision because he believed that the new league would fail if it simply served as a straitjacket designed to freeze the status quo based on military expediency as opposed to justice. A new league could survive only as a moral authority and not because it was based on force. In his view, peace identified as a static position assured war.

Maintenance of peace, Dulles believed, required facilitation of change based on just and equitable arrangements. "We must avoid attempted miracles. . . . But we need not go to the other extreme of setting up a League with a mandate to sustain, by force, if need be, any status irrespective of judgment as to whether it is just or unjust." That possibility led to his objection—hence Dewey's opposition voiced in the campaign—to the veto power afforded the permanent members of the Security Council. Austin took the position that forces assembled by an international structure for any purpose would be limited to "prevent or suppress danger to international security and peace." Further, no state should have the right to veto a council action if charged with aggression. "The law should rule."[16]

As the campaign opened, Hull, Dulles, and Dewey ruled out public discussion of the American delegate's right to commit the nation to the use of force without congressional approval as well as the broader issue of the availability of armed forces to the Security Council. It was generally agreed, at least by the internationalists, that the absence of such authority in the original League charter obliged that organization to rely on condemnation of aggression and leave it to the democracies to act. As a result, aggressor nations could pursue their objectives unrestrained and unconcerned about possible action by League members. Accordingly, Austin favored American commitment to the Security Council if it should call for armed forces in order to assure peace and security. This raised a contentious issue: Was such authority to be incorporated in the American delegate's power or was it necessary for the executive to consult Congress before any such action could be taken?

In a carefully calibrated statement for the *March of Time* newsreel as the campaign drew to a close, Austin recommended that Congress empower the delegate to the United Nations "to commit limited armed forces for interposition to prevent war." While only Congress could declare war, such interposition, he claimed, would preserve peace. "The remote hazard of war occurring from the act of interposition is the lesser of two hazards. The alternative is war anyway."

Just before Election Day, Minnesota's Republican senator Joseph Ball, an internationalist, put the issue of the level of authority that should be enjoyed by the American delegate to Dewey and Roosevelt in a public challenge. Roosevelt decided that the "town hall" possessed no authority without a policeman. Dewey failed Ball's test when he required that the American delegate could not commit the nation's military to action without the consent of Congress. Taft supported Dewey's position on the ground that the Dumbarton Oaks draft afforded a veto to the Big Four, thus nullifying international law and the purpose of the contemplated organization. Vandenberg vacillated. Wary of being accused of bad faith by his colleagues should he wave their right to declare war, he seconded Dewey's position and then changed his mind, suggesting that the American representative could commit forces to a League action based on presidential authority.[17]

Roosevelt's margin of victory over Dewey by a vote of nearly 25 million to 22 million likely reflected the electorate's confidence in Roosevelt's wartime leadership. "The people were not willing to change a leader in the midst of a victorious war," Taft conceded. He also deplored the fact that Dewey "seems to be entirely surrounded by New Yorkers," a reference no doubt to Dewey's internationalism and willingness to endorse a national old-age pension scheme, minimum-wage legislation, and other New Deal social legislation. In the event, the mechanical, controlled nature of Dewey's speeches did not play well against FDR's ease and presence as commander in chief in wartime. Dulles attributed Dewey's loss to the "dismal record" of the party's congressional wing during the previous four years. Austin was gratified that some of the avid isolationists, among them Hamilton Fish and Stephen Day in the House, and Nye, Danaher, and James Davis in the Senate, were voted out of office. In the event, Dewey's comparatively strong showing, his youth and centrist policies, earned him another chance in 1948.

Before the vote, the prolific and liberal journalist Gerald Johnson had noted: "The bald fact is that we face an election without definitely formulated issues, for the old issues are dead and the new ones not yet here." The South was in flux, but had not yet turned against Roosevelt and the New Deal. Dewey's charge of mismanagement could not be substantiated so far as the military conduct of the war was concerned, especially since Allied victory was considered a certainty. And once more, the Republican Party could not win an election based largely on hatred of "that man in the White House" and the New Deal. Americans feared a postwar depression, and the GOP offered few alternatives to FDR's program other than self-reliance or dependence on the locality.[18]

While Dulles, Hull, Vandenberg, and Austin negotiated among themselves the terms of agreement on an international organization, Herbert Brownell, anointed Republican national chairman by Dewey, raised issues such as control of the Democratic convention and the Roosevelt administration by the CIO's Political Action Committee; the legality of the PAC's politicking under the Hatch Act; Sidney Hillman's youthful proclivities toward radicalism; and the endorsement of Roosevelt by Earl Browder, leader of the Communist remnant. In an address delivered in Boston late in the campaign, Dewey picked up the theme of Hillman as labor radical and Browder's support of Roosevelt—widely circulated in an article published by the conservative *Reader's Digest*. Such desperate charges failed to carry weight in wartime; nor did they reflect well on the Republican candidate among liberal eastern Republicans.[19]

The president carried the Electoral College by a vote of 433 to 99. There were major gains in counties won by the Republican Party between the Hoover and Dewey campaigns: from 372 in 1932 to 1,344 in 1944. The Democratic Party won a majority of voters in 1944 in 1,750 counties, 1,221 of these in the South. Party membership in the House of Representatives showed a considerable shift in these years, with the Republicans improving from 117 in the 1932 campaign to 199 in 1944; in the Senate, the gain was most pronounced between 1936 an 1944, 16 to 38. The Democratic Party won the Deep South and the urban centers, the latter ascribed to the vote of labor and African Americans. Roosevelt also won a substantial majority of votes cast by the military. The Republicans took the north central states (upper Midwest) and the middle Atlantic states. Roosevelt won New York's electoral votes with the aid of the American Labor Party and the Liberal Party (825,600 votes). Wisconsin's Progressive Party virtually disappeared.[20]

During these months, Vandenberg followed the strategy of keeping a foot in both camps of the party, dealing respectfully with Austin but, one surmises, not with enthusiasm. Indeed, in May, when Secretary Hull invited Senate Democratic majority leader Tom Connally to assemble a committee of six to confer with him on postwar peace plans, it turned into the Committee of Eight. When Vandenberg insisted on the inclusion of Robert La Follette, Connally appointed the Republican Austin to balance Vandenberg's selection of the isolationist Progressive from Wisconsin. Vandenberg, it must be noted, was satisfied with Hull's support for allowing a veto power for the Big Four, while Hull agreed with the proposition that there would be no commitment of American forces to a military action absent congressional approval. Accordingly, the new League as proposed by Hull "was anything but a wild-eyed internationalist dream of a World state."

In a series of meetings between Hull and the Committee of Eight, the secretary of state requested a letter for his use in future negotiations with Churchill and Stalin agreeing to his plan for a new international organization. "It is a good plan," Vandenberg hedged, but he could not commit the next Republican president to an agreement reached by a Senate subcommittee; nor could he agree to any plan without knowing the nature of the peace. Hull, he noted, wanted to go ahead with establishing a League first. "If so, it will fail." The senators agreed to preliminary conversations for a "general plan for an international organization as the ultimate means to implement a just and satisfactory peace."

In the process, Vandenberg allied with the isolationists on the committee, particularly La Follette and Guy Gillette of Iowa. They would give Hull a letter approving of his desire to enter into negotiations, but no more. They would not sign a "blank check" until they were informed of the nature of the peace, meaning the contents of secret agreements reached by Roosevelt with Stalin and Churchill at their wartime conference, particularly the acceptance of Soviet occupation of eastern Europe and continuation of the British Empire. An angry Hull was dissatisfied with the strings attached to the senators' response. Austin sided with Hull.

The Hull–Senate committee discussions were further complicated by an article published in the *Saturday Evening Post* by Forest Davis confirming the suspicions of the Vandenberg–La Follette cohort regarding concessions made to Stalin by FDR. In a lengthy meeting on May 29, Hull explained: "We cannot stop in the midst of the war to quarrel with Russia with regard to peace terms." Vandenberg reiterated his insistence that the committee did not have available to it commitments made at higher levels. In the end, the group and Hull agreed to preparations and discussion for "an effective postwar international organization to keep the peace and prevent aggression." Beyond this, unaware of the substance of behind-the-scenes commitments, the senators refused to provide a written statement underwriting Hull's diplomatic exchanges.[21]

Upon resumption in late August of the exchanges between Hull and the Senate committee, with the Dumbarton Oaks Conference under way, the secretary of state raised the issue of the use of cooperative force by the new international structure. Effectively, what should be the authority of the United States delegate to commit armed forces to a United Nations mission? Vandenberg insisted on a clear distinction between the immediate availability of American forces to assure the demilitarization of Germany and Japan as opposed to the authority of the American representative to the new League Council in other situations. With the exception of minor disturbance, it was agreed, the American delegate would need to secure the consent of the president and the Congress "to . . . put us into joint war." "I said," Vandenberg recalled, "that I would never consent that our delegate on the new League Council should have the power to vote us into a major military operation (tantamount to declaring war) without a vote of the Congress as required by the Constitution."

Effectively, Vandenberg and La Follette carried the committee on their insistence that they would not agree to the details of a new League without complete knowledge of the commitments made at wartime conferences.[22]

Vandenberg's January 10, 1945, Senate address, viewed in the press as a turning point in his disposition toward American participation in world order, did not represent an epiphany. Rather it suggested a gradual conversion to the notion that isolationism was unrealistic in light of the destructive potential of modern warfare. The address also signaled public affirmation of his fear that the Soviet Union intended to occupy eastern Europe, violating the assumptions expressed in the Atlantic Charter that underlay American entry into the European war. Acknowledging Russian apprehension regarding the resurgence of a militaristic Germany, he assured the Soviets that the United States, distinct from the Dumbarton Oaks proceedings, would join in preventing a reincarnated militaristic Reich; and also that such intervention would be the prerogative of the chief executive. In short, Russia did not require a buffer in eastern Europe. The United States, he insisted, had not entered the conflict to ensure the subjugation of small nations, in effect a Soviet Empire built on the ashes of World War II.[23]

A congratulatory letter from Austin elicited a succinct summary of Vandenberg's views. He was troubled by three aspects of Dumbarton Oaks. He abhorred "surrender to the Russian idea that all of the permanent members of the [Security] Council shall be immunized against discipline." He wanted injustices in the peace treaty subjected to review by the new League. And he regarded presidential authority to use force in the absence of congressional approval as unconstitutional, except to prevent the remilitarization of the Axis powers. To Dulles, he confided: "I still do not know what to do about the latitudes to be allowed our peace delegate in respect to military commitments; and I still lack a practical formula to implement the constitutional requirement that only Congress can declare war."

Vandenberg and especially Taft offered a protectionist response in the event of a postwar recession. The 1944 party platform promised shelter for local labor and manufacturing from cheap overseas competition and limitation of agricultural exposure to the world market. Whereas the party leaders were prepared to reverse the earlier rejection of United States membership in a League of Nations, their outlook had not advanced beyond the economic proscriptions of the New Economic Era. When Vandenberg requested elucidation of a platform plank that supported assistance by direct credits in reasonable amounts to liberated nations facilitating their recovery, Taft explained that the plank in question focused on limitations. Thus, assistance by direct credits would exclude "the idea of a . . . stabilization fund or United Nations bank, which . . . will cost us much more money, with no control, because we have only twenty-five percent voting strength." Further, the credits would be used strictly for American-made goods and used only for emergency loans.

Vandenberg and Taft apparently gave little attention to the economic meaning attached to the fact that some 50 percent or more of gross national product worldwide originated in the United States. The time had come for American assumption of the role once exercised out of London—the financing of world trade and maintenance of monetary stability. Yet, when the administration offered Vandenberg membership in the United States delegation to the International Monetary Conference in June, he declined on the ground that the plan formulated by Harry Dexter White placed too substantial a burden on the United States. Then, in late July, he indicated that he opposed the creation of the International Monetary Fund since it permitted member nations to engage in competitive currency depreciation and offered no clear commitment to gold.[24]

As the war came to a conclusion, Taft hoped to reverse the New Deal's interventionist program. He told Bruce Barton, a politician and advertising executive: "There is only one fundamental issue in this country today. That is whether we maintain reasonable freedom . . . or turn quickly to an all-powerful Socialist State." He desired repeal of the Hull trade treaties. He opposed support prices and commodity loans for agriculture and proposed abolition of the Agricultural Adjustment Administration. Attacks by the CIO-PAC in the course of his bitterly fought reelection campaign in 1944 "left him grimly resolved to curb the power of organized labor in the future." Taft followed Hoover's advice "to take up the cudgels for the A.F.L. as against the C.I.O." In an address before that union in Cleveland on October 7, he rejected the assertion of the CIO Political Action Committee that he opposed labor as unfounded and a Communist smear. He countered with a detailed recitation of support for the American Federation of Labor, also noting that "the labor unions certainly do not wish to permit the Communists to use the form of labor union for political purposes." Nor would labor benefit from the centralizing tendencies of the federal government as it gave increasing authority to boards and bureaus. "Labor would benefit, more than anyone else, from the Republican policy of stimulating full employment through free enterprise."

Once elected, albeit by a surprisingly small margin, Taft fought Senate approval of the large sums required to underwrite the Bretton Woods proposals for the World Bank and International Monetary Fund, institutions intended to serve as the economic equivalent of the United Nations, initially to service the reconstruction of Europe. These institutions, he held, could prevent neither trade restrictions nor currency warfare. Then again, currency stabilization did not assure prosperity or increase trade, while the creation of the World Bank usurped the lending authority of Congress. United States guarantee of private investment abroad was unwise, since recipients viewed such investments with suspicion. Unsound loans for reconstruction would lead to default, stimulate inflation, and result in "pouring dollars down a rat-hole." Instead, he proposed stabilization of the dollar and the pound; congressional management of direct loans; and substantial funding of the Export-Import Bank, which would lend abroad at market rates. In the realm of international economics, Taft remained committed to "the policy of America first."[25]

In the last analysis, it is questionable whether Vandenberg permanently bridged the gap between midwestern nationalists and the eastern internationalists, commentators, and intelligentsia. Taft considered international security as "poppycock." Efforts to move the nation back to the mind-set of the New Economic Era retained their appeal to a large segment of the party. Taft argued that the Gallup poll should not shape party policy. "Party principles first and if you are right . . . the people will come back to you." An appeal limited to the middle class was "absolutely wrong." The Ohioan proffered a narrow construction of the Constitution.

Taft rejected the "theory of restoring prosperity through government spending and deficit financing." He favored a balanced budget and lower taxes. He characterized the New Deal, particularly the efforts of the National Resources Planning Board, as an attempt to introduce a planned economy, which he equated with "state socialism without the slightest regard for the freedom of the individual, of local government or of the Congress." He regarded federal agencies as responsible for excessive accumulation of authority and thereby repressive and urged abolition of those that were unnecessary.

Taft deplored the president's control over the value of the currency and challenged the executive's overregulation of the farmer, business, the worker, and the consumer. He urged greater financial accountability of public corporations. In the matter of social legislation, whereas Dulles viewed the Beveridge Plan as "exceedingly modest" and Dewey affirmed the need for enlarged government functions in a modern economy and certain of the New Deal social program including minimum wages, unemployment insurance, provision for pensions, and stabilization of interest rates, Taft rejected "an American Beveridge plan," claiming that excessive public expenditure would choke private investment and employment. He supported social insurance for old age, unemployment, low-cost housing, and medical care so long as these programs were administered at the state level.

In the years under consideration, Willkie—through the agency of internationalist-minded senators and governors—prodded an insular party toward some awareness of the responsibilities required of the world's leading power. Once membership in an international body for maintenance of the peace was accepted by the Republicans in the Mackinac Declaration and jointly with the Democratic Party in the Connally Resolution, the way was paved for the Moscow accord negotiated by Cordell Hull, Dumbarton Oaks, and the San Francisco Conference, which created the United Nations. Vandenberg served as the mediator between the nationalists concentrated in the nation's midsection and the Eastern Seaboard's internationalist elite. Yet, neither Hoover, nor Vandenberg, nor Taft provided the party with a program appropriate to the weight of the American economy in world markets. Rather Taft, the party's leader in shaping domestic policy in the mold of Hoover, favored an economy protected from a world ravaged by the destruction of the Second World War.

In domestic matters, Willkie proved unsuccessful in prodding the party toward meeting the complexities of the twentieth century. The mind-set of Hoover and Taft prevailed, with a large segment of a divided Republican Party in a quest for a return to the New Economy of the 1920s. Hoover originated the pursuit of a return to limited intervention in the economy, given his distrust of federal authority and his defense of his presidency as having resolved the economic and banking crises of the early 1930s only to have his successes reversed by the Roosevelt policies. A strong component of the party returned in time to the economic mantra of the Hoover-Taft wing: self-sufficiency sustained by protectionism; budget balance; devolution of administrative responsibility for a national economy to the locality and the states; a weak presidency; and opposition to the very concept of domestic and international interdependence.[26]

The arguments of Tugwell, Hansen, and Keynes merited careful examination, but not total rejection. The worker required protection from the vicissitudes of the business cycle and the impact of an industrial-technological economy. Hansen's approach to planning exceeded American willingness to replicate Europe's adoption of the welfare state and overhead economic management, but planning was a necessity in a modern economy. Over the longer term, abhorrence of expertise in government led to the questioning of central banking, disinterest in the funding of scientific education and research, and limited investment in infrastructure associated with an advanced economy. The failure of Hoover and Taft to advance beyond the strictures of the interwar era left an indelible imprint on not-so-modern Republican thought.

NOTES

ABBREVIATIONS

Acheson Papers   Dean Acheson Papers, Yale University Library, New Haven,
                        Conn.
Austin Papers   Warren R. Austin Papers, University of Vermont,
                        Burlington
Baker Papers   Newton D. Baker Papers, Manuscript Division, Library of
                        Congress, Washington, D.C.
Barnard Papers   Ellsworth Barnard Papers, Lilly Library, University of Indi-
                        ana, Bloomington
Baruch Papers   Bernard M. Baruch Papers, Seeley Mudd Manuscript
                        Library, Princeton University, Princeton, N.J.
Berle Papers   Adolf A. Berle Papers, FDRL, Hyde Park, N.Y.
Berry Papers   Don L. Berry Papers, Iowa State University, Ames
The Bible   The Collected Speeches of Herbert Hoover, HHPL
Byrnes Papers   James F. Byrnes Papers, Robert Muldrow Cooper Library,
                        Clemson University, Clemson, S.C.
Chamberlain Papers   Neville Chamberlain Papers, Birmingham University,
                        United Kingdom
Commerce Papers   HHPL
Daniels Papers   Josephus Daniels Papers, Manuscript Division, Library of
                        Congress, Washington, D.C.
DGFP   Documents on German Foreign Policy
Dirksen Collection   Everett McKinley Dirksen Papers, Dirksen Center, Pekin,
                        Ill.
Dodd Papers   William E. Dodd Papers, Manuscript Division, Library of
                        Congress, Washington, D.C.
du Pont, Irénée, Papers Irénée du Pont Papers, Hagley Library, Wilmington, Del.
du Pont, Pierre S., Papers Pierre du Point Papers, Hagley Library, Wilmington, Del.
FDRL   Franklin D. Roosevelt Library, Hyde Park, N.Y.
Eccles Papers   Marriner S. Eccles Papers, University of Utah, Salt Lake
                        City
Fletcher Papers   Henry P. Fletcher Papers, Manuscript Division, Library of
                        Congress, Washington, D.C.
Flynn Papers   John T. Flynn Papers, University of Oregon, Eugene
FO   Foreign Office, British Foreign Office Papers, Kew, London

Glass Papers	Carter Glass Papers, Alderman Library, University of Virginia, Charlottesville
Hamilton Papers	John D. M. Hamilton Papers, Manuscript Division, Library of Congress, Washington, D.C.
Hansen Papers	Alvin Hansen Papers, Pusey Library, Harvard University, Cambridge, Mass.
Henry Papers	John M. Henry Papers, HHPL
HHPL	Herbert Hoover Presidential Library, West Branch, Iowa
Hope Papers	Clifford Hope Papers, Kansas Historical Society, Topeka
Joslin Diary	Theodore Joslin Papers, HHPL
Lamont Papers	Thomas W. Lamont Papers, Baker Library, Graduate School of Business, Harvard University, Cambridge, Mass.
Landon Papers	Alf M. Landon Papers, Kansas Historical Society, Topeka
Leffingwell Papers	Russell Leffingwell Papers, Yale University Library, New Haven, Conn.
McAdoo Papers	William Gibbs McAdoo Papers, Manuscript Division, Library of Congress, Washington, D.C.
McNary Papers	Charles McNary Papers, Manuscript Division, Library of Congress, Washington, D.C.
Mills Papers	Ogden Mills Papers, Manuscript Division, Library of Congress, Washington, D.C.
Moley Papers	Raymond Moley Papers, Hoover Institution Archives, Stanford University, Stanford, Calif.
Nye Papers	Gerald P. Nye Papers, HHPL
OF	Official File, FDRL
Pew Papers	Pew Family Papers, Sun Oil Collection, Hagley Library, Wilmington, Del.
PPF	President's Personal File, FDRL
PPI	Post-Presidential Individual, HHPL
PPS	Post-Presidential Subject, HHPL
PRO	Public Records Office, Kew, London
PSF	President's Secretaries File, FDRL
Raskob Papers	John J. Raskob Papers, Hagley Library, Wilmington, Del.
Rickard Diary	Edgar Rickard Papers, HHPL
Rosen Papers	Elliot A. Rosen Papers, HHPL
Sachs Papers	Alexander Sachs Papers, FDRL
Shouse Papers	Jouett Shouse Papers, Hagley Library, Wilmington, Del.
Stimson Diary	Henry L. Stimson Papers, Yale University, New Haven, Conn.
Strauss Papers	Lewis Strauss Papers, HHPL
Taft, Charles, Papers	Charles P. Taft Papers, Manuscript Division, Library of Congress, Washington, D.C.
Taft, Robert, Papers	Robert A. Taft Papers, Manuscript Division, Library of Congress, Washington, D.C.
Tugwell Papers	Rexford G. Tugwell Papers, FDRL
Vandenberg Papers	Arthur Vandenberg Papers, University of Michigan, Ann Arbor

Waymack Papers	William Wesley Waymack Papers, Iowa Historical Society, Iowa City
Warburg Papers	James P. Warburg Papers, John F. Kennedy Library, Columbia Point, Boston, Mass.
White Papers	William Allen White Papers, Manuscript Division, Library of Congress, Washington, D.C.
Willkie Papers	Wendell L. Willkie Papers, Lilly Library, University of Indiana, Bloomington
Witte Papers	Edwin E. Witte Papers, Wisconsin Historical Society, Madison

INTRODUCTION

1. Gene Smiley, *Rethinking the Great Depression* (Chicago, 2002), 128.

2. Tugwell to author, May 5, 1964.

3. Charles Kindleberger, *The World in Depression, 1929–1939* (Berkeley and Los Angeles, 1973), is regarded as the source of hegemonic theory; see Adam Tooze, *The Wages of Destruction: The Making and Breaking of the Nazi Economy* (New York, 2007), as the basis for my conclusions. For a contrary view, see George H. Nash, ed., *Freedom Betrayed: Herbert Hoover's Secret History of the Second World War and Its Aftermath* (Stanford, Calif., 2011).

1 | HERBERT HOOVER AND THE ARK OF THE COVENANT

1. Theodore Joslin Diary, June 28, 30, 1932, box 10, Joslin Papers. A detailed analysis of the factors responsible for Roosevelt's nomination is found in Rosen, "Baker on the Fifth Ballot? The Democratic: Alternative: 1932," *Ohio History* 75, no. 4 (Autumn 1966): 226–46, 273–77. Until 1936, the Democratic Party nomination required a two-thirds vote of the convention.

2. William Gibbs McAdoo to George F. Milton, Jan. 19, 1932, box 348, McAdoo Papers. Jonathan Daniels to Josephus Daniels, Feb. 19, 1932, box 660; David F. Houston to Josephus Daniels, May 8, 1932, box 665, both in Daniels Papers. William E. Dodd to Newton D. Baker, March 24, 1932, box 87; Allan Nevins to Baker, April 15, 1932, box 162, both in Baker Papers. Carl Becker to Dodd, Nov. 29, 1932, box 39, Dodd Papers. George Creel, *Rebel at Large: Recollections of Fifty Crowded Years* (New York, 1947), 270. Adolf A. Berle Jr. to Ralph Hayes, July 6, 1932, box 8, Berle Papers. Robert Jackson to author, memorandum, Feb. 24, 1966; Raymond Moley, interview by author, Sept. 1963, both in Rosen Papers. Walter Lippmann, "The Candidacy of Franklin D. Roosevelt," *New York Herald Tribune*, Jan. 9, 1932; Paul K. Conkin, *The New Deal*, 2nd ed. (Arlington Heights, Ill., 1975), chap. 1.

3. Raymond to Nell Moley, April 12, 1932, in Moley, *After Seven Years* (New York, 1939), 11. Don L. Berry to John Spargo, Nov. 10, 1937, box 1, Berry Papers. Clifford Hope to Berry, July 12, 1937, box 62, Hope Papers. Verne Marshall to Herbert Hoover, May 25, 1933, box 143, PPI.

4. Ellis W. Hawley, "Herbert Hoover, the Commerce Secretariat, and the Vision of an Associative State," *Journal of American History* 61 (June 1974): 116–40. Herbert Hoover to Gerard Swope, draft of letter, October 1926, box 190, Commerce Papers. Hoover address, "Some Phases of the Government in Business," Cleveland Chamber of Commerce, May 7, 1924, Public Statements File; Hoover address, "Republican Policies,"

Republican County Committee, New York City, Oct. 16, 1928, The Bible, 26, no. 648, all in HHPL.

5. "Summary of Statement of Secretary Hoover to the Super Power Conference," New York City, Oct. 13, 1923, box 162; William Hard, "Giant Negotiations for Giant Power: An Interview," *Survey Graphic*, March 1924, 577–80, box 162; radio address, Hoover to Convention of National Electric Light Association, Atlantic City, May 21, 1924, box 162; [Hoover], "Power Development Not a Function of Government," n.d., not used, box 590; Hoover address, "Why the Public Interest Requires Local Rather Than Federal Regulation of Electric Public Utilities," National Association of Railroad and Utilities Commissioners," Washington, D.C., Oct. 14, 1925, box 591; McGraw Hill summary of Hoover views on state vs. federal control of water power, box 591, all in Commerce Papers. Hoover address, "Republican Policies," Republican County Committee, New York City, Oct. 16, 1928, The Bible, 26, no. 648; "Portion of Gridiron Club Address," Dec. 14, 1933, box 138, PPS. Paul A. Sexson, Arizona Secretary [to Barry Goldwater], to Bernice Miller, Jan. 19, 1960, box 202, PPI.

6. Kendrick A. Clements, *The Life of Herbert Hoover: Imperfect Visionary, 1918–1928* (New York, 2010), 131–47; "Campaign Speech at Madison Square Garden, New York City, Oct. 31, 1932, The Campaign a Contrast between Two Philosophies of Government, (Analysis of Democratic Proposals as dangerous to the foundations of American Life)," in *The State Papers and Other Public Writings of Herbert Hoover*, ed. William Starr Myers (Garden City, N.Y., 1934), 2: 408–28; David Burner, *Herbert Hoover: A Public Life* (New York, 1972), 164–66, 282. Hoover to Ogden Mills, Feb. 2, March 2, May 7, 1933, box 151; Hoover to Lewis Strauss, April 4, 1933, box 224, all in PPI.

7. Hoover to Mark Sullivan, Sept. 1, 1934, box 229, PPI.

8. Hoover to Frank B. Knox, March 22, 1935, box 115, PPI.

9. Hoover to Ogden L. Mills, Feb. 22, May 7, 1933, box 151; Hoover to Senator J. G. Townshend (Delaware), April 4, 1933, box 237; Hoover to Frank B. Knox, April 5, 1933, box 115; Hoover to Henry P. Fletcher, April 11, 1933, box 60; Hoover to Walter F. Brown, April 25, 26, Oct. 22, 1933, box 25; Inflation File, sent to Harry Chandler, Edwin Kemmerer, and Mark Sullivan, April 27, 1933, box 34; Hoover to Simeon D. Fess, April 27, May 9, 1933, box 58; Hoover to Walter Ewing, April 27, 1933, box 56; Hoover to Simeon D. Fess, April 27, 1933, box 328; Hoover to Adolph Miller, Federal Reserve Board, Aug. 25, 1933, box 149; Hoover to Arch W. Shaw, Sept. 12, 1933, Gen. Acc. 285/2; Hoover to Henry L. Stimson, Oct. 3, 1933, box 222; Hoover to J. C. O'Laughlin, Oct. 12, 1933, box 166; Hoover to David A. Reed, Oct. 23 and Nov. 15, 1933, box 183, all in PPI. Edgar Rickard Diary, Sept. 24–27, 1933.

10. Henry L. Pritchett, Carnegie Foundation for the Advancement of Teaching, to Mark L. Requa, May 5, 1933, box 180; Henry L. Stimson to Hoover, June 23, 1933, box 222; "Dictated: My recollection of his [Elihu Root's] words: 'The Sins of the Republican party,'" box 196; Mills to Hoover, Nov. 21, 1933, box 151, all in PPI. Gary Dean Best, "Herbert Hoover as Titular Leader of the G.O.P., 1933–35," *Mid-America* 61, no. 2 (April-July 1979): 86–89. Stimson Diary, Sept. 21, 1933.

11. Hoover to Arch W. Shaw, Sept. 12, Nov. 13, 16, 1933; Shaw to Hoover, Sept. 12, Nov. 12, 13, 16, 28, 1933, Gen. Acc. 282/2, box 207; Hoover to Edwin Kemmerer, Oct. 12, 1933, box 108; Kemmerer to Hoover, Oct. 13, 1933, box 108; Hoover to Harrison E. Spangler, Dec. 28, 1933, box 219, all in PPI. Rickard Diary, Sept. 24–27, 1933.

12. Hoover to William Allen White, May 11, 1934, box 252, PPI.

13. Leffingwell to John Maynard Keynes, July 28, 1922, box 4; Leffingwell to the Editor, *Manchester Guardian Commercial,* July 28, 1922, box 4; Leffingwell to J. P. Morgan, Sept. 10, 1923, box 6; Morgan to Leffingwell, Oct. 15, 1923, box 6; Leffingwell to E. C. Grenfell, Feb. 6, 1925, box 3; Leffingwell to Thomas Lamont, Oct. 25, 1926, March 8, 1929, July 21, Aug. 29, 1931, July 27, Nov. 15, 1932, box 4; Leffingwell to B. S. ("Bunny) Carter, Oct. 3, 1931, Feb. 16, 1932, box 1; Leffingwell to Walter Lippmann, Dec. 18, 30, 1931, Feb. 16, April 13, Oct. 25, 1932, box 5; Leffingwell to Carter Glass, Nov. 7, 1932, box 3, all in Leffingwell Papers.

14. Leffingwell to Carter Glass, Jan. 8, 1932, box 3; Leffingwell to Walter Lippmann, May 4, 1932, box 5; Leffingwell to Frank[lin D. Roosevelt], Dec. 6, 1932, box 7, all in Leffingwell Papers. Series D57–71, Industrial Distribution of Gainful Workers, 1820–1940, *Historical Statistics of the United States: Colonial Times to 1957* (Washington, D.C., 1960).

15. Hoover to Frank Knox, Sept. 1, 1933, box 115; Hoover to Theodore Roosevelt Jr., Sept. 10, box 196; Hoover to Alan Fox, Oct. 8, box 62; Hoover to Silas H. Strawn, Oct. 15, 1934, box 222, all in PPI. Lewis Strauss to Hoover, n.d. [1934], Strauss Papers. The expression "Ark of the Covenant" appears in Hoover to Henry J. Allen, Oct. 17, 1934, box 4, PPI.

16. Walter Lippmann, "The Permanent New Deal," *Yale Review* 24 (June 1935): 649–67.

17. Herbert Hoover, *The Challenge to Liberty* (New York, 1934), 1, 8n1, 13, 15–16, 20–21, 40–41, 47–49, 76–79, 86–114, 122–27, 133–34. Hoover to Charles C. Teague, Nov. 19, 1934, box 234; Hoover to A. H. Kirchhofer, June 28, 1935, box 112, both in PPI. Edward Berkowitz and Larry DeWitt, "Social Security from the New Deal to the Great Society: Expanding the Public Domain," in *Conservatism and American Political Development,* ed. Brian J. Glenn and Steven M. Teles (New York, 2009), 59.

18. Hoover to David A. Reed, and attached speech by Reed, box 183; Hoover to Mrs. Vernon (Charlotte) Kellogg, box 107; Hoover to Ashmun Brown, box 24; Hoover to Lester J. Dickinson, box 47, all Nov. 9, 1934; Hoover to Franklin W. Fort, Nov. 17, 1934, box 61; Henry M. Robinson to Hoover, Oct. 21, 1933, box 193; Theodore Joslin to Hoover, ca. April 1, 1934, box 103; Harry D. Hatfield to Hoover, Nov. 13, 1934, Jan. 4, 1950 [1951]; Hoover to Hatfield, Jan. 15, 1951, box 81, all in PPI. Best, "Hoover as Titular Leader," 90–91.

19. Franklin D. Roosevelt to Charles L. McNary, April 11, 1933, box 33; McNary statements, Aug. 3, 1933, Jan. 1, 1934, August 1934, box 23; radio broadcast, June 8, 1934, box 23; McNary to James Couzens, Sept. 14, 1934, box 5; Couzens to McNary, Sept. 18, 1934, box 5, on his support for social security legislation; McNary to Mr. and Mrs. J. J. Hamilton, April 8, 1936, box 5, all in McNary Papers. Clyde P. Weed, *The Nemesis of Reform: The Republican Party during the New Deal* (New York, 1994), 49–52; James T. Patterson, *Congressional Conservatism and the New Deal* (Lexington, Ky., 1967), 16–17; George H. Mayer, "Alf M. Landon, as Leader of the Republican Opposition, 1937–1940," *Kansas Historical Quarterly* 32 (Autumn 1966): 2 (online). Robert S. Allen to William Allen White, Dec. 20, 1933, ser. C, box 201, White Papers.

20. Henry C. Warner to Everett M. Dirksen, Nov. 10, 1936, folders 3–4; Dr. Andy Hall to Dirksen, Nov. 11, 1934, folders 3–4; Verle V. Kramer to Dirksen, Nov. 11, 1936, folders 3–4; F. H. Gillen to Dirksen, Nov. 12, 1936, folders 3–4; Benjamin H. Miller to Dirksen, Nov. 20, 1936, folders 3–4; "Buck Strawn Rides Again," memorandum, folder

485; Illinois Republican Citizens Organization to Dear Sir, March 6, 1937, folder 485, Politics Series, all in Dirksen Collection.

21. National Economy League to Henry P. Fletcher, Sept. 23, 1932, box 15; Fletcher to Mark Sullivan, Feb. 28, 1934, box 16; Fletcher to Hoover, Aug. 31, 1934, box 16; Alexander Biddle to Fletcher, July 16, 1934, box 16; *Baltimore Sun,* June 6, 1934, box 19, all in Fletcher Papers. Mayer, "Landon," 2–3. H. Alexander Smith to Mills, June 7, 1934, box 80A, Mills Papers.

22. William Allen White to David Hinshaw, Feb. 16, 1933, ser. C, box 203, White Papers. Arthur H. Hyde to Hoover, Nov. 19, 1934, box 98; Hoover to Hyde, Nov. 29, 1934, box 98; Hyde to Theodore G. Joslin, Dec. 8, 1934, box 103; Verne Marshall to Hoover, March 27, 1935, box 143; Hoover to Gould Lincoln, Aug. 22, 1935, box 124; Hoover to Tim J. Campbell, Jan. 3, 1936, box 29, all in PPI. Rickard Diary, June 9–12, 28, July 30, Aug. 12–15, 1935.

23. Hoover to William Allen White, Sept. 12, 1934, box 252; Hoover to Ashmun Brown, June 21, 1935, box 24; Hoover handwritten note, n.d., box 90; Walter Newton to Hoover, June 25, 27, July 25, 1935, box 162, all in PPI. Hoover manuscript, "The Bank Crisis and Interregnum, 1932–33," Flynn Papers. Rickard Diary, Oct. 9, 1935.

24. Hoover to William L. Hennold, Jan. 22, 1935, box 85; Hoover to Ashmun Brown May 3, June 21, July 25, 1935, box 24; Brown, "The Day in Washington," *Providence Journal,* June 12, 1935, box 24; Charles B. Goodspeed to Hoover, Sept. 13, 1935, box 71, all in PPI. Hoover to Lewis Strauss, May 10, 1935, note attached to *New York Times* editorial, box 34, Strauss Papers. "Creed Approved by 'Grass Root' Republicans," n.d., Hamilton Papers. Theodore C. Wallen, *New York Herald Tribune,* March 27, 1935; Robert Mason, *The Republican Party and American Politics from Hoover to Reagan* (New York, 2012), 56–57.

25. [Hamilton], Memorandum of conference held at Kansas City, Feb. 17, 1935; William Allen White to John D. M. Hamilton, May 6, 1935; excerpt copied from Mr. White's letter to Mr. Hoover, Hamilton to White, May 9, 1935; White to Hamilton, May 11, 1935; Hamilton to White, May 13, 1935; White to Hamilton, May 14, 24, 1935, all in box 1, Hamilton Papers. William Allen White to Ogden L. Mills, June 19, July 3, 1934, box 170, Mills Papers.

26. Frank Knox to Hoover, May 6, 1935, box 115; Hoover to Ogden Mills, July 20, 1935, box 151, both in PPI. C. B. Goodspeed to John Hamilton, Feb. 29, 1936, box 78, Landon Papers.

27. Rickard Diary, Nov. 4, 11, 13, Dec. 4, 1935. "Sacramento, Dec. 9," box 197; Walter Newton to Hoover, Dec. 9, 1935, box 162; Paul Sexson to Robert G. Simmons, Jan. 7, 1936, box 202; Alan Fox to Hoover, Jan. 18, 1936, box 62, all in PPI. Lewis Strauss to Hoover, Nov. 27, 1935, box 34, Strauss Papers. William Allen White to Arthur Capper, April 2, 1934, ser. C, box 214, White Papers.

2 | LANDON OF KANSAS

1. G. (Grace Tully), "Memo for Mary, for President's locked drawer," PSF178. E. E. Lincoln, "Federal Non-Recoverable Relief Expenditures by States, Compared with Internal Revenue Collections, July 1, 1933, to June 30, 1937 . . ." and accompanying table, file 771, box 1, Pierre du Pont Papers. "Summary Operations Report of Federal Funds Loaned and Expended from New and Emergency Appropriations, March 4,

1933, through December 31, 1937," *Cong. Record,* Senate, 75th Cong., 3rd sess., vol. 83, April 14, 1938.

2. Alexander J. Field, "The Most Technologically Progressive Decade of the Century," *American Economic Review* 93 (Sept. 2003): 1399–414; Field, *A Great Leap Forward* (New Haven, Conn., 2011), 1–23; John Kendrick, *Productivity Trends in the United States* (Princeton, N.J., 1961), table A–XXII, XXIII, 334–35, 339–40. For a more complete study of the New Deal public-works programs and their import, see Jason Scott Smith, *Building New Deal Liberalism: The Political Economy of Public Works, 1933–1956* (New York, 2009), 1–28, 87, 94, 103–22.

3. Donald R. McCoy, *Landon of Kansas* (Lincoln, Neb., 1966), 3–196. Clifford R. Hope to F. M. Arnold, April 29, 1936, box 235, Hope Papers.

4. William Allen White to Theodore Roosevelt Jr., Dec. 5, 1933, box 204, White Papers. White to Ogden L. Mills, July 3, 1934, box 170, Mills Papers. White to John D. M. Hamilton, May 11, 14, 24, 1935, box 1, Hamilton Papers. White to Herbert Hoover, July 1, 1936, box 252, PPI. William L. White, "The Last Two Decades," in *The Autobiography of William Allen White* (New York, 1946), 638–40.

5. Ogden L. Mills to Owen D. Young and George Harrison, Dec. 16, 1932, box 9; Mills, "Where Do We Go from Here?" address, Kansas Day Club, Jan. 29, 1934, box 139; Alf M. Landon to Lee Cowden, Feb. 2, 1934, box 11, all in Mills Papers.

6. Ogden L. Mills to James H. Douglas, Oct. 27, 1933, box 170; Mills to Everett Sanders, Oct. 19, Nov. 21, 1933, box 11; "The Speech of Ogden Mills," editorial, *Hartford Courant,* Jan. 1, 1934, box 163; Alf M. Landon to Mills, Nov. 28, 1933, box 161; Mills to Landon, March 12, 1934, box 161; Landon to Mills, March 16, 1934, box 161; Russell Leffingwell to Stanley P. Davies, Feb. 26, 1934, box 96; memorandum from Mr. Davies, General Director, Charity Organization Society, to Mr. Page, Sept 20, 1934, box 96; Mills to Kenneth B. Walton, Oct. 1, 1934, box 163; Russell Leffingwell to Mills, Oct. 24, 1934, box 96; Mills to Leffingwell, Oct. 29, 1934, box 96; H. Alexander Smith to Mills, June 7, 1934, box 80A; Henry P. Fletcher to Mills, Sept. 18, 1934, box 161; Mills to George H. Lorimer, Nov. 9, 1934, box 11; Mills to Harold L Varney, Dec. 10, 1934, box 11; Mills, "The Road to Recovery," address, *Town Hall of the Air,* June 27, 1935, box 140; "Unemployment," address, Rotary Club, Chicago, Nov. 12, 1935, box 140; Henry J. Haskell to Mills, Dec. 28, 1935, box 12; Mills to Haskell, Dec. 30, 1935, box 12; address before San Francisco Group Northern California Bankers Association, March 16, 1936, box 143; Mills to Mrs. Burnett Malcom, May 27, 1936, box 52; O. Glenn Saxon to Mills, Nov. 11, 1936, box 170; Landon to Mills, Jan. 10, 1937, box 52, all in Mills Papers. Ogden L. Mills, *What of Tomorrow?* (New York, 1935), 1–5, 141–45; *Liberalism Fights On* (New York, 1936), 103, 121–23.

7. Clyde Reed to Arch W. Jarrell, May 7, 1933, sec. C, box 204, White Papers.

8. Landon, "The Nation Needs Better Housekeeping," address, Kansas Day Club, Topeka, Jan. 29, 1936, box 80, Landon Papers.

9. Landon to W. W. Kiplinger, April 9, 1935, box 78; Irwin House to Landon, Feb. 11, 1936, box 56, both in Landon Papers. Clifford Hope to Landon, June 15, 1936, box 53, Hope Papers. Robert F. Burk, *The Corporate State and the Broker State: The Du Ponts and American National Politics, 1925–1940* (Cambridge, Mass., 1990), 153–54; Weed, *The Nemesis of Reform,* 76, 204n4.

10. Stanley High to Landon, Sept. 9, Oct. 1, 24, 1935, Feb. 15, 1936, box 56; Landon to

High, Sept. 17, Oct. 9, Nov. 4, 26, 1935, box 56, all in Landon Papers. McCoy, *Landon of Kansas,* 293; Arthur M. Schlesinger Jr., *The Politics of Upheaval* (Boston, 1960), 573–74.

11. Raymond Gram Swing to Landon, Dec. 31, 1935, Jan. 25, May 19, 1936; Landon to Swing, Jan. 15, Feb. 2, May 15, 1936, all in box 54, Landon Papers. McCoy, *Landon of Kansas,* 305–6.

12. Edward L. Schapsmeier and Frederick H. Schapsmeier, *Henry A. Wallace of Iowa: The Agrarian Years, 1910–1940* (Ames, Iowa, 1968), 214–20; Richard Kirkendall, *Social Scientists and Farm Politics in the Age of Roosevelt* (Columbia, Mo., 1966), 145–46; Henry Steele Commager, ed., *Documents in American History,* 7th ed. (New York, 1963), vol. 2, document no. 478, 246–53; Gilbert C. Fite, *American Farmers: The New Minority* (Bloomington, Ind., 1984), 60.

13. William D. Rowley, *M. L. Wilson and the Campaign for the Domestic Allotment* (Lincoln, Neb., 1970), 142–43, 153, 166–67; Kirkendall, *Social Scientists and Farm Politics,* 40–41; Hoover, *Challenge to Liberty,* 85–88. Clifford Hope to Harry W. Abrams, July 9, 1932, box 232; Hope to Keith Cox, Nov. 18, 1932, box 232; Hope to C. F. Spillman, July 13, 1932, box 233; Hope to B. Shaklett, Nov. 10, 1932, box 233; Hope to J. L. Horlacher, March 18, Nov. 17, 1932, box 39; Hope to W. T. Caldwell, May 10, 1933, box 39; Hope to W. G. Clagston, Sept. 20, 1934, box 234; Hope to Hal Harlan, Sept. 28, 1934, box 234; Hope to Lester McCoy, May 17, 1935, box 45; Whitney Austin to Hope, Sept. 21, 1934, with *Hutchison Herald* editorial attached, "Life of:" box 236; Harrison Spangler to Hope, Oct. 25, 1935, box 236; Hope to W. D. Means, Aug. 17, 1936, box 236; "Excerpts from the Address of Clifford R. Hope," [ca. 1935–36], box 236; speech draft beginning "A prosperous and stable agriculture," [1936], box 238; all in Hope Papers.

14. Benjamin M. Anderson to Landon, Nov. 18, 1935, box 53, Landon Papers. Hope to Homer Hoch, Jan. 21, 1936, box 52; Hope to George H. Hutchison, Jan. 25, 1936, box 52; Hope to E. J. Laubengayer, Sept. 18, 1935, box 53; Landon to Hope, Dec. 4, 1935, March 28, April 29, 1936, box 53; Hope to Landon, Jan. 10, Jan. 15, April 22, 1936, box 53; Hope to George N. Peek, Jan. 24, 1936, box 53; Hope to Edmond E. Lincoln, April 23, 1936, box 53; Hope to David W. Peck, May 15, 1936, box 53; F. D. Farrell to Landon, Jan. 17, 1936, box 53; E. H. Taylor to Hope, Jan. 17, 1936, Wednesday, n.d. [Jan. 22], Thursday, n.d. [ca. Jan. 24–26], Jan. 31, Feb. 17, March 31, April 28, 1936, box 54; Hope to Taylor, Jan. 29, April 10, May 9, June 25, 1936, box 54; "Some Observations on the Taylor Plan," [1936], box 54; "E. H. Taylor," box 54; Hope to Samuel R. Guard, Nov. 14, 1936, box 57; Don L. Berry to Walter Lippmann, Oct. 5, 1936, box 235; Hope to Wiley Blair Jr., Oct. 6, 1936, box 235; Hope to Earl C. Michener, Aug. 17, 1936, box 236; Republican National Committee Farm Division Release, Sept. 17, 1936, memorandum, "agriculture," n.d., box 236; "Miscellaneous Speeches," box 237, all in Hope Papers. Francis W. Schruben, *Kansas in Turmoil, 1930–1936* (Columbia, Mo., 1969), 166; "Republican Platform for 1936," in *National Party Platforms, 1840–1972,* comp. David Bruce Johnson and Kirk H. Porter (Urbana, Ill., 1975), 367–68.

15. *New York Times,* Sept. 23, Oct. 4, 1936; U.S. Department of Commerce, Bureau of the Census, *Historical Statistics of the United States, Colonial Times to 1957* (Washington, D.C., 1960), ser. Y, 258–63, 712. Benjamin Anderson to Landon, Dec. 24, 1935, box 53; Anderson to Henry Haskell, Jan. 7, 1936, box 53; "Acceptance Speech of Gov. Alf M. Landon," Topeka, Kansas, July 23, 1936, box 58, all in Landon Papers. McCoy, *Landon of Kansas,* 305.

16. *New York Times,* Sept. 25, 1936; Schapsmeier and Schapsmeier, *Henry A. Wallace*

of Iowa, 237. George Peek, "As I See the Farm Program," reprint, box 207, Charles Taft Papers. Newton D. Baker to John W. Davis, Sept. 30, 1936, box 97; Baker to William Allen White, Oct. 19, 28, 1936, box 234; White to Baker, Oct. 31, 1936, box 234, all in Baker Papers.

17. Warburg to Landon, July 17, 1936, box 10; Warburg to Judge George McDermott, July 27, 1936, box 10; McDermott to Warburg, Aug. 15, 1936, box 10; William Cumberland to Warburg, Aug. 10, 1936, box 10; Warburg to Landon, Sept. 1, 11, 14, 1936, box 11; second speech draft, "Foreign Relations," box 11, all in Warburg Papers. David W. Peck to Landon, April 1, box 54; H. Alexander Smith to Landon, Oct. 18, 1936, box 59, both in Landon Papers. Baker to White, Oct. 19, 1936, box 234; Baker to Henry James, Oct. 24, 1936, box 132, both in Baker Papers.

18. McCoy, *Landon of Kansas,* 325. Landon to Raymond Clapper, Dec. 30, 1935, box 78, Landon Papers. Warburg to Mills, Oct. 8, 1936, box 10; Warburg to Frank Knox, Oct. 5, 1936, box 10; Warburg to Hull, Oct. 13, 1936, box 10; Warburg to Dean Acheson, Oct. 13, 1936, box 13; Warburg to O. Glenn Saxon, Oct. 13, 1936, box 17; Acheson to Warburg, Oct. 19, 1936, box 13; Warburg to James Cox, Oct. 20, 1936, box 14, all in Warburg Papers. Otis Glenn Saxon, professor of economics at Yale and director of the Landon campaign, claimed that the antireciprocity planks of the party platform and the Minneapolis speech had been "forced upon [his] . . . advisors by Landon himself under the influence of [Earl] Zack Taylor [an antistatist and nationalist]" (Stimson Diary, April 14, 1937, vol. 28, p. 55).

19. Dean G. Acheson, address, Churchmen's Club of Maryland, May 8, 1934, box 13; Acheson to Warburg, Oct. 8, 1935, box 13; Acheson to editor, *Baltimore Sun,* Oct. 17, 1936, box 13; Acheson to Warburg, Oct. 19, 1936, box 13; Acheson to James Cox, Oct. 20, 1936, box 14; Warburg to Pierre S. du Pont, Nov. 2, 1936, box 9, all in Warburg Papers. Acheson to Alexander Sachs, Jan. 10, 1935, box 28, and generally file 3, box 2, Acheson Papers. Burk, *The Corporate State and the Broker State,* 123, 215; James Chace, *Acheson: The Secretary of State Who Created the American World* (New York, 1998), 63–70.

20. Henry J. Haskell, "The Reciprocity Agreements," *Kansas City Times-Star,* Sept. 25, 1936, reprinted in William S. Culbertson, *Reciprocity* (New York, 1937), 280–82.

21. Charles P. Taft, *You and I—and Roosevelt* (New York, 1936), 40–46. Taft, "[Speech draft] prepared for A.L.," box 207; W.R.C., "Notes on New Deal Foreign Policy," n.d., box 208, both in Charles Taft Papers. *New York Times,* "Text of Governor Landon's Indianapolis Address on Peace and Foreign Policies," Oct. 24, 1936.

22. "Address at Chautauqua, New York, August 14, 1936," in *The Public Papers and Addresses of Franklin D. Roosevelt,* comp. Samuel Rosenman (New York, 1938), 5: 285–92; McCoy, *Landon of Kansas,* 325. Baker to Frederic R. Coudert, Oct. 20, 1936, box 78; Baker to Henry James, Oct. 24, 1936, box 132, both in Baker Papers. Membership, Committee on Economic Policy, box 75, Waymack Papers. Economic Policy Committee, Statement of Purposes, n.d., box 291; Taft to Raymond L. Buell, Dec. 13, 1937, box 291; George Fort Milton to Taft, Dec. 27, 1937, box 291; Economic Policy Committee, January 13, 1938, box 291, Charles Taft Papers.

23. Landon to W. W. Kiplinger, Aug. 16, 21, 1935, box 78, Landon Papers. *New York Times,* Oct. 10, 1936; *Chicago Sun-Times,* Oct. 16, 1936; Peter Fearon, "Taxation, Spending, and Budgets: Public Finance in Kansas during the Great Depression," *Kansas History* 28, no. 4 (Winter 2005–6): 230–45.

24. McCoy, *Landon of Kansas,* 305–6; *New York Times,* September 27, 1936. "Ad-

dress of Miss Grace Abbott, September 29, 1936, Columbia Broadcasting System, box 80; Landon to Raymond Clapper, Nov. 13, 1936, box 78, both in Landon Papers. "You're Sentenced to a Weekly Pay Reduction for All Your Working Life," Industrial Division Republican National Committee, box 236, Hope Papers.

25. Robert H. Zieger, *American Workers, American Unions, 1920–1985* (Baltimore, 1986), 44–46; McCoy, *Landon of Kansas,* 274–75. "Acceptance Speech of Governor Alf M. Landon, Topeka, Kansas, July, 23, 1936," Republican National Committee, Chicago, box 58; Norman Thomas to Landon, July 24, Aug. 1, 1936, box 59; Landon to Thomas, July 29, 1936, box 59, all in Landon Papers. *New York Times,* Sept. 6, 1936; Stanley Vittoz, *New Deal Labor Policy and the American Industrial Economy* (Chapel Hill, N.C., 1987), 137–52.

26. *New York Times,* July 24, Sept. 6, 1936. Raymond Gram Swing to Landon, Dec. 31, 1935, box 54; Landon to Swing, July 30, 1936, box 59; Swing to Landon, Aug. 6, 7, Sept. 21, 1936, box 59; Grenville Clark to Landon, Aug. 3, 1936, box 54; Hill Blackett to Landon, Oct. 6, 1935, box 78, all in Landon Papers.

27. McCoy, *Landon of Kansas,* 310; Edgar Eugene Robinson, *They Voted for Roosevelt* (Stanford, Calif., 1947), 25; William H. Harbaugh, *Lawyer's Lawyer: The Life of John W. Davis* (New York, 1973), 354–55; "Ex-Gov. Smith Declares for Landon," *New York Times,* Oct. 3, 1936; "[William Green] Says 90% of Labor Is for Roosevelt," *New York Times,* Oct. 5, 1936; Arthur Krock, "Makings of Class War Seen in Pennsylvania," *New York Times,* Oct. 4, 1936; "Colby Says Reds Back Roosevelt," *New York Times,* Oct. 7, 1936, "Candidate Goldwater," Jan. 5, 1964, *New York Times.* William T. Wollman to Landon, May 25, 1936; box 54; Henry Breckinridge to Landon, Aug. 10, 1936, box 54; both in Landon Papers. "Remarks of Charles P. Taft at Cincinnatus Association Meeting," Nov. 24, 1936, box 207; "Letter of Charles P. Taft to Mr. C. G. Marshall," Dec. 1, 1936, box 207; Raymond Leslie Buell, "Casual Observations on the State of the Union," n.d., box 208, all in Charles Taft Papers. Earl Taylor to Don Berry, Nov. 11, 1936, box 2, Berry Papers. Bernard Sternsher, "The Emergence of the New Deal Party System: A Problem in Historical Analysis of Voter Behavior," *Journal of Interdisciplinary History* 6 (Summer 1975): 142–43.

3 | FORGING AN ANTISTATIST CONSENSUS

1. Louise Overacker, "Campaign Funds in the Presidential Election of 1936," *American Political Science Review* 31, no. 3 (June 1937): 479, 492–93, 495; Overacker, "Labor's Political Contribution," *Political Science Quarterly* 54, no. 1 (1939): 56–68; Overacker, *Presidential Campaign Funds* (Boston, 1946), 14–17, 32; Michael J. Webber, *New Deal Fat Cats: Business, Labor, and Campaign Finance in the 1936 Presidential Election* (New York, 2000), 7, 10–12, 17–22, 26–28, 57–62.

2. Burk, *The Corporate State and the Broker State,* 1–15, 271; Webber, *New Deal Fat Cats,* 22; Alfred D. Chandler Jr. and Stephen Salsbury, *Pierre S. du Pont and the Making of the Modern Corporation* (New York, 1971), 38–587; William S. Dutton, *Du Pont: One Hundred and Forty Years* (New York, 1942), 261–377; Leonard Mosley, *Blood Relations: The Rise and Fall of the Du Ponts of Delaware* (New York, 1980), 77–153, 165–94; Martin J. Sklar, *The Corporate Reconstruction of American Capitalism, 1890–1916* (New York, 1988), 34–35. Pierre S. du Pont Writings, "New Industries, 1915–1920," ser. B, file 517; "Investments and P. S. du Pont's recollections, 1951," ser. B, file 63; Lammot to Pierre S. du Pont, May 17, 1932, file 418, box 6; "Christiana Securities," Nov. 1940, ser. B, file 55;

Special Report, . . . *Gemeinschaft Farbenindustrie A.g.*, letter no. 219, Nov. 9, 1926, file 418, box 5; Pierre to E. E. Lincoln, Nov. 27, 1936, file 418, box 6; Report of the Federal Trade Commission on Du Pont Investments, Feb. 1, 1926, files of Lammot du Pont; "Memorandum of Conference with Mr. Pierre S. du Pont at Wilmington," Jan. 17, 1951, 36–37, file 418–26; table of assets, sales, and earnings, n.d., file 418, box 7; E. I. du Pont de Nemours& Co., Acquisitions, n.d., "Holdings of Du Pont common stock," Feb. 18, 1938, file 418–26, box 8; all in Pierre du Pont Papers. File E. I. du Pont de Nemours & Co., Welfare Plans, Miscellaneous, Raskob Papers. Rexford G. Tugwell, "A Third Economy," address before the Rochester, N.Y., Teachers Association, April 9, 1935, box 38, Tugwell Papers. Tugwell, "The Fourth Power," *Planning and Civic Comment*, April-June 1939, pt. 2, 1–31.

3. Chandler and Salsbury, *Pierre S. du Pont and the Making of the Modern Corporation*, 394–423; Dutton, *Du Pont*, 2233–57; Mosley, *Blood Relations*, 268–71; Burk, *The Corporate State and the Broker State*, 6–10, 12–15, 51–56, 64–66. Raskob to Pierre du Pont, April 16, 1920, file 681, box 1; Raskob to Roosevelt, Oct. 28, 1928, Sept. 11, 1930, folder, F. D. Roosevelt; radio address, National Broadcasting Company, Oct. 27, 1930, Personal File; undated newspaper clipping, 1931, box AAPA Correspondence, 1933, all in Raskob Papers. Matthew and Hannah Josephson: *Al Smith: Hero of the Cities* (London, 1970), 353–57; Rosen, *Hoover, Roosevelt, and the Brains Trust: From Depression to New Deal* (New York, 1977), 16–17, 23–24, 27–33, 107–8, 212–20.

4. "Dinner at the Metropolitan Club," April 28, 1932; Lewis E. Pierson to Pierre S. du Pont, Apr. 29, 1932; Alfred P. Sloan to du Pont, May 2, 1932; Pierre du Pont to W. W. Atterbury, May 3, 1932; Pierre du Pont to Sloan, May 9, 1932; [Du Pont] Notes and acceptances to dinner, Metropolitan Club, May 11, 1932; Pierre du Pont to E. V. Walsh, Dec. 19, 1932; Daniel C. Roper to Pierre S. du Pont, June 9, 1933; Pierre du Pont to Roper, June 14, 1933; "List of businessmen who agreed to serve on the Advisory Committee, Department of Commerce," June 21, 1933, all in file 1173, Pierre du Pont Papers.

5. Pierre S. du Pont to George A. Sloan, Jan. 29, 1934, file 1173–6, Pierre du Pont Papers.

6. Burk, *The Corporate State and the Broker State*, 112–29; U.S. Government Printing Office, *Decisions of the National Labor Board, August 1933–March 1934* (Washington, D.C., 1934), v–vi, 1–2; Vittoz, *New Deal Labor Policy*; Irving Bernstein, *Turbulent Years: A History of the American Worker, 1933–1941* (Boston, 1969), 174.

7. H. F. Sedgwick to all Works Managers, "Employee Representation not a Company Union," to all Department Heads, Presidents of Subsidiaries, Plant Managers, Nov. 2, 1933, file 1173–5; Gerard Swope, Chairman, Business Advisory and Planning Council, Nov. 2, 1933, Committee on Industrial Relations; Walter C. Teagle, in "Digest of Reports of Progress of Committees of the Business Advisory and Planning Council, meeting of Nov. 3, 1933," file 1173–3, all in Pierre du Pont Papers.

8. Craig Phelan, *William Green: Biography of a Labor Leader* (Albany, N.Y., 1989), vii–xi, 29–47, 54–71; Burk, *The Corporate State and the Broker State*, 127–28; "Text of President Roosevelt's Clarification of Section 7(a) . . . ," Oct. 19, 1933, file 1173–6, box 4; [Johnson's interpretation of executive order of Feb. 1, 1934], Feb. 2, 1934. file 1173–5, box 1; National Labor Board, Houde Engineering Company and United Automobile Workers Federal Labor Union, March 1934, file 1173–5; "Address by Milton Handler," general counsel, National Labor Board, file NRA: Industrial Advisory Board, 1934, file 1173–6, box 3, all in Pierre du Pont Papers. J. Joseph Huthmacher, *Senator Robert F. Wagner and*

the Rise of Urban Liberalism (New York, 1968), 189–98; Franklin D. Roosevelt, Executive Order No. 6580, Feb. 1, 1934, in *Decisions of the National Labor Board* (Washington, D.C., 1934), vii; Sidney Fine, *Sit-Down* (Ann Arbor, Mich., 1969), 30; Rosemary Feurer, *Radical Unionism in the Midwest, 1900–1950* (Urbana, Ill., 2006), 104–5.

9. John C. Rumm, "The Du Pont Company and the Special Conference Committee, 1919–1939," paper presented at the Duquesne History Forum, Oct. 1983.

10. Lammot to Pierre du Pont, Feb. 28, 1934, file 418, box 6; Jouett Shouse, address, Bond Club of New York, file 771–2, both in Pierre du Pont Papers.

11. R. R. M. Carpenter to John J. Raskob, March 16, 1934; Raskob to Carpenter, March 20, 1934, both in file 1173–6, Pierre du Pont Papers. Raskob to Frank R. Hope, Aug. 22, 1934, file 61, box 1; "Executive Committee of the American Liberty League," [Nov. 1934], Minutes of meeting, executive committee, Dec. 20, 1934, file 61, box 1, all in Raskob Papers. "New Deal Tax Laws," transmitted to Irénée du Pont by secretary to Mr. Shouse, July 7, 1936, file no. 292, Irénée du Pont Papers. Lewis H. Brown to Alfred P. Sloan Jr. et al., cc to Raskob, Nov. 11, 1935, file 1624, Raskob Papers. *New York Times,* Jan. 26, 1936. Raoul Desvernine to Irénée du Pont, Oct. 20, 1934; [Desvernine] Memorandum Re: General Welfare Clause, n.d., both in box: American Liberty League, Shouse Papers. William H. Harbaugh, *Lawyer's Lawyer: The Life of John W. Davis* (New York, 1973), 344–55.

12. Burk, *The Corporate State and the Broker State,* 157–58. Subscribers to the American Liberty League, n.d., file 61, box 1; National Association of Manufacturers, "Congress of American Industry Documents," Dec. 1, 1934, Washington, D.C., file 462; Alfred P. Sloan Jr. to Raskob, Sept. 1, 1934, file 61, box 1; *San Francisco Argonaut,* Nov. 23, 1934, box 1; American Liberty League press release, June 6, 1934, file 61, box 2; Pierre du Pont to Raskob, April 16, 1935, file 61, box 2; Jouett Shouse to Raskob, May 8, June 2, 1935, box 2; "A Summary Analysis of Pending and Proposed Legislation Which Has Been Proposed by the American Liberty League," June 14, 1935, National Lawyers Committee of the American Liberty League, n.d., file 61, box 2; R. E. Desvernine to Raskob, Aug. 15, 1935, file 61, box 2; "Declaration of . . . Conference of the National Jeffersonian Democrats," August 1936, file 602, box 13, all in Raskob Papers. American Liberty League, "The National Recovery Administration," doc. 11, January 1935, file 1173–6, box 1; Pierre to William Z. Ripley, Dec. 1, 1936, box 2, both in Pierre du Pont Papers. *New York Herald Tribune,* Sept. 18, 1935; *Time,* Sept. 18, 1935.

13. *New York Times,* Jan. 26, 1936. Jouett Shouse to Roy Roberts, Oct. 14, 1936, box: Corresp. 1932–1934, Shouse Papers. George Wolfskill, *The Revolt of the Conservatives: A History of the American Liberty League, 1934–1940* (Boston, 1962), 150–52; Burk, *The Corporate State and the Broker State,* 212–21.

14. August Giebelhaus, *Business and Government in the Oil Industry: A Case Study of Sun Oil, 1876–1945* (Greenwich, Conn., 1980), 31–41, 94–162, 231. J. Howard Pew to Raskob, Jan. 4, 1935, file 61, box 2, Raskob Papers. Joseph N. Pew to Pierre du Pont, Jan. 23, 1936, file 765, box 2, Pierre du Pont Papers. Paul Ward, "Washington Weekly," *Nation,* June 27, 1936, 831–32; *New York Times,* Oct. 4, 1936. John D. M. Hamilton, "Notes on the Republican Convention and Campaign of 1936," box 1; Heywood Broun column, press clippings, "[Hamilton] Offers Resignation," *Galveston Daily News,* box 1, both in Hamilton Papers.

15. Karl A. Lamb, "The Opposition Party as Secret Agent: Republicans and the

Court Fight, 1937," *Papers of the Michigan Academy of Science, Arts, and Letters,* 1961 (1960 meeting), 540–48.

16. Address of John Hamilton, Alabama Republican State Convention, Birmingham, June 22, 1938, box 2, Hamilton Papers.

17. Raymond Leslie Buell, "Casual Observations on the State of the Union," May 13, 1937, box 208, Charles Taft Papers. Clifford Hope to Don Berry, Nov. 13, 1936, Jan. 4, 1937, box 52, Hope Papers.

18. Weed, *The Nemesis of Reform,* 165, 170–80; Ronald L. Feinman, *Twilight of Progressivism: The Western Republican Senators and the New Deal* (Baltimore, 1981), xii, 1–16, 68–75, 94–95, 111, 117, 123–43; Malcolm Moos, *The Republicans: A History of Their Party* (New York, 1956), 394; Otis L. Graham Jr., *An Encore for Reform: The Old Progressives and the New Deal* (New York, 1967), 60–61.

19. Feinman, *Twilight of Progressivism,* 2–4, 7, 137. James Couzens to Charles McNary, Oct. 29, Nov. 19, 1934, box 5; McNary to J. J. Hamilton, Apr. 8, 1936, box 5; McNary to Asabel N. Bush, July 23, 1937, box 5; McNary to Hiram W. Johnson, Aug. 3, 1938, box 6, all in McNary Papers.

20. Vandenberg to Carter Glass, July 13, 1933, box 267, Glass Papers. Vandenberg to Herbert Hoover, Sept. 10, 1931, Vandenberg Scrapbooks, vol. 4, pp. 4–5, 44B–45; Vandenberg to Roy A. Young, Vandenberg Scrapbooks, vol. 5, p. 1, both in Vandenberg Papers. Milton Friedman and Anna J. Schwartz, *A Monetary History of the United States, 1867–1960* (Princeton, N.J., 1971) 134–35.

21. Vandenberg to L. S. Birely, Feb. 6, 1934, box 1; Vandenberg to Lois B. Ward, Nov. 15, 1934, box 1; Vandenberg to F. N. Bores, April 8, 1936, box 1; Vandenberg's Record [1936], box 5, all in Vandenberg Papers. Speech, "Reckless, Wasteful, Corrupting, and Inadequate Relief," *Congressional Record,* 74th Cong., 2nd sess., Senate, May 12, 1936, copy in box 225, Baker Papers. Rosen, "The Midwest Opposition to the New Deal," in *The New Deal Viewed from Fifty Years,* ed. Lawrence E. Gelfand and Robert J. Neymeyer (Iowa City, 1983), 55–90.

22. C. David Tompkins, *Senator Arthur H. Vandenberg: The Evolution of a Modern Republican, 1884–1945* (East Lansing, Mich., 1970), 3, 15, 21–134; George H. Mayer, *The Republican Party, 1854–1964* (New York, 1964), 439, 441. *Detroit News,* May 8, 1934, Vandenberg Scrapbooks, vol. 6, p. 40; Vandenberg to F. N. Bores, April 8, 1935, box 1; address, "No Tariff Dictatorship," March 18, 1934, *Congressional Record,* 73rd Cong., 2nd sess., box 1; address, Jackson, Mich., July 7, 1934, box 3; address, Grand Rapids, July 4, 1936, box 3; "Constitution Address," Sept. 17, 1936, box 3; editorial, "Cases Altered," *Baltimore Sun,* June 2, 1936, box 5, all in Vandenberg Papers. Harold B. Hinton, "And What About Vandenberg's Record?," *New York Times Magazine,* May 17, 1936; "Vandenberg: Minority Hope in the Senate," *Christian Science Monitor,* Nov. 21, 1936; William J. Novak, "The Myth of the 'Weak' American State," *American Historical Review* 113, no. 3 (June 2008): 752–72.

4 | THE GOP AND THE PRELUDE TO WAR

1. David Reynolds, *From Munich to Pearl Harbor: Roosevelt's America and the Origins of the Second World War* (Chicago, 2001), 6–43, 172–78; Leonard P. Liggio, introduction to *Watershed of Empire: Essays on New Deal Foreign Policy,* ed. Liggio and James J. Martin (Colorado Springs, 1976), xiii; Derek H. Aldcroft, *The Inter-War Economy: Britain,*

1919–1939 (New York, 1970), 20–21; Sir Charles Morgan-Webb, *The Money Revolution* (New York, 1935); Barry Eichengreen, *Golden Fetters: The Gold Standard and the Great Depression, 1919–1939* (New York, 1992), 4–7, 216–20; D. E. Moggridge, *British Monetary Policy, 1924–1931* (London, 1972), 1–96. Patrick Karl O'Brien, "The Pax Britannica and American Hegemony: Precedent, Antecedent or Just Another History?," 3–66; Robert Gilpin, "The Rise of American Hegemony," 165–67; Angus Maddison, "The Nature of US Economic Leadership: A Historical and Comparative View," 184–91, all in *Two Hegemonies: Britain, 1846–1914 and the United States, 1941–2001,* ed. O'Brien and Armand Clesse (Burlington, Vt., 2001), 29–36. Tooze, *The Wages of Destruction,* xxi–xvi, 8–9, 17–18, 21–25, 32, 38, 56, 140–63, 268–69, 282–83; B. J. C. McKercher, *Transition of Power: Britain's Loss of Global Pre-eminence to the United States, 1930–1945* (Cambridge, U.K., 1999), 5–11, 14, 22, 48–49, 126, 178–77, 180–88; Arnold Offner, *American Appeasement: United States Foreign Policy and Germany, 1933–1938* (Cambridge, Mass., 1969), 20–50; Angus Maddison, *Economic Growth in the West: Comparative Experience in Europe and North America* (New York, 1964), tables no. I–1 (p. 28), I–2 (p. 29), H–1 (p. 231), H–2 (p. 232); Frank Castigliola, *Awkward Dominion: American Political, Economic, and Cultural Relations with Europe, 1919–1933* (Ithaca, N.Y., 1984), 218–20, 263–64; Christopher Thorne, *The Limits of Foreign Policy: The West, the League and the Far Eastern Crisis of 1931–1933* (New York, 1972), 58–60; Bruce M. Russett, *No Clear and Present Danger: A Skeptical View of the U.S. Entry into World War II* (New York, 1972), 11–12, 17–36, 41–62; Saul Friedlander, *Prelude to Downfall: Hitler and the United States, 1939–1941* (New York, 1967), 3–4, 7–123, 171, 194–201, 252, 255; David A. Lake, *Power, Protection, and Free Trade: International Sources of U.S. Commercial Strategy, 1887–1939* (Ithaca, N.Y., 1988), 184–86, 235; Charles P. Kindleberger, *The World in Depression, 1929–1939* (Berkeley and Los Angeles, 1973), 29, 292.

2. Vansittart to Ronald Lindsay, Sept. 24, 1934, FO 115/3405/1934; Lord Lothian, "Interview with the President," draft, October 1934, FO 115/3405/1934, both in PRO.

3. Tooze, *Wages of Destruction,* 69–71, 81–91; McKercher, *Transition of Power,* 206–15. Neville Chamberlain, "Cabinet: The Naval Conference and Our Relations with Japan. Memorandum Circulated by the Chancellor of the Exchequer," September, 1934," NC 8/19/2, Chamberlain Papers. Benjamin D. Rhodes, "British Diplomacy and the Congressional Circus, 1929–1939," *South Atlantic Quarterly* 82, no. 3 (Summer 1983): 301, 305.

4. Rhodes, "British Diplomacy," 307; R. Douglas Hurt, *The Great Plains during World War II* (Lincoln, Neb., 2008), 1–31; Walter Millis, *Road to War, America, 1914–1917* (Boston, 1935), 13–14; Offner, *American Appeasement,* 131–32, 156–57; Justus D. Doenecke, *Not to the Swift: The Old Isolationists in the Cold War Era* (Lewisburg, Pa., 1979), 21; Wayne S. Cole, *Roosevelt & the Isolationists* (Lincoln, Neb., 1983), 6–9, 141–62; Robert A. Divine, *The Illusion of Neutrality* (Chicago, 1962), 68–70, 81–121; C. David Tompkins, *Senator Arthur H. Vandenberg: The Evolution of a Modern Republican, 1884–1945* (East Lansing, Mich., 1970), 124–27; John Edward Wiltz, *In Search of Peace: The Senate Munitions Inquiry, 1934–1936* (Baton Rouge, La., 1963), 14, 207, 221–37. Vandenberg speech, "Take the Profits Out of War," April 12, 1934, 73rd Cong., 2nd sess., box 3, file 64; Vandenberg, "How We Can Bankrupt the God of War," *Liberty,* Sept. 1, 1934, Vandenberg Scrapbooks, vol. 6, p. 86, both in Vandenberg Papers. *Munitions Industry, Report on Existing Legislation, Special Committee on Investigation of the Munitions Industry,* 74th Cong., 2nd sess., Senate Report no. 944, pt. 5, June 5, 1936; *Muni-*

tions Industry, Supplemental Report of the Adequacy of Existing Legislation of the Special Committee on Investigation of the Munitions Industry, 74th Cong., Senate Report no. 944, pt. 6, June 16, 1936; Betty Glad, *Key Pittman: The Tragedy of a Senate Insider* (New York, 1986), 231–35; Wayne S. Cole, "Gerald P. Nye and Agrarian Bases for the Rise and Fall of American Isolationism," in *Three Faces of Midwestern Isolationism,* ed. John N. Schacht (Iowa City, 1981), 1–10; Daniel Rylance, "A Controversial Career: Gerald P. Nye," *North Dakota Quarterly* 36 (Winter 1968): 5–29. Nye Proposal to Committee Members, n.d., box 23; W. T. Stone, Memorandum: "Profits of Industries Engaged in the Manufacture of Arms, Munitions or War Materials," n.d., box 43; "Address by Brigadier General William Mitchell, . . . Foreign Policy Association, . . . on Profiteering in Preparedness-Should Private Manufacture of Munitions be Abolished," March 3, 1934, box 43; Frank B. Kellogg to Nye, Aug. 1, 1934, box 24, Emergency Peace Campaign, "Nation-wide Mobilization Against War . . . ," Oct. 25, 1936, box 48; John R. Williams, "Gerald P. Nye: A Biographical Study," pp. 2, 18, box 48, all in Nye Papers.

5. Frederick C. Adams, *Economic Diplomacy: The Export-Import Bank and American Foreign Policy, 1934–1939* (Columbia, Mo., 1976), 66, 80–88; Gilbert Fite, *George N. Peek and the Fight for Farm Parity* (Norman, Okla., 1954), 270–85; Cordell Hull, *Memoirs* (New York, 1948), 353–54, 357–60, 370–74; Harold James, *The End of Globalization* (Cambridge, Mass., 2001), 134–35; Lake, *Free Trade,* 209–12. Cordell Hull to the president, Nov. 28, 1934, accompanied by [Francis B. Sayre] memorandum, "The United States Trade Agreements Program and Most Favored Nation Treatment," [1934], and Hull "Memorandum on Concessions," [1934], all in PSF 87. Peek to the president, and draft of Foreign Trade Board Bill, July 16, 1935, both in PSF 73. Peek to Bernard M. Baruch, Aug. 26, 1935, General Correspondence, box 190; "Explanation of Foreign Trade Board Bill," General Correspondence, box 190; Peek address, "The Foreign Trade Problem of the United States," National Industrial Conference Board, New York City, Oct. 24, 1935, General Correspondence, box 190, all in Baruch Papers. "America's Choice," address before the War Industries Board Association, New York City, Nov. 11, 1935, PSF 73. *Detroit News,* Feb. 14, 1934, Vandenberg Scrapbooks, vol. 6, p. 30; "Take the Profit Out of War," U.S. Senate, April 12, 1934, *Cong. Record,* 73rd Cong. 2nd sess., box 3, all in Vandenberg Papers.

6. Vandenberg address, "Republican Responsibilities for 1934," Feb. 19, 1934, box 3; "No Tariff Dictatorship," May 18, 1934, box 3; "International Trade Relations of the United States," May 8, 1935, box 3, all in Vandenberg Papers. George N. Peek with Samuel Crowther, *Why Quit Our Own?* (New York, 1936), 220–33. Herbert Hoover to Silas R. Strawn, Nov. 20, 1938, PPI 522.

7. Newton D. Baker to Ralph W. Smith, n.d., box 176, Baker Papers. Harold B. Hinton, "Again the Vexatious Tariff Draws Fire," *New York Times Magazine,* Aug. 2, 1936; "Vandenberg: Minority Hope in the Senate," *Christian Science Monitor,* Nov. 21, 1936. Vandenberg to Ferndale Teachers Club, May 19, 1938, box 1, file 29, Vandenberg Papers. Tompkins, *Vandenberg,* 127–29, 159; Divine, *The Illusion of Neutrality,* 66–67, 165–67, 185–86, 191–94; Cole, *Roosevelt and the Isolationists,* 223, 230–34; Rhodes, "British Diplomacy," 311; Reynolds, *Munich to Pearl Harbor,* 66. Wilbur M. Brucker to Hoover, Sept. 11, 1939, box 26, PPI. Friedlander, *Prelude to Downfall,* 41–45; "Neutrality Act, Pulled by Peace vs. Prosperity, Stretches," *Literary Digest,* June 19, 1937; Russett, *No Clear and Present Danger,* 26.

8. Russett, *No Clear and Present Danger,* 19–20; Manfred Jonas, *Isolationism in*

America, 1935–1941 (Ithaca, N.Y., 1966), 1, 6–7, 100, 170. John Callan O'Laughlin to Hoover, June 25, 1941, box 169; Herbert Hoover to Mrs. Ogden Reid, March 10, 1942, box 184, both in PPI. Reynolds, *Munich to Pearl Harbor,* 13.

9. Divine, *Illusion of Neutrality,* 69, 163. A. W. D. [Allen W. Dulles], Confidential Memorandum for Newton D. Baker, Feb. 18, 1936, box 251; Hamilton Fish Armstrong to Newton D. Baker, Aug. 21, 1936, box 97, both in Baker Papers.

10. Christopher Thorne, *The Illusion of Neutrality: The West, the League and the Far Eastern Crisis of 1931–1933* (New York, 1973), 13, 55–59; Elting E. Morison, *Turmoil and Tradition: A Study of the Life and Times of Henry L. Stimson* (Cambridge, Mass., 1960), 462–66. Stimson Diary, Dec. 1938–June 1939, vol. 30, p. 3.

11. Henry L. Stimson to the *New York Times,* October 11, 1935; Stimson radio address, "Preserve American Security by Repealing the Embargo," Oct. 5, 1939; Stimson to Herbert Hoover, June 19, 1940; "Messrs. Stimson and Knox . . . ," n.d., 1940, all in box 222, PPI. Stimson Diary, June 25, 1940, vol. 30, p. 55. Jonas, *Isolationism,* 1.

12. *New York Times,* Oct. 7, 1937, March 7, April 5, 1939, Stimson Diary, June 25, 1940, vol. 30, p. 55.

13. Paul Shoup to Hoover, June 21, 1940, box 209, PPI. *New York Times,* June 22, July 9, 10, 1940. Warren Austin, Memorandum re Nomination of Honorable Henry L. Stimson to be Secretary of War, box 20, Austin Papers.

14. Hadley Cantril, *Public Opinion, 1935–1946* (Westport, Conn., 1978), 1075–76, 1081, 1101–2, 1168.

15. Hoover to John C. O' Laughlin, July 18, 1939, box 168; Hoover to Walter Newton, Jan. 25, 1941, box 162; Karl Mundt to Hoover, June 9, Oct. 20, 1941, box 159, all in PPI.

16. Warren Austin, "Memorandum . . . Luncheon . . . at the Home of Honorable William Castle," box 20, Austin Papers.

17. Hoover memorandum of conversation with Joseph P. Kennedy, Nov. 22, 1940, box 110, PPI.

18. Herbert Hoover, *American Individualism* (Garden City, N.Y., 1923), 1–8. Hoover to H. Alexander Smith, Jan. 26, 1938, box 215; Hill Blackett to Boake Carter, Oct. 8, 1937, box 309; Hoover to Carter, July 8, 14, Dec. 11, 1941, box 309; Hamilton Fish to Hoover, Jan. 17, 1938, box 59, all in PPI. Hoover to J. C. O'Laughlin, Sept. 4, 1939, PPI 457C. Hoover to O'Laughlin, Jan. 5, 26, 1941, box 169, PPI. William Allen White to Hoover, Oct. 11, 1939, Oct. 21, 23, 28, 1940; White to Hoover, n.d. [1940], telegram; Hoover to White, Jan. 6, 1941; Hoover to White, Oct. 21, 1939, Jan. 8, 1941, all in box 252, PPI. Hoover to Arthur Vandenberg, Oct. 12, 1939; Vandenberg to Hoover, Nov. 6, 1939, both in PPI 541. Hoover to Sol Bloom, Jan. 15, 1941, box 19; John G. Mott to Hoover, Sept. 10, 1941, box 157; Hoover to Walter Newton, May 5, 20, 1941, box 162, all in PPI. Hoover to John G. Mott, Sept. 12, 18, 1941, box 152; Hoover to Wallace H. White, Nov. 5, 1941, box 252; Hoover to Robert E. Wood, Nov. 12, 1941, June 16, 1945, box 259; Wood to Hoover, June 22, 1945, box 259; Hoover to William R. Castle, Dec. 8, 1941, box 31, all in PPI. George Nash, *Freedom Betrayed* (Stanford, Calif., 2011), 198–99; Wayne S. Cole, *America First* (New York, 1971), 104–5; Robert Dallek, *Franklin D. Roosevelt and American Foreign Policy, 1932–1945* (New York, 1979), 200–205; James T. Patterson, *Mr. Republican: A Biography of Robert A. Taft* (Boston, 1972), 243; Warren F. Kimball, *The Most Unsordid Act: Lend-Lease, 1939–1941* (Baltimore, 1969), 151–57.

19. Kimball, *The Most Unsordid Act,* 151–57; Reynolds, *Munich to Pearl Harbor,* 102–12.

20. Hoover to Charles G. Dawes, May 1, 1941, box 45; Hoover to Joseph Kennedy, July 1, 1941, box 110; Hoover to James Grafton Rogers, Sept. 23, 1942, box 195; Robert M. Hutchins to Hoover, June 29, 1941, box 97; Hutchins to Hoover, July 11, 1941, Hutchins working draft, n.d., box 155; Hoover to Felix Morley, July 18, 1941; "Statement as Generally Approved," box 155, all in PPI. George C. Herring Jr., *Aid to Russia, 1941–1946; Strategy, Diplomacy, the Origins of the Cold War* (New York, 1973), 6–7.

21. [Hoover], "Conversation with Bob Taft," April 20, 1940; Hoover to Taft, June 3, 1940; Taft to Hoover, Feb. 25, 1941; "Summary of Proposed, Senate Amendments to H.R. 1776, April 2, 1941, all in box 232, PPI. Hoover to John C. O'Laughlin, June 26, 1941, box 169; Hoover to Igor I. Sikorsky, July 8, 1941, box 209, both in PPI.

5 | PARTY OF THE BOURBONS

1. Hoover to Frank Kent, June 2, 1937, box 10; Kent, "The Great Game of Politics," *Baltimore Sun*, June 6, 1937, box 110; Hoover to William Allen White, May 11, 1937, box 252, all in PPI. *New York Times*, Feb. 13, 1938. Alexander Sachs, "Danger Issues Confronting Willkie," Aug. 21, 1940, box 89, Sachs Papers.

2. Hoover, "The Crisis and the Political Parties," *Atlantic Monthly*, Sept. 1937, copy in PPI 282. Hoover to J. C. O'Laughlin, Feb. 26, 1937, box 168; Hoover to John W. Bricker, Nov. 1, 1937, box 22, both in PPI. "Hoover 'Vindication' Doomed," *Babson Confidential Report*, March 28, 1938, cited in Hoover to Roger W. Babson, May 19, 1938, box 34, Strauss Papers.

3. William Starr Myers, *The True Republican Record*, reprinted from *The Guide: The Women's National Political Review* (New York, 1939); McCoy, *Landon of Kansas*. "Drew Pearson and Robert S. Allen, "Daily Washington Merry Go Round, Hyde Campaign Seeks Hoover as G.O.P. Head," June 23, 1937, box 98, PPI. "Would Draft Hoover to Revitalize Party," *New York Times*, June 27, 1937; "Capper Hits Hoover Plan," *New York Times*, Nov. 1, 1937. Hoover to Mrs. George Lorimer, Feb. 13, 1937, box 127; "draft given to Mrs. Lorimer," Sept. 30, 1937, box 127; Arthur Hyde to Alan Fox, May 12, 1937, box 98; Hyde to Jacob O. Allen, May 7, 1939, box 98; Charles F. Adams to Hoover, May 18, 1937, box 1; Hoover to Robert G. Simmons, Aug. 24, 1937, box 210; Simmons to Hoover, Aug. 30, 1937, box 210; Hoover to Thomas J. Down, Sept. 4, 1937, box 50; Hoover to Frank O. Lowden, Oct. 8, 1937, box 127; Hill Blackett memorandum, Oct 8, 1937, box 18; Hoover to Harrison Spangler, Oct. 29, 1937, with untitled memorandum drafted by "Congressional opponents," Nov. 3, 1937, box 219; Lawrence Richey to Spangler, Nov. 8, 1937, box 219, all in PPI. Herman Siebert to Hoover, Nov. 26, 1937, with Block Newspapers editorial, PPI 282. John Hamilton to Alf M. Landon, Nov. 1, 1937, box 75; Hamilton to Hoover, Nov. 19, 1937, box 75; Joseph W. Martin Jr., "Released for the Morning Papers," Nov. 4, 1937, box 143; Frank Knox, "Better Safe Than Sorry," editorial, *Chicago Daily News*, Nov. 4, 1937, box 115; Hoover to Knox, Nov. 6, 1937, box 115; Knox to Hoover, Nov. 9, 1937, box 115; Hoover to O. Glenn Saxon, Jan. 3, 1938, box 190; Lewis L. Strauss to Hoover, April 4, 1938, with *Babson Confidential Forecast*, March 28, 1938, box 224; Chester H. Rowell to Hoover, Aug. 14, 1938, box 197; Hoover to Glenn Frank, Sept. 7, Dec. 23, 26, 1938, Jan. 21, 1939, box 62; Hoover to Sewell Avery, May 5, 1939, box 8, all in PPI.

4. *New York Times*, Nov. 13, 30, 1938; Richard Norton Smith, *Thomas E. Dewey and His Times* (New York, 1982), 217, 220, 240, 276–77: Andrew E. Busch, "The New Deal Comes to a Screeching Halt in 1938," online, May 2006, Ashbrook Center for Public Affairs; Leroy D. Brandon under the direction of South Trimble, Clerk of the House

of Representatives, "Statistics of the Congressional Election of November 8, 1938";
David A. Horowitz, *Beyond Left and Right: Insurgency and the Establishment: Insurgency & the Establishment* (Urbana and Chicago, 1997), 159; David R. Mayhew, *Major Realignments: A Critique of an American Genre* (New Haven, Conn., 2002).

5. Arthur Krock, "Taxpayers Revolt," *New York Times,* Nov. 10, 1938; Fine, *Sit-Down,* 336–38.

6. *Congressional Quarterly Weekly,* Nov. 14, 1958, 1441–42; Neil McNeil, *Dirksen: Portrait of a Public Man* (New York, 1970), 22–40, 43, 58–60, 67–68; William B. Furlong, "The Senate's Wizard of Ooze: Dirksen of Illinois," *Harper's,* Dec. 1959, 44–49; "Congressman: A Case History," *Fortune,* April 1943. Dirksen, "The Congressional Front," Jan. 6, 10, 20, Mar. 23, 34, 1934, Mar. 25, July 13, 1935, April 11, 1936, May 13, July 19, 1939, Remarks and Releases; address, Republican State Convention, Peoria, Illinois, May 22, 1936, Addresses; "Pattern of Tomorrow," Sept. 27, 1937, Dirksen Notebooks; "The Congressional Front," Jan. 6, 20, 1934, May 13, July 19, 1939, Remarks and Releases; "Buck Strawn Rides Again," Mar. 6, 1937, folder 485; "Voting Record of Congressman Dirksen, [1940], folder 493; Press Releases, 1938, "Congressman Everett M, Dirksen . . . ," folder 486; Dirksen, "The Grand Canyon of Illinois," Extension of Remarks, *Congressional Record,* Mar. 30, 1938, folder 488, all in Politics Series; "Rundschau," Survey of the 75th Congress, 1939, folder 26a, 240–45, "The Issue," folder 26b, 105, "The Long and Tortuous Road," [1940], folder 26b; address, "Back to Private Initiative," folder 26b, Dirksen Notebooks, Dirksen Collection. Silas Strawn to Hoover, Dec. 22, 1933, Oct. 10, 1934; "Business Confidence," [1934]; Strawn, Confidential Memorandum, Oct. 15, 1934, all in box 224, PPI.

7. Waymack to Henry Hazlitt, Nov. 22, 1938, box 8; Waymack to J. H. Frandsen, Nov. 13, 1940, box 14, both in Waymack Papers. Weed, *The Nemesis of Reform,* 197; Horowitz, *Beyond Left and Right,* 159; Edgar Eugene Robinson, *They Voted for Roosevelt: The Presidential Vote, 1932–1944* (Stanford, Calif., 1947), 53.

8. Vandenberg to Donald Despain, April 27, 1937, box 1, file 25; Despain to Vandenberg, May 3, 1937, box 1, file 25; Vandenberg to John W. Blodgett, Nov. 22, 1937, box 1, file 27; Vandenberg to Pat Harrison, May 18, 1938, box 1, file 29; to Vandenberg to Despain, June 8, 1938, box 1, file 30; Vandenberg to Martin J. Gillen, June 28, 1938, box 1, file 30; Vandenberg to William Barbour, July 20, 1938 box 1, file 31; Vandenberg to Mrs. Robert L. Bacon, Aug. 15, 1938, box 1, file 31; Vandenberg to D. W. Dunlap, Aug. 28, 1938, box 1, file 31; Vandenberg to Walter S. Goodspeed, Aug. 29, 1938, box 1, file 31; Vandenberg to H. C. Pratt, Sept. 12, 1938, box 1, file 32; Vandenberg to Frank S. Gould, Dec. 10, 1938, box 1, file 36; William Green to Vandenberg, Dec. 1, 1938, box 1, file 36; [Profit-Sharing Report, April, 1939], box 1, file 38, all in Vandenberg Papers. *New York Times,* March 13, Nov. 26, 1938; Huthmacher, *Wagner,* 234.

9. Vandenberg to S. D. Lipham, June 2, 1939, Vandenberg Scrapbooks, vol. 11, pp. 56, 56b, 128b, Vandenberg Papers. "Note on Industrial Insurance," Nov. 15, 1939, PSF 97. *New York Times,* Nov. 16, 1939; Edwin E. Witte, "Social Security–1940 Model," *American Labor Legislation Review,* Sept. 1939, 101–9. Witte to Wilbur J. Cohen, March 30, 1939, box 5; Witte to Thomas MacMahon, March 31, 1939, box 5; Witte to George Robinson, March 23, 1949, box 35, all in Witte Papers.

10. Vandenberg, "The Truth about the Coalition Manifesto," Dec. 1937, Vandenberg Scrapbooks, vol. 10, p. 23; Vandenberg to W. P. Lovett, Feb. 17, 1938, box 1, f. 28, both in

Vandenberg Papers. James T. Patterson, *Congressional Conservatism and the New Deal* (Lexington, Ky., 1967), 188–210; *New York Times,* Dec. 17, 21, 1937.

11. Patterson, *Mr. Republican,* 49–51, 162–66. Robert A. to William Howard Taft, Dec. 4, 1918, box 18; Robert Taft to Hoover, Dec. 24, 1934, box 34, both in Robert Taft Papers. Ronald Radosh, *Prophets on the Right: Profiles of Conservative Critics of American Globalism* (New York, 1975), 120.

12. Robert Taft, "What Do I Want to Work Out?," Aug. 25, 1933, box 1291, Robert Taft Papers.

13. Taft to W. H. Stayton, Nov. 9, 1934, box 101; address, Warren, Ohio, Chamber of Commerce, "The New Deal: Reform, Recovery, and Revolution," April 1935, possibly at Columbia University, 1936, box 1291; Taft to Charles C. Burlingham, Jan. 30, 1936, box 103; Taft notes, Taft to Judson King, May 8, 1936, box 105; Taft to Arthur A. Craven, June 30, 1936, box 105; address, Women's Club of New Hampshire, April 30, 1936, box 105; "Something for Nothing," folder: Speeches, 1936, box 1291, Robert Taft Papers.

14. Patterson, *Mr. Republican,* 174–79; Fine, *Sit-Down,* 337–38.

15. T. V. Smith and Robert A. Taft, *Foundations of Democracy* (New York, 1939), v, 13–21, 109, 137–40, 146–49, 175–92, 222–33, 265.

16. Richard V. Gilbert, ed., *An Economic Program for American Democracy, by Seven Harvard and Tufts Economists* (New York, 1938); "The Annual Budget Message, January 5, 1939," in *The Public Papers and Addresses of Franklin D. Roosevelt: 1939 Volume,* ed. Samuel Rosenman (New York, 1939), 36–53; Marriner C. Eccles, "Controlling Booms and Depressions," *Fortune,* April 1937, 88a–88d, 178–82. Taft radio address, Lincoln Day Dinner, Netherland Plaza Hotel, Feb. 11, 1939, box 142, Robert Taft Papers.

17. William J. Barber, *From New Era to New Deal: Herbert Hoover, the Economists, and American Economic Policy, 1921–1933* (New York, 1988), 155–57, 224–25; J. Ronnie Davis, "Chicago Economists, Deficit Budgets, and the Early 1930s," *American Economic Review* 58, no. 3 (June 1968): 476–82; Joseph Dorfman, *The Economic Mind in American Civilization, 1918–1933* (New York, 1959), 5: 769–70. Lauchlin Currie, "Comments on Pump Priming," Nov. 30, 1934, "Federal Employment Stabilization Board," appended to Currie Memorandum on "Confidence" (1934), box 72; "A Suggested Works Program," March 6, 1935, box 72; "The Present Status and Problems of the Recovery Movement," Dec. 22, 1936, box 72; "The Transition Problems in Compensatory Fiscal Policy," Oct. 29, 1938, box 72; "Memorandum on the Question: The Claim Is Made That Private Industry by Itself Cannot Profitably Absorb Current Savings," April 19, 1939, box 72; "Notes on Fiscal Policy," April 26, 1939, box 72; "A Tentative Program to Halt the Business Recession," Oct. 13, 1937, box 73; "The Current Situation," Oct. 16, 1937, box 73; "Causes of the Recession," April 1, 1938, box 73; "Statement Submitted to the Temporary National Economic Committee," May 16, box 73, all in Eccles Papers. Currie's testimony, U.S. Cong., Senate, Temporary National Economic Committee, Investigation of Concentration of Economic Power, Hearings, 76th Cong., 1st sess., pts. 7–9, March–May 1939, 3520–58; Herbert Stein, *The Fiscal Revolution in America* (Washington, D.C., 1996), 108–13. Lauchlin Currie, "Causes of the Recession," April 1, 1938, box 73, Eccles Papers.

18. *New York Times,* June 23, 1939; "The Lending Plan," *Washington Post,* July 24, 1939; Clarence E. Wunderlin Jr., *The Papers of Robert A. Taft* (Kent, Ohio), 2: 62n2; William J. Barber, *Designs within Disorder: Franklin D. Roosevelt, the Economists, and*

the Shaping of American Economic Policy, 1933–1945 (New York, 1996), 128–31; Perry G. Mehrling, *The Money Interest and the Public Interest* (Cambridge, Mass., 1997), 81–134; Alan Sweezy, "The Keynesians and Government Policy, 1933–1939," *American Economic Review* 62, no. 2 (May 1972): 122; U.S. Cong., Senate, TNEC, Hearings, 76th Cong., 1st sess., March-May 1939, pts. 7–9, 3493–3518, 3538–59, 3837–59: "Statement of Testimony of Dr. Alvin H. Hansen . . . before the Temporary National Economic Committee at Hearings on Savings and Investment, May 16, 1939." Marriner S. Eccles, "Address before the Ninth Annual Special Meeting of the Harvard Business School," June 16, 1939, pre-1940, Willkie Papers.

19. Taft, "Citizens of the United States of America, Spend-Lend for the Floor," n.d., [Edmund E. Lincoln, memorandum] to Members of the [DuPont] Executive Committee, "Federal Spending, Industrial Production, and Wholesale Prices," June 16, 19, 1939, box 809; "Estimated Trends in Industrial Production," July 18, 1939, box 809; Lincoln to Taft, July 21, Aug. 1, Aug. 3, 1939, box 809; Taft to Lincoln, Aug. 5, 1939, box 493, all in Robert Taft Papers.

20. U.S. Bureau of the Census, *Historical Statistics of the United States, Colonial Times to 1957* (Washington, D.C., 1960), 132–33, 139, 712, 718, 724; James D. Savage, *Balanced Budgets and American Politics* (Ithaca, N.Y.), 169, 290; Mehrling, *The Money Interest,* 121–23; Herbert Stein, *The Fiscal Revolution in America* (Washington, D.C., 1990), 34–38, 57, 61.

21. J. M. Keynes to Alvin Hansen, Sept. 29, 1941, HUG (FP)-3.10, box 1; Roy Harrod to Seymour Harris, [?] 25, 1968, HUG (FP)-3.10, box 1; "General Procedure with Respect to the Setting up of International Economic Machinery," Feb. 11, 1942, HUG (FP)-3.42, box 5, all in Hansen Papers. *Economist,* April 3, 2010, 75.

22. Voting Record, 1939–1942, box 855, "Record of Robert A. Taft," [1944], box 159, Robert Taft Papers.

23. Robert C. Albright, "No Crooner, Taft Thumps Drums of Fact," *Washington Post,* 1939, box 129; S. 2721, A Bill to amend the Social Security Act, June 28, 1939, box 777; Taft address, "The Farmer and America's Future," Feb. 24, 1940, box 786; Taft to Vincent Starzinger, March 29, 1940, box 125, all in Robert Taft Papers.

24. Smith and Taft, *Foundations of Democracy,* 185–92; Taft address, Indianapolis Bar Association, Oct. 30, 1939, box 1292; radio address, April 25, 1939, "Foreign Relations-Congress or the President," box 1292; "Taft's Policies," file political, 1940, box 148, all in Robert Taft Papers.

6 | THE INTERLOPER

1. Drew Pearson and Robert S. Allen, "Washington Daily Merry-Go-Round," *Washington Times-Herald,* Nov. 18, 1939, PPI 373. Parke Brown, "Hoover Backers Work to Obtain His Nomination," *Chicago Tribune,* Dec. 17, 1939; Arch W. Shaw to Walter Hope, Jan. 28, 1939; "Dinner, Saturday night" (May 20), Shaw to Hoover, Aug. 21, 1939; Jacob D. Allen to Ben S. Allen, Sept. 11, 1939; Orville Bullington to Hoover, Nov. 21, 1939; Bullington to Orville Taylor, Nov 21, 1939; Bullington to Lawrence Richey, May 10, 1940, all in box 207, PPI. Orville J. Taylor to Hoover, "Those indicating interest and willing to work," Dec. 7, 1939; Taylor to Hoover, Dec. 18, 1939; Hoover to Taylor, June 29, 1940, all in box 234, PPI. Jacob Allen to Hoover, Dec. 15, Dec. 16, 1939, Jan. 23, 1940, all in box 4, PPI. Hoover to Sewell Avery, May 5, Nov. 4, 1939, both in box 8, PPI. Walter Newton to Hoover, Oct. 9, 1939, box 162; Hoover to Lawrence Richey, June

21, 1939, box 188; Hoover to Robert G. Simmons, Aug. 28, 1939, box 210; Feb. 17, 1940, box 210; Hoover to Frank Fetzer, Aug. 28, 1939, box 58; Hoover to Jacob D. Allen, Sept. 11, 16, 28, Oct. 7, Dec. 15, 16, 28, 1939, all in box 5; James B. Howell to Hoover, Sept. 12, 1939, box 93; Hoover to R. B. Creager, Aug. 28, 1939, box 41; Hoover to Thomas E. Campbell, Sept. 14, 1939, box 29; Hoover to Campbell, on uninstructed delegations, April 5, 1940, box 29, all in PPI. Herbert W. Clark to Hoover, Aug. 29, 1939, Feb. 5, April 11, May 28, 1940, Hoover to Clark, Feb. 7, April 25, 1940, all in box 36 PPI. Report of Republican Program Committee Submitted to Republican National Committee, *A Program for a Dynamic America: A Statement of Republican Principles*, Feb. 16, 1940, PPI 452. "Hoover Manuscript on the Bank Crisis and Interregnum, 1931–1933," Flynn Papers. Gary Dean Best, *Herbert Hoover: The Post-Presidential Years, 1933–1964* (Stanford, Calif.), 131–32. Paul H. Graves to Henry R. Luce, Aug. 28, 1940, Willkie Papers. Smith, *Thomas E. Dewey*, 280.

2. Richard Wilson, "Dewey Has Ideas," *Des Moines Register*, April 30, 1939. Harrison Spangler to Hoover, April 17, 1939, box 219; Claude Robinson, Opinion Research Corporation, to James P. Selvage, "The Political Outlook for 1940," May 21, 1940, box 202, both in PPI.

3. Harrison E. Spangler to Lawrence Ritchey, May 27, 1940, box 219; John C. O'Laughlin, memorandum, April 28, 1940, box 168; James P. Selvage to Hoover, "Wendell Willkie, Presidential Candidate His Record," n.d. [June 1940], box 202; Hoover to Robert G. Simmons, June 7, 1940, box 210, all in PPI.

4. Hoover to Harrison E. Spangler, June 20, 1939, box 219; Herbert W. Clark to Hoover, April 20, 1940, box 36; Hoover to Clark, April 24, 26, 1940, box 36; Hoover to Walter Newton, March 1, 1940, box 162, all in PPI. Frank I. Fetzer to Hoover, April 24, 1940; Hoover to Fetzer, April 26, June 18, 1940, all in box 58, PPI 329. Ickes is quoted in Smith, *Thomas E. Dewey*, 289.

5. "Inside Stuff–Real History," [1940 Republican Party Convention], Vandenberg Scrapbooks, vol. 12, p. 134, Vandenberg Papers. Hoover, "Memorandum on telephone conversation with Tom Dewey, June 27, 1940," box 47; Charles Heberd, memorandum, [1947], box 83, both in PPI. A. Willis Robertson to Taft, April 22, 1940, box 145, Robert Taft Papers.

6. Ronald Radosh, "Robert A. Taft: A Non-Interventionist Faces War," in Radosh, *Prophets on the Right* (New York, 1973), 119–45. Taft to Maurice Leon, Jan. 27, 1939, Willkie Papers. Patterson, *Taft*, 163–64, 198–200, 213–22, 242. Richard B. Scandrett to Taft, May 15, 1940, box 130; Scandrett to Forest Davis, June 13, 1940, box 143A; Willis Robertson to John B. Hollister, May 27, 31, 1940, box 146; [John B. Hollister], "Summary of Part in Taft Nomination Campaign," n.d., box 146, all in Robert Taft Papers. Turner Catledge, "Strict Neutrality Demanded by Taft," *New York Times*, May 21, 1940; Turner Catledge, "War's Turn Upsets Republican Race," *New York Times*, May 26, 1940; Richard C. Bain and Judith H. Parris, *Convention Decisions and Voting Records* (Washington, D.C., 1973), 254–56; John Moser, "Principles without Program: Senator Robert A. Taft and American Foreign Policy," *Ohio History* 108, no. 2 (1999): 177–92; George Nash, ed., *Freedom Betrayed: Herbert Hoover's Secret History of the Second World War and Its Aftermath* (Stanford, Calif., 2011), 239; Wayne Cole, *America First: The Battle Against Intervention* (New York, 1971), 169.

7. Newton D. Baker to Ellen Gowen Hood, April 6, 1935, box 121, Baker Papers.

8. "What's What of Wendell Willkie," Sept. 26, 1929, box: W.L.W.; Willkie to George

Heighway, file 16, Mrs. W. L. Love to Willkie, June 20, 1939, file 27, pre-1940, all in Will-kie Papers. Gwyneth H. Meyer to Ellsworth Barnard, April 26, 1953, file 1953; Barnard, interview by Turner Catledge, Nov. 1, 1960, file 8; "The Candidate," *Times Literary Sup-plement*, June 2, 1966, copy in file 19, all in Barnard Papers. Steve Neal, *Dark Horse: A Biography of Wendell Willkie* (Lawrence, Kans., 1989), 1–2, 14.

9. Philip H. Willkie to Ellsworth Barnard, Nov. 21, 1960, file 1960–61; Barnard Mss Notes, file 4, both in Barnard Papers. Mark H. Leff, "Strange Bedfellows: The Utility Magnate as Politician," in *Wendell Willkie: Hoosier Internationalist*, ed. James H. Madi-son, 22–43 (Bloomington, Ind., 1992). "Investigation of Executive Agencies of the Gov-ernment," report to the Select Committee to Investigate the Executive Agencies of the Government, No. 4, *Report on Government Activities in the Field of Mineral Resources and Power Prepared by the Brookings Institution* (Washington, D.C., 1937), 109–11, in file: "June 1937, National Power Policy Proposal," pre-1940, Willkie Papers.

10. Richard Lowitt, "The TVA, 1933–1945," 35–44, in *TVA: Fifty Years of Grass Roots Bureaucracy,* ed. Edwin C. Hargrove and Paul K. Conkin (Urbana, Ill., 1983; Ellsworth Barnard, *Wendell Willkie: Fighter for Freedom* (Marquette, Mich., 1966), 78–109, 195, 111, 115, 117, 118–19; Thomas P. Hughes, *Networks of Power Electrification in Western So-ciety, 1880–1930* (Baltimore, 1983), 393–401. Willkie to James P. Warburg, Sept. 7, 1934, box 22, Warburg Papers. David Lillienthal to Willkie, April 25, 1936, 63; Willkie to Lillienthal May 5, 1936, box 63; Alexander Sachs, "Highlights from . . . Eventual Plan for Southeastern Cooperative Pool for Publicly and Privately Owned Utilities," Sept. 29, 1936, box 63; Willkie to Roosevelt, Sept. 30, 1936, box 89; Lillienthal to Willkie, Jan. 29, 1937, box 89; Willkie to Lillienthal, Feb. 1, 1937, box 89, all in Sachs Papers. "TVA Joint Conferences Discontinued by President, Jan. 26, 1937, file June 1937, National Power Policy Proposal," pre-1940, Willkie Papers.

11. E. T. Weir, Lammot du Pont et al. to Willkie, April 7, 1936, file: Corres., pol., Oct. 1929–Dec. 1939; [Willkie memorandum], "The last time I saw the President . . . ," Nov. 23, 1937, file 37, pre-1940, both in Willkie Papers. Raymond Moley, interview by author, 1963–64.

12. Neal, *Dark Horse,* 37–55. Willkie to Moley, July 11, 1934, box 59, Moley Papers. Moley to Willkie, Oct. 12, 1936, with address, "How Much Government Can American Business Stand?," Oct. 7, 1937, Corres-Misc, Oct-Dec 1937, pre-1940; Willkie to Nor-man Beasley, July 2, 1937, file 1937; "The Back Door to Government Ownership," file: Correspondence, 1937, Willkie Manuscripts–Barnard Materials; Willkie to Mrs. Robert Bell, Dec. 17, 1937, Willkie pre-1940 correspondence, Jan.-Feb. 1937; Willkie to Jules G. Kiplinger, Nov. 1, 1935, file 15, "Report of the National Jeffersonian Democrats on the Detroit Conference," Aug. 7 and 8, 1936, May-Sept. 1936; Willkie to Bainbridge Colby, Oct. 31, 1936, Corres-Misc., Oct.-Dec. 1936; Colby to Willkie, Nov. 28, 1938, file 22; Will-kie to Oswald Garrison Villard, April 11, 1939, file 26, pre-1940; Willkie, "New Deal Power Plan Challenged," copy, *New York Times Magazine,* file *New York Times; Inves-tigation of Executive Agencies of the Government,* report to the Select Committee to Investigate the Executive Agencies of the Government, No. 4, *Report on Government Activities in the Field of . . . Power Prepared by the Brookings Institution* (Washington, D.C., 1937); Message from the President of the United States, *Report of National Power Policy Committee with Respect to the Treatment of Holding Companies,* March 12, 1935, 74th Cong., 1st sess., file: June, 1937, 109–16; Frank R. McNinch and Federal Power Commission, file National Power Pooling Proposal, June 1937, pre-1940, all in Willkie

Papers. Philip H. Willkie to Ellsworth Barnard, Oct. 14, Nov. 21, 1960, file 1960–61, Barnard Papers. Willkie, "Set Enterprise Free," *Christian Science Monitor,* March 2, 1940.

13. Willkie to Raymond Moley, Feb. 22, 1939, file 25, pre-1940, Willkie Papers. Pierre S. du Pont to Senator John G. Townshend, June 27, 1940, file 765–11; Pierre du Pont to Harry L. Cannon, Oct. 30, 1940, file 765–11; [Jouett Shouse?], Memorandum No. 597, Dec. 18, 1940, file: Political-Presidential Campaigns, 1940, all in Pierre du Pont Papers. [Benjamin Cohen], "Conversation at luncheon with Mr. Wendell Willkie," Dec. 11, 1939, PSF 140. Thomas L. Lamont to Ellsworth Barnard, May 7, 1952, file: 1952; Russell Davenport interview by Barnard, New York, June 5, 1952, Barnard Mss Notes, folder 5, p. 21, all in Barnard Papers. Neal, *Dark Horse,* 54–56.

14. *New York Times,* May 29, 1940.

15. [Jouett Shouse?], Memorandum No. 532, June 27, 1940, file 771, Pierre du Pont Papers. Frank D. McKay to Ellsworth Barnard, Oct. 14, 1952, file 1952, Barnard Papers. Bain and Parris, *Convention Decisions,* 251–56, part C, "The Voting Records"; Donald Bruce Johnson and Kirk H. Porter, *National Party Platforms, 1840–1972* (Urbana, Ill., 1975), 390. Sinclair Weeks, "Notes on the Willkie Campaign for the Presidential Nomination," box 4, Hamilton Papers. Drew Pearson and Robert S. Allen, "Washington Daily Merry-Go-Round," July 3, 1940, box 141; Charlie [Charles Taft] to Mrs. Wm. H. Taft, July 9, 1940, box 864, both in Robert Taft Papers. Patterson, *Mr. Republican,* 223–31.

16. John D. M. Hamilton, "The Nomination of Senator Charles L. McNary as the Candidate for Vice-President," April 3, 1967, box 3, Hamilton Papers.

17. Hamilton, "The Balloting in the 1940 Campaign," Feb. 4, 1959, box 3; Hamilton, interview by Murray Friedman, Oct. 27, 1945, box 4, both in Hamilton Papers. Charles Peters, *Five Days in Philadelphia: 1940, Wendell Willkie and the Political Convention that Freed FDR to Win World War II* (New York, 2005), 120–21; John M. Henry, "Autobiography," manuscript, 154–55, Henry Papers. E. E. Willkie to Barnard, Aug. 5, 1952, file: 1952; Gardner Cowles, interview by Barnard, Jan. 23, 1952; Russell Davenport, interview by Barnard, June 5, 1952; Phillip Willkie, interview by Barnard, Rushville, Aug. 5, 1952, folder 6, Mss Notes, all in Barnard Papers. "The Republican Party: Up from the Grave," file: Republican Policies, 1938–41, box 786, Robert Taft Papers. Mason, *The Republican Party and American Politics,* 72–73.

18. *New York Times,* Aug. 12, 1940; McCoy, *Landon of Kansas,* 447–48; Neal, *Dark Horse,* 130–31.

19. Willkie address, "Wendell Willkie Speaks to the Negroes," Chicago, Sept. 13, 1940, Willkie Papers.

20. "Speech of Acceptance," in *This Is Wendell Willkie,* ed. Stanley Walker (New York, 1940), 259–80; Barnard, *Willkie: Fighter for Freedom,* 210. Taft to Willkie, Aug. 13, 1940, box 142, Robert Taft Papers.

21. Barnard, *Willkie: Fighter for Freedom,* 210–11; Johnson, *White,* 532–33; Neal, *Dark Horse,* 139–40; Mark Lincoln Chadwin, *The Warhawks: American Interventionists before Pearl Harbor* (New York, 1968), 79–81. Dorothy Thompson to Wendell Willkie, July 23, 1940, box 263; Grenville Clark to Lewis W. Douglas, Oct. 30, 1940, box 263, both in Douglas Papers.

22. Hoover to John C. O'Laughlin, Sept. 3, 1940, box 169, PPI 457. Willkie address, Pittsburg, Kans., Sept. 16, 1940, Speeches and Writings, Willkie Papers. Dallek, *Franklin D. Roosevelt,* 250; *Historical Statistics of the United States,* 65.

23. David Reynolds, *From Munich to Pearl Harbor* (Chicago, 2001), 100–101; Robert A. Divine, *Roosevelt & World War II* (New York, 1979), 37–38; *New York Times,* Sept. 22, 23, Oct. 9, 1940; Barnard, *Willkie: Fighter for Freedom,* 248–68. "Interventionism vs. Isolationism," Mss Notes, file 10, Barnard Papers. Hoover to John C. O'Laughlin, Oct. 11, 1940, box 169, PPI. Neal, *Dark Horse,* 165; Edgar Eugene Robinson, *They Voted for Roosevelt: The Presidential Vote, 1932–1944* (Stanford, Calif., 1947), 7, 15. Claude Robinson, "The Roosevelt-Willkie Campaign: A Study of the Primary Social and Economic Determinants of the 1940 Presidential Election," Opinion Research Corporation, Princeton, N.J., Feb. 6, 1941, box 264, Douglas Papers.

7 | REPUBLICAN RESURGENCE

1. Richard Thurlow, *Fascism in Britain* (New York, 1998), 145; Gerry Kearns, *Geopolitics and Empire: The Legacy of Halford Mackinder* (New York, 2009), 15, 18–19, 155; Geoffrey Parker, *Geopolitics* (London, 1998), 26–45; Immanuel Wallerstein, "Three Hegemonies," in *Two Hegemonies,* ed. O'Brien and Clesse, 357–61; Robert Gilpin, "The Rise of American Hegemony," in *Two Hegemonies,* ed. O'Brien and Clesse, 165–69; Randall Bennett Woods, *A Changing of the Guard: Anglo-American Relations: 1941–1946* (Chapel Hill, N.C., 1990), 1–3.

2. Tooze, *Wages of Destruction,* 223, 302–3, 313, 383–505; Alan S. Milward, *War, Economy and Society* (Berkeley, 1979), 4–306; Mark Harrison, "The Economics of World War II," in *The Economics of World War II: Six Great Powers in International Comparison,* ed. Harrison, 1–22 (New York, 2000); Patrick J. Hearden, *Roosevelt Confronts Hitler: America's Entry into World War II* (DeKalb, Ill., 1987), 121; Timothy Snyder, *Bloodlands: Europe between Hitler and Stalin* (New York, 2010), 156–66; Mark Mazower, *Dark Continent: Europe's Twentieth Century* (New York, 1999), 150–81; Richard J. Evans, "Immoral Rearmament," review of *Wages of Destruction,* by Adam Tooze, *New York Review,* Dec. 20, 2007.

3. Ritchie Ovendale, *Anglo-American Relations in the Twentieth Century* (New York, 1998), 28–49. Jay G. Hayden, "G.O.P. Nearing Showdown," North American Newspaper Alliance, box 864, Robert Taft Papers. Herbert Hoover to Honorable Sol Bloom, Jan. 16, 1941, box 19; John Callan O'Laughlin to Hoover, and attached revision of Hoover statement, Jan. 25, 1941, box 169; William D. Mitchell to Hoover, Feb. 11, 1941, box 153, all in PPI 441.

4. Taft to Maurice Leon, Jan. 27, 1939, copy, Willkie Papers. Taft to Phyllis B. Tinckler, Sept. 18, 1940, box 863; Hoover to Taft, June 27 1941, box 1286; Taft to Hoover, July 3, 1941, box 1286, all in Robert Taft Papers.

5. Statement by Robert A. Taft, Feb. 26, 1941, box 710; Address by Senator Taft . . . Cincinnati, Ohio, March 27, 1941, box 664, both in Robert Taft papers.

6. Taft speech notes, "Convoys," handwritten, n.d., box 867; Taft, Statement on Foreign Policy, n.d., box 710; Taft, "Shall the United States Enter the European War?" May 17, 1941, box 860; Taft speech notes, "Foreign Policy Today," n.d., box 867; Taft to Mrs. C. A. Dykstra, March 1, 1951, box 34, all in Robert Taft Papers. Grenville Clark to Wendell Willkie, March 18, 1941, Willkie Papers.

7. R. Douglas Stuart Jr. to Taft, April 16, box 860; Stuart to Taft, Oct. 28, 1941, box 863; Edward S. Thurston to Taft, Sept. 23, 1941, box 860; Taft to Thurston, n.d., box 860, all in Robert Taft Papers. Patterson, *Taft,* 242, 247; Wayne Cole, *America First* (New York, 1971), 12, 143–53, 167.

8. Richard B. Scandrett to Taft, June 9, 29, 1941, box 860, Robert Taft Papers.

9. Colby Chester to Taft, fragment, n.d.; Taft to Chester, Aug. 12, 1942; both in box 162, Robert Taft Papers.

10. Taft, *A Foreign Policy for Americans* (Garden City, N.Y., 1951), 18.

11. Mark Foote, "Vandenberg for Lease-Lend, but Balks at Commitments," May 25, 1943, Vandenberg Scrapbooks, vol. 15, p. 43b; Jay Hayden, "Threat in the Trade Pacts," Vandenberg Scrapbooks, vol. 15, p. 23b, both in Vandenberg Papers. Richard E. Darilek, *A Loyal Opposition in Time of War: The Republican Party and the Politics of Foreign Policy from Pearl Harbor to* Yalta (Westport, Conn., 1976), 58–89; Vandenberg, "Extending the Trade Agreements Act," *Cong. Record,* Senate, 78th Cong., 1st sess., May 14, 1943.

12. John Moser, "Principles without Program: Senator Robert A. Taft and American Foreign Policy," *Ohio History* 108 (Sept. 2001): 177–92. Taft, "National Resources Planning Board, Proposal," box 728, Robert Taft Papers. Arthur Vandenberg, "Why Not Deal Congress In?" *Coronet,* July 1943. Address of Robert A. Taft, March 26, 1943, PPI 528.

13. Phillip W. Warken, introduction to *A History of the National Resources Planning Board, 1933–1943* (New York, 1979); Marion Clawson, *New Deal Planning* (Baltimore, 1981), 40–43; C. E. Merriam, "Government and Society," in *Recent Social Trends in the United States* (Westport, Conn., 1970), 2: 1521–22, 1534; Barry Karl, *Charles E. Merriam and the Study of Politics* (Chicago, 1974), 261–82; Patrick D. Reagan, *Designing a New America: The Origins of New Deal Planning, 1890–1943* (Amherst, Mass.), 78–81; Alan Brinkley, *The End of Reform: New Deal Liberalism in Recession and War* (New York, 1995), 216–17.

14. "6. National Resources Planning Board," box: Legislation, 1833–41, file: Ra–Reorganization, Byrnes Papers. Cong. Record, Senate, 78th Cong., 1st sess., vol. 89, pt. 4, 4946.

15. "Report of the Conference of the National Resources Planning Board with the President at the White House," Oct. 17, 1939, box 3; Delano memorandum to the president, Dec. 30, 1941, with appendices, box 4; Delano to the president, July 23, 1941, box 4; Delano to the president, April 4, 1941, box 6, all in OF 1092. Warken, *History of the National Resources Planning Board,* 201–2.

16. National Resources Planning Board, *After Defense—What? Post Defense Planning* (Washington, D.C., 1941). Charles W. Eliot [to Hansen], and "Agenda, War-Time Planning for Continuing Full Employment, NRPB," Feb. 20, 1942, HUG (FP)-3.16, box 2, Hansen Papers. Alvin Hansen, *After the War: Full Employment* (Washington, D.C., 1942).

17. Hansen, "National Resources Planning Board," "Preliminary Assignments for War-time Planning Agenda," Feb. 19, 1942; "War-time Planning for Continuing Full Employment, National Resources Planning Board," Feb. 20, 1942, both in HUG (FP)-3.16, box 2, Hansen Papers. Landon R. Y. Storrs, "Red Scare Politics and Suppression of Popular Front Feminism: The Loyalty Investigation of Mary Dublin Keyserling," *Journal of American History* 90, no. 2 (Sept. 2003): 4; Reagan, *Designing a New America,* 220–22.

18. Storrs, "Red Scare Politics," 21; White House memorandum, "Mr. Corrington Gill Called," Jan. 13, 1943; James F. Byrnes to the president, March 12, 1943; FDR to Carter Glass, March 24, 1943, all in OF 1092. James T. Kloppenberg, *The Virtues of Liberalism* (New York, 1998), 106–8. Taft speech notes, "National Resources Planning Board,"

n.d., file: New Dealism Truce, box 728, Robert Taft Papers. "Toward Security," PSF 175. *Washington Review,* sec. 3, March 13, 1943, copy in box 5, OF 1092. Warken, *History of the National Resources Planning Board,* 216–23.

19. *National Resources Development Report for 1943,* pt. 1, *Post-War Plan and Program* (Washington, D.C., 1943), 29–39. Hansen, "Postwar Controls: Fate of Private Enterprise Hinges on Successful Postwar Reconversion and Full Employment," *Chicago Journal of Commerce,* Aug. 31, 1942, HUG (B)-H 145.72, box 2, Hansen Papers. Hansen to Taft, Jan. 22, 1943, box 529, Robert Taft Papers. Taft address, "We Need a Courageous and Independent Congress," *Cong. Record,* Appendix, 78th Cong., 1st sess., vol. 89, pt. 9, A32–A35; Alvin H. Hansen and Guy Greer, "Toward Full Use of Our Resources," *Fortune,* Nov. 1942.

20. Ronald L. Heinemann, *Harry Byrd of Virginia* (Charlottesville, Va., 1996), 254; Patterson, *Taft,* 260; *Cong. Record,* Senate, 78th Cong., 1st sess., vol. 89, pt. 4, 4924, Appendix, pt. 10, A2623; Harold G. Moulton, *The New Philosophy of Public Debt* (Washington, D.C., 1943), 90–93; "Senators Guard Postwar Policy: Form Own Group to Weigh Problems," Vandenberg Scrapbooks, vol. 15, pp. 25b, 26b, 27, Vandenberg Papers.

8 | CHALLENGING ISOLATION

1. *New York Times,* Nov. 12, 1940; Arthur Krock, Vandenberg's Stand a Political Paradox," *New York Times,* Jan. 14, 1945; Cole, *America First,* 167–72.

2. "Willkie Offers Republicans His Idea of Platform Needs," June 12, 1944, box 164, Robert Taft Papers. Willkie to Harold Stassen, Nov. 28, 1941; Stassen to Willkie, Dec. 2, 1941, both in Willkie Papers.

3. Thomas W. Lamont to Willkie, Suggestions for Willkie speeches, file 24, box 123; Lamont to Russell Leffingwell, Nov. 24, 1941, both in Lamont Papers. Leffingwell to Walter Lippmann, April 23, 1941, box 5; Leffingwell to Lamont, Dec. 2, 1941, box 4; Leffingwell to Clinton Crane, Dec. 27, 1949, box 1, all in Leffingwell Papers. Grenville Clark to Willkie, March 18, 1941, Willkie Papers.

4. Elizabeth R. Valentine, "A Defeated Candidate Remains a Leader: The Willkie of Today," *New York Times Magazine,* June 1, 1941; "Willkie Says G.O.P. Can Win Next Year," *New York Times,* Aug. 11, 1943.

5. James Roosevelt and Sidney Shalett, *Affectionately, F.D.R.* (London, 1959), 291; Neal, *Dark Horse,* 191; Joseph Alsop, Memorandum, "I dined last night at Irita Van Doren's," Jan. 16, 1941, PSF 194. Willkie Statement, Jan. 12, 1941, file: Henry Luce, 1943, Willkie Papers.

6. Vandenberg Scrapbooks, Jan. 7, 1941, vol. 13, p. 46, Vandenberg Papers. Roscoe Drummond to Ellsworth Barnard, July 23, 1957, file 1957–58, Barnard Papers. *New York Times,* Jan. 2, 1941.

7. *New York Times,* Feb. 7, 1941.

8. Willkie, "Statement before Senate Foreign Relations Committee, Feb. 11, 1941, Willkie Papers. Kimball, *Lend-Lease,* 217, 240–41; George C. Herring Jr., *Aid to Russia, 1841–1946* (New York, 1973), 5; *New York Times,* Jan. 31, Feb. 9, 11, March 9, 1941; Arthur Vandenberg Jr., ed., *The Private Papers of Senator Vandenberg* (Boston, 1952), 9–11. Vandenberg speech, "H.R. 1776," U.S. Senate, Feb. 18, 1941, box 4, file 13, Diary Notes, March 8, 1941, vol. 13, p. 59, Vandenberg Papers. Vandenberg to John W. Blodgett, March 13, 1941; Vandenberg to Reverend Leland Sumner, Chairman, America First Committee, Grand Rapids, March 21, 1941; Vandenberg to Francis K. Glew, Aug. 13, 1941, all in Van-

denberg Correspondence, 1941, Vandenberg Papers. Mira Wilkins, *The History of Foreign Investment in the United States, 1914–1945* (Cambridge, Mass., 2004), 472. Hoover to Vandenberg, Oct. 29, 1941, Vandenberg Scrapbooks, vol. 13, p. 95B, Vandenberg Papers. John W. Marlsberger, *From Obstruction to Moderation: The Transformation of Senate Conservatism, 1938–1952* (Selingsgrove, Pa., and Cranbury, N.J., 2000), 76.

9. Vandenberg to Gerald L. K. Smith, Oct. 11, 1941; Vandenberg to General John K. Schouton, Oct. 11, 1941; Vandenberg to John J. Stalker and John J. Ferry, Oct. 18, 1941; Vandenberg to Wallace Hook, Nov. 4, 1941, all in Vandenberg Correspondence, 1941, Vandenberg Papers. James A. Gazell, "Arthur H. Vandenberg, Internationalism and the United Nations," *Political Science Quarterly* 88, no. 3 (Sept. 1973): 379.

10. Wendell Willkie, "The Cause of Human Freedom, We Cannot Appease the Forces of Evil," address, Madison Square Garden, New York City, May 7, 1941, Willkie Speeches, Willkie Papers. Herbert Hoover, "We Are Not Prepared for War," radio address, May 11, 1941, *Vital Speeches,* May 15, 1941; Grenville Clark to Willkie, March 18, 1941, all in Willkie Papers. Raymond Moley, interview by Elliot Rosen, ca. 1959; R. J. Overy, *The Nazi Economic Recovery, 1932–1938* (New York, 1996), 1–4; Maddison, *Economic Growth in the West,* 28.

11. *New York Times,* Sept. 14, 1941. Jay G. Hayden, "Willkie Embarked on Anti-Isolationist Crusade . . . Imposing List of Republicans Are on the List, Sept. 4, [1941], Vandenberg Correspondence, Vandenberg Papers.

12. Robert to Hulbert Taft, April 27, 1942; James A. Haggerty, "Willkie Wins Republicans to His Anti-Isolation Stand," *New York Times,* April 21, 1942; *New York Herald Tribune* editorial, *Chicago Sun,* April 21, 1942; George E. Sokolsky, "These Days," April 23, 1942; "Proposed Republican Resolution," "Resolution Proposed by Wendell L. Willkie," "Report of the Committee on Resolutions," all in box 785, Robert Taft Papers. "Proposed Resolution for the Republican National Committee, April 17, 1942, Willkie Papers. Johnson, *Republican Party,* 204–8; Darilek, *A Loyal Opposition,* 44–45, 61–64; "Text of the Republican Resolution," *New York Times,* April 21, 1942; Robert A. Taft, *A Foreign Policy for Americans* (Garden City, N.Y., 1951), 5–36.

13. "Statement to PM," Feb. 5, Roosevelt to Willkie, Feb. 21, Willkie to Roosevelt, March 6, 1942, Willkie Papers.

14. Wayne Cole, *Roosevelt and the Isolationism, 1932–45* (Lincoln, Neb., 1983), 405, 538; Darilek, *A Loyal Opposition,* 53, 61–65; *New York Times,* April 19, 1942.

15. Dorothy Hays to Lem, June 21, 1942; Willkie to Drew Pearson, June 26, July 2, 1942, all in Willkie Papers. *Time,* June 29, 1942; Philip Willkie interview, Aug. 6, 1953, Barnard Mss notes, file 10, Barnard Papers.

16. *Washington Sunday Star,* Dec. 13, 1942, Willkie Papers. Johnson, *Republican Party,* 224–26; Best, *Hoover: Postpresidential Years,* 1: 21, 23, 38–39, 59, 87–90.

17. Barnard, *Willkie: Fighter for Freedom,* 384–85. Barack Mattingly to Willkie, June 15, 1942; Willkie to Henry Luce, Nov. 10, 1942; A. L. Miller to Willkie, Jan. 7, Aug. 13, 1943; Willkie to Miller, Jan. 8, 1943, all in Willkie Papers.

18. Austin Memorandum, "The Republican Conference," Jan. 19, 1943, box 20, Austin Papers.

19. Austin to Lt. Colonel Harold W. Mason, March 15, 1943, carton III, Correspondence, Harrison E. Spangler; Statement, Creation of a Republican Postwar Advisory Council, May 31, 1943, box 15; Leo Casey to Austin, June 23, 1943, box 15; Spangler to Austin, June 23, 1943, box 15; Austin to Spangler, July 8, 12, 1943, box 15, all in Austin Pa-

pers. Darilek, *A Loyal Opposition,* 94–99. Deneen Watson to Members and Republican Leaders, July 19, 1943, box 622; Harrison Spangler to Taft, July 31, 1943, box 622, both in Robert Taft Papers.

20. Mark Foote, "Vandenberg for Lease-Lend, but Balks at Commitments," February 1943, vol. 15, p. 23b; Jay Hayden, "Threat in the Trade Pacts," May 25, 1943, vol. 15, p. 43b, both in Vandenberg Correspondence, Vandenberg Papers. Darilek, *A Loyal Opposition,* 58–89; Vandenberg, "Extending the Trade Agreements Act," *Cong. Record,* Senate, 78th Cong., 1st sess., May 14, 1943. Vandenberg to Warren R. Austin, June 29, 1943, box 25; Austin to V. Orton, July 28, 1943, box 15, both in Austin Papers.

21. Taft address, "Peace or Politics," American Bar Association, Chicago, Aug. 26, 1943, box 622, Robert Taft Papers. Vandenberg to George Fielding Eliot, Feb. 10, 1943; Vandenberg to Cordell Hull, March 24, 1943; Vandenberg to Walter George, March 27, 1943; Eliot to Hull, March 26, 1943, all in Vandenberg Correspondence, Vandenberg Papers. Turner Catledge, "Republican Group Put to Test at Mackinac," *New York Times,* Sept. 5, 1943; Willkie, "After the War—What?," *Look,* April 2, 1943; Darilek, *A Loyal Opposition,* 94–98; Barnard, *Willkie Fighter for Freedom,* 417; S. Res. 114, 78th Cong., 1st sess. Sen. Con. Res. 16, Vandenberg-White Resolution, with Austin's holographic commentary, box 20, Austin Papers.

22. Austin to Manchester Boddy, Jan. 19, 1943, box 10; Vandenberg to Austin, June 29, 1943, and holograph notes written by Austin on S. Con. Res. 16, box 20; Austin to Wallace White, July 22, 1943, Austin Papers. Gould Lincoln, "Vandenberg-White Cooperation Move Serves 2 Purposes," Vandenberg Scrapbooks, July 19, 1943, vol. 15, p. 49b; Sen. Con. Res. 16, 79th Cong., 1st sess., July 2, 1943; Vandenberg to Henry K. Dellson, July 6, 1943, Vandenberg Correspondence, all in Vandenberg Papers.

23. Herbert Hoover and Hugh Gibson, *The Problems of Lasting Peace* (New York, 1942), 278–79. Hoover to John Bricker, Aug. 30, 31, 1943, box 22; Hoover to John Cowles, Sept. 6, 1943, box 40; Taft to Hoover, Sept. 23, 1943, 233; Hoover to Taft, Sept. 25, 1943, all in PPI. Hoover to Lewis Strauss, Dec. 13, 1943, document posted online by the Gallery of History; Smith, *Thomas E. Dewey,* 386; *Time,* Sept. 13, 1943; Best, *Hoover: Postpresidential Years,* 236–42. Document beginning "The result which people of goodwill . . . ," box 15, file 8, Austin Papers.

24. "Rep. Charles G. Eaton of NJ, Foreign Policy," with Austin emendations in hand, n.d., Austin proposals, including holograph notes inscribed across "Advice by Republican Postwar Advisory Council to Republican National Committee," marked as follows: "Senator's original copy," Aug. 30, 1943, Austin's copy of Vandenberg Proposal as amended," n.d. box 15; Austin to Roy L. Patrick, April 3, 1944, box 25, all in Austin Papers. Darilek, *A Loyal Opposition,* 92–93, 209–19; Richard Norton Smith, *Thomas E. Dewey and His Times* (New York, 1982), 385; James Reston, "The Education of a Statesman," *New York Times,* April 20, 1952. Republican National Committee, "Resolution on Foreign Policy and International Relations Adopted Unanimously by the Republican Postwar Advisory Council," Sept. 7, 1943, box 158, Robert Taft Papers. Patterson, *Taft,* 290; *New York Times,* Sept. 7, 8, 1943; Roscoe Drummond, "Why of Doubts RE: Mackinac Charter," *Christian Science Monitor,* Sept. 17, 1943. The Eaton and Austin drafts can be compared in their entirety in Austin to Walter E. Higgins, Nov. 29, 1943, box 14, file 5, Austin Papers.

25. Arthur Krock, "In the Nation: The Hope of Political Unity Made Stronger," *New*

York Times, Sept. 10, 1943. Taft to Arthur Krock, Sept. 18, 1943, box 158, Robert Taft Papers. Willkie to Austin, Sept. 20, 1943, Willkie Papers.

26. Holographic notes, Taft's hand, Hotel Harding, Marion, Ohio, n.d., Republican National Committee, "Mackinac Declaration of Domestic Policy," Sept. 7, 1943, box 158, Robert Taft Papers.

9 | WILKIE'S LEGACY AND THE GOP

1. Turner Catledge, "Willkie Gains Ground in G.O.P. Preliminaries," Sept. 26, 1943; Arthur Krock, "Major Political Camps Are Torn by Conflict," *New York Times,* Dec. 12, 1943; Darilek, *A Loyal Opposition* 142–43; Barnard, *Willkie: Fighter for Freedom,* 427–28.

2. Barnard, *Willkie, Fighter for Freedom,* 428–30; *New York Times,* Sept. 21, 1943; Elmo Roper, *You and Your Leaders: Their Actions and Reactions, 1936–1956* (New York, 1957), 100–101.

3. "Wendell Willkie Speaks on Labor," address at Forbes Field, Pittsburgh, Oct. 3, 1940, Willkie Papers. Taft to Hugh S. Johnson, Nov. 5, 1940, box 142, Robert Taft Papers. Barnard, *Willkie: Fighter for Freedom,* 437, 440.

4. *Time,* May 18, 1936, Jan. 30, 1939; *St. Louis Commerce Magazine,* Dec. 1999; Edgar M. Queeny, *The Spirit of Enterprise* (New York, 1943), 34–109; John MacCormack, "A Defense of Private Enterprise," *New York Times,* Aug. 8, 1943. Joseph N. Pew Jr. to Lee Ellmaker, Aug. 14, 1944; Pew to John Cowles, Nov. 8, 1944, Personal, both in box 4, ser. 21B, Pew Papers, Sun Oil Collection.

5. *New York Times,* Dec. 7, 1939. Joseph N. Pew Jr. to A. L. Shultz, Nov. 16, 22, 1943, box 4, ser. 21E; Pew to Raymond Henle, Oct. 6, 1943, box 4, ser. 21B; Pew to Wendell P. Dodge, Feb. 28, 1944, box 4, ser. 21B; Pew to Felix Morley, June 16, 1944, box 4, ser. 21B; Pew to Lt. Col. Jay Cooke, June 16, 1944, box 4, ser. 21B; "Decentralize for Liberty," manuscript, n.d., box 5, ser. 21B; Pew to Edgar Queeny, Nov. 26, 1943, box 27, ser. 21B, all in Pew Papers. Overacker, *Presidential Campaign Funds,* 14–15. Taft to J. B. Doan, Feb. 24, 1944, box 161, Robert Taft Papers.

6. Edgar M. Queeny to Willkie, April 14, 16, 1941, March 26, June 11, 12, 16, 17, 1942, Jan. 25, March 8, 1943; Queeny interview, *St. Louis Globe-Democrat,* Oct. 31, 1943, all in Willkie Papers. Cole, *America First,* 177.

7. List of six questions, Charles J. Graham to Queeny, Sept. 28, 1943; *St. Louis Post-Dispatch,* Sept. 12, 1943; *St. Louis Globe-Democrat, St. Louis Star-Times,* Sept. 14, 1943; Representative Louis E. Miller, "What Missouri Asks of Mr. Willkie," *Cong. Record,* House, Oct. 11, 1943, all in Willkie Papers.

8. Edgar M. Queeny to Hoover, April 27, May 6, Dec. 18, 1942, Jan. 18, 1943, April 8, Sept. 27, 1943; Hoover to Queeny, May 2, Dec. 29, 1942, Jan. 29, 1943, all in box 182, PPI.

9. Queeny, "Why Missouri Questioned Willkie"; Willkie to Queeny, Oct. 6, 1943, both in Willkie Papers.

10. Willkie address, "America's Purposes," Opera House, Kiel Municipal Auditorium, St. Louis, Oct. 15, 1943, Willkie Papers. That Queeny endorsed the position of William Sentner, a labor radical, on union control of the workplace after the war, as claimed by Rosemary Feurer, *Radical Unionism in the Midwest* (Urbana, Ill., 2006), 155, is doubtful. Queeny desired, as did most entrepreneurs, liberation from government controls after the war.

11. Richard Polenberg, *War and Society* (Philadelphia, 1972), 167–71, 203–6; Over-

acker, *Presidential Campaign Funds*, 55–71; Howell John Harris, *The Right to Manage: Industrial Relations Policies of American Business in the 1940s* (Madison, Wisc., 1982), 37, 42–43, 70–73, 94, 106–8; Turner Catledge, "The Elephant Smells Lush Pastures," *New York Times*, Nov. 14, 1843.

12. Alfred P. Sloan Jr. to Willkie, March 24, 1942; Willkie to Sloan, March 30, 1942, both in Willkie Papers.

13. Michaela Hoenicke-Moore, *Know Your Enemy: The American Debate on Nazism, 1933–1945* (New York, 2010), 41–96, 342–43; Johnson, *Republican Party*, 271–72; Arthur Krock, "Major Political Camps Are Torn by Conflict," *New York Times*, Dec. 12, 1943; Willkie, "Don't Stir Distrust of Russia," Jan. 2, 1944, *New York Times*; Kate Zernike, "As Goes Wisconsin," *New York Times*, March 6, 2011; McCoy, *Landon of Kansas*, 501–4; Best, *Hoover: Postpresidential Years*, 250–54. Willard R. Smith to Willkie, May 7, 1944; Willkie to Bruce Bliven, May 8, 1944, Willkie to Henry Luce, May 9, 1944, all in Willkie Papers. "Memorandum to WW on the Polish-American attitude," March 17, 1944; Willkie to Helen Reid, April 10, 1944; Willkie to Ruth Kivett, April 16, 1944, all in Willkie Papers. Lem Jones to Ellsworth Barnard, file 1960–61; Don Anderson and William Evjue, interviews by Barnard, May 23, 1953, "Notes on Interview with Milton Polland," March 23, 1954, file 8, all in Barnard Papers.

14. Willkie, *An American Program* (New York, 1944), 3–36. Willkie to Edwin L. James, June 8, 1944, Willkie Papers. *New York Times*, July 2, 11, 1944; *Washington Post*, Sept. 12, 1944. "Willkie Offers Republicans His Idea of Platform Needs," June 12, 1944, box 164, Robert Taft Papers.

15. *New York Times*, April 30, 1952; Samuel Rosenman, *Working with Roosevelt* (New York, 1952), 463–70. Roosevelt to Willkie, July 13, 1944; Willkie to Roosevelt, never mailed, July 30, 1944; "Press Statement," Aug. 25, 1944; Willkie to Lev [Leverett Saltonstall], Sept. 27, 1944; Henry Luce to Willkie, n.d., all in Willkie Papers. Leo Crowley to Ellsworth Barnard, July 9, July 25, 1956; Barnard to Crowley, July 21, 1956; Barnard memorandum, "Willkie and Roosevelt," Manuscript Notes, all in file 20, Barnard Papers.

10 | SOURCES OF MODERN REPUBLICAN PARTY IDEOLOGY

1. Joseph N. Pew Jr. to A. L. Schulz, March 10, 1944, ser. 21B, Personal, box 4, Pew Papers. *New York Times* March 18, May 28, July 9, 1944. Robert E. Wood to Taft, April 12, May 2, 1944, box 161, all in Robert Taft Papers. Turner Catledge, "Isolationists Look for a Protagonist," *New York Times*, May 2, 1944.

2. Gabriel Kolko, *The Politics of War: The World and United States Foreign Policy, 1943–1945* (New York, 1968), 269–71.

3. Diary, June 4, 1942, Vandenberg Scrapbooks, Vandenberg Papers.

4. Austin memorandum, "Note Historical," June 1, 1942, box 20, Austin Papers. Vandenberg to James Kennedy, Feb. 11, 1943; Vandenberg to George Fielding Eliot, March 26, 1943; Vandenberg to Cordell Hull, March 27, 1943; Vandenberg to Harold Titus, April 23, Vandenberg to Frank Janussowski, Nov. 19, 1943, Vandenberg Correspondence, Vandenberg Papers.

5. Mark Foote, "Vandenberg for Lend-Lease, but Balks at Commitments," press clipping, Feb. 1943, Scrapbooks, vol. 15, p. 23B. Vandenberg, "Why Not Deal Congress In?" *Coronet*, July 1943, Scrapbooks, vo. 15, p. 44B, both in Vandenberg Papers.

6. Vandenberg to Nellie Hayes, Aug. 3, 1943; Vandenberg to Thomas W. Lamont,

Aug. 4, 1943; Vandenberg to Samuel Pettengill, Aug. 24, 1943; Vandenberg Correspondence, Vandenberg Papers.

7. Frank Gannett to Vandenberg, Jan, 7, 1944; John Hamilton to Vandenberg, Jan. 5, 1944; Vandenberg to Hamilton, Jan. 7, 1944; Vandenberg to Lansing Hoyt, Jan. 26, 1944; Vandenberg to Robert E. Wood, Feb. 11, April 30, 1944; Hoyt to Vandenberg, Feb. 16, 1944; Vandenberg to Austin, March 6, 1944; Austin to Vandenberg, March 10, 1944, all in Vandenberg Correspondence, Vandenberg Papers.

8. Vandenberg to Dewey, March 30, May 22, 1944, plus attachment; Dulles to Vandenberg, June 12, 1944; Vandenberg to Dulles, June 14, 1944, all in Vandenberg Correspondence, Vandenberg Papers. Vandenberg to Austin, May 22, 27, 1944; Austin-Dulles draft, June 10, 1944, both in carton III, Correspondence, Austin Papers.

9. Austin to Howard C. Rice, Feb. 22, 25, 1944, box 10; Austin to Francis P. Locke, March 18, 25, 1944, box 10, carton III; member of Austin's staff to World Peace Foundation, April 7, 1944; Austin to Herbert Butcher, April 22, 1944, box 10, all in Austin Papers. Brinkley, *End of Reform,* 140; Turner Catledge, "Midwest Is Drawn to Nationalism," *New York Times,* Oct. 7, 1943; Darilek, *A Loyal Opposition,* 97–98.

10. Vandenberg to Dewey, May 10, 1944, Vandenberg Correspondence, Vandenberg Papers (italics in original).

11. Austin, "The Use of External Sovereignty for Security," *Cong. Record,* May 2, 1944, copy in Austin Speech File, No. 302. Frederic Coudert, a highly regarded attorney and member of the New York State Senate and subsequently elected from Manhattan's "Silk Stocking District" to the House of Representatives, followed up Austin's presentation in a lengthy letter to the *New York Times.* Agreements to end war, Coudert claimed, could not end conflict. Peace and the rule of law could only be achieved when nations "use their might against the aggressor." In the event, no nation was "sovereign" in the face of an organized community of nations. Sovereignty, in short, was useless against the preponderance of power. Coudert argued further that "international law properly applied and sanctioned must override national law."

12. "Problem for Republicans," *Baltimore Evening Sun,* May 17, 1944; Darilek, *A Loyal Opposition,* 67–68; Donald Bruce Johnson and Kirk H. Porter, *National Party Platforms* (Urbana, Ill., 1975), 411. Edmund E. Lincoln to Joseph Martin, May 3, 1944, box 161, Robert Taft Papers.

13. Vandenberg to Austin, July 18, 25, 1944; Austin to Dulles, July 20, 1944; Austin to Vandenberg, July 20, 1944; Dulles to Austin, July 25, 1944, all in carton III, Correspondence, Austin Papers. Smith, *Thomas E. Dewey,* 280, 286–99, 366–433. "Condensation of an Address by Herbert Hoover on 'Freedom in America and the World,'" June 27, 1944; Taft to Raymond E. Willis, July 1, 1944, both in box 162, Robert Taft Papers.

14. Smith, *Thomas E. Dewey,* 412.

15. Townsend Hoopes, *The Devil and John Foster Dulles* (Boston, 1973), 56; Richard H. Immerman, *John Foster Dulles: Piety, Pragmatism, and Power in U.S. Foreign Policy* (Wilmington, Del., 1999), 23–26; Dulles, "The American People Need to be Imbued with a Righteous Faith," and "Statement of Guiding Principles," in William Paton, introd., *A Just and Durable Peace* (London, 1943), 11–20, 137–41.

16. Dulles to Austin, Aug. 11, 1944; Austin to Dulles, Aug. 14, 1944, both in carton III, Correspondence; [Dulles] memorandum with Austin, and Austin's marginal note, n.d., box 24, Austin Papers.

17. Austin to Robert Lucas, Oct. 28, 1944, Austin Papers. Smith, *Thomas E. Dewey,*

414–15; Cordell Hull, *Memoirs* (New York, 1948), 2: 1694–99; "Senator Taft Made the Following Statement," Oct. 26, 1944, box 778, Robert Taft Papers. Vandenberg to Hull, Aug. 29, 1944, Vandenberg Scrapbooks, vol. 16, p. 77b, Vandenberg Papers.

18. Darilek, *A Loyal Opposition,* 170–71. Dulles to Austin, Nov. 9, 1944, carton III, Correspondence, Austin Papers. Robinson, *They Voted for Roosevelt,* 1–182. Taft to Landon, Aug. 11, box 162; Taft to Julius Klein, Nov. 22, 1944, box 34, Robert Taft Papers. Marlsberger, *From Obstruction to Moderation,* 113–14.

19. "Brownell Pictures New Deal Rule by PAC with Labor in Revolt," *New York Times* Aug. 30, 1944; "Davenport Predicts Defeat of Dewey," *New York Times,* Nov. 7, 1944; Smith, *Thomas E. Dewey,* 409–10, 433–34; Alexander Barmine, "The New Communist Conspiracy," *Reader's Digest,* Oct. 1944, 27–33.

20. Dulles to Austin, Nov. 9, 1944, box 24, Austin Papers. Robinson, *They Voted for Roosevelt,* 7–46. Arthur Krock, "Aspects of the Election Are Open to Argument," *New York Times,* Nov. 12, 1944. Taft memorandum, "The Republican Party," n.d., box 161, Robert Taft Papers.

21. Memoranda, May 2–29, Vandenberg Scrapbooks, vol. 16, pp. 44–46B; Jay G. Hayden, "G.O.P. Waits—Vandenberg," June 1, 1944, Vandenberg Scrapbooks, vol. 16, p. 49, both in Vandenberg Papers.

22. Vandenberg memorandum, Aug. 25, 1944, Vandenberg Scrapbooks, vol. 16, p. 49, Vandenberg Papers.

23. Vandenberg, "Let's Win Both the War and the Peace," address, *Cong. Record,* Jan. 10, 1945, 79th Cong., 1st sess., copy in box 4, Vandenberg Papers.

24. Wayne Cole, *America First* (New York, 1951), 158; Arthur Vandenberg Jr. and Joe Alex Morris, *The Private Papers of Senator Vandenberg* (Boston, 1952), 109–10. Vandenberg to James P. Wolcott, July 27, 1944; Vandenberg to Allen Schoenfeld, July 2, 1944, both in Vandenberg Correspondence, Vandenberg Papers. Mark Harrison, ed., *The Economics of World War II* (Cambridge, U.K., 1998), 10, table 1.3, "Wartime GDP of the Great Powers, 1939–1945, in International Dollars and 1990 Prices." Vandenberg to Taft, July 8, 1944; Taft to Vandenberg, July 14, 1944, both in box 162, Robert Taft Papers.

25. Hoover to Taft, June 17, box 161; "Taft Expresses His Views on Labor," Cleveland, Ohio, Oct. 7, 1944, box 159, Robert Taft Papers. Patterson, *Taft,* 291–95; Justus D. Doenecke, *Not to the Swift: The Old Isolationists In the Cold War Era* (Lewisburg, Pa., 1959), 5. Quotation, Taft to Bruce Barton, in Gareth Davies, "Education Policy from the New Deal to the Great Society: The Three Rs—Race, Religion, and Reds," in *Conservatism and American Political Development,* ed. Glenn and Teles, 90; Benn Steil, *The Battle of Bretton Woods; John Maynard Keynes, Harry Dexter White and the Making of the Modern World* (Princeton, N.J., 2013), 259, 292.

26. Dulles to Taft, Aug. 2, 1944, box 162, Robert Taft Papers. Malsberger, *From Obstruction to Moderation,* 113–14; "Senator Taft on the Issues," *New York Times,* Sept. 3, 1944.

INDEX

Page numbers in italics refer to illustrations.